CROSS-CULTURAL RESEARCH IN HUMAN DEVELOPMENT

Photo credit: Maric Productions

CROSS-CULTURAL RESEARCH IN HUMAN DEVELOPMENT

_____ Life Span _____
Perspectives

EDITED BY
Leonore Loeb Adler

PRAEGER

New York
Westport, Connecticut
London

Library of Congress Cataloging-in-Publication Data

Cross-cultural research in human development : life span perspectives
/ edited by Leonore Loeb Adler.
  p.   cm.
  Bibliography: p.
  Includes index.
  ISBN 0-275-93048-3 (alk. paper)
  1. Developmental psychology—Cross-cultural studies.
  2. Ethnopsychology. I. Adler, Leonore Loeb.
  BF713.C74   1989   88-15536
  155—dc19

Library of Congress Catalog Card Number: 88-15536
ISBN: 0-275-93048-3

First published in 1989

Praeger Publishers, One Madison Avenue, New York, NY 10010
A division of Greenwood Press, Inc.

Printed in the United States of America

The paper used in this book complies with the
Permanent Paper Standard issued by the National
Information Standards Organization (Z39.48-1984).

10 9 8 7 6 5 4 3 2 1

This book is dedicated to my wonderful family: to my husband, Helmut; to our son Barry Peter, his wife Karen, and their children Beth and Derek; to our daughter Beverly Sharmaine, her husband Madison, and their son Harrison; to our daughter Evelyn Renee, her husband Pedro, and their daughters Lynnette and Annette; and to my sister Margo and her husband Eric.

Contents

Acknowledgments   xi

Foreword
Marshall H. Segall   xiii

Introduction
Leonore Loeb Adler   xv

PART ONE: FOCUS ON CHILDHOOD

1. *REPRESENTATIONS OF TRADITIONAL AND MODERN ATTITUDES IN FRUIT-TREE DRAWINGS BY CHILDREN FROM 29 COUNTRIES*
   Leonore Loeb Adler   3

2. *THE DEVELOPMENT OF NUMBER, SPACE, QUANTITY, AND REASONING CONCEPTS IN SUDANESE SCHOOL-CHILDREN*
   Ramadan A. Ahmed   17

3. *APPLICATION OF A TEACHER RATING SCALE IN THE ASSESSMENT OF EARLY AND LATER DATES OF DEVELOPMENT IN YOUNG SCHOOLCHILDREN IN DIFFERENT CULTURES*
   Peter F. Merenda   27

4. *THE CULTURAL DIFFERENCE MODEL AND APPLIED BEHAVIOR ANALYSIS IN THE DESIGN OF EARLY CHILDHOOD INTERVENTION*
   Junko Tanaka-Matsumi   **37**

5. *THE CONSEQUENCES OF FATHER ABSENCE: A CROSS-CULTURAL PERSPECTIVE*
   Mitchell W. Robin and Regina C. Spires   **47**

PART TWO: FOCUS ON ADOLESCENCE

6. *PERCEPTIONS OF PARENTAL BEHAVIOR AND THE DEVELOPMENT OF MORAL REASONING IN JAMAICAN STUDENTS*
   Uwe P. Gielen, Claudette Reid, and Joseph Avellani   **61**

7. *SOME THOUGHTS ON SELF-ACTUALIZATION IN ADOLESCENTS*
   Machiko Fukuhara   **74**

8. *UNDERSTANDING THE BRAIN-DAMAGED ADOLESCENT: BEHAVIOR AND TREATMENT*
   Manny Sternlicht   **78**

9. *THALIDOMIDE ADOLESCENTS AND PREADOLESCENTS IN BRAZIL*
   Jefferson M. Fish, Saulo Monte Serrat, and Maria Emilia Tormena Elias   **85**

10. *THERAPEUTIC MANAGEMENT OF SOCIOECONOMIC CONFLICT IN A SUBURBAN CULTURE: DEVELOPMENTAL STAGES IN ADDICTION EPIDEMIOLOGY*
    Justin P. Carey and Alice T. Carey   **93**

PART THREE: FOCUS ON ADULTHOOD

11. *ETHNIC AND GENDER COMPARISONS IN DOMINANCE AND ASSERTION*
    Florence L. Denmark and Elaine C. Bow   **103**

12. *COMPARISON OF PROJECTED SOCIAL DISTANCES TO STIMULI WITH ASCRIBED CALM AND EMOTIONAL BEHAVIOR WITH EITHER ENGLISH OR HINDI INSTRUCTIONS*
Nihar R. Mrinal, Leonore Loeb Adler, Gwendolyn Stevens, Usha Kumar, and Jean G. Graubert   112

13. *EFFECTS OF LENGTH OF STAY IN THE UNITED STATES ON HOW THE CHINESE FULFILLED THEIR FILIAL OBLIGATIONS*
Lucy C. Yu and Shu-Chen Wu   121

14. *MOTHER-IN-LAW, SON, AND DAUGHTER-IN-LAW: A DEVELOPMENTAL ANALYSIS OF THE RELATIONSHIPS IN THE HINDU SOCIAL CONTEXT*
Usha Kumar   131

15. *FROM THE PSYCHOANALYSIS OF A GRECO-AMERICAN MAN: DEATH OF THE FATHER*
C. Edward Robins   143

16. *STAGES AND AGES IN ADULT DEVELOPMENT: A COMMENTARY AND RESEARCH NOTE*
John D. Hogan and Gary G. F. Yorke   155

17. *PERCEPTIONS OF MIDDLE AGE AND OLD AGE*
Leonore Loeb Adler, Nihar Ranjan Mrinal, Helmut E. Adler, William M. Davis, Joan Goldberg, and S. Patricia Walsh   164

18. *CROSS-CULTURAL AND INTERDISCIPLINARY PERSPECTIVES IN THE RESEARCH ON HUMAN RELIGIOSITY*
Halina Grzymala-Moszczynska   173

PART FOUR: FOCUS ON OLD AGE

19. *REAL-IDEAL RESIDENCE ENVIRONMENT: PERCEPTIONS OF OLDER WOMEN RELIGIOUS*
S. Patricia Clark   179

20. *FRIENDS OF OLDER BLACK AND WHITE WOMEN*
Hedva Lewittes and B. Runi Mukherji   193

21. *CROSS-CULTURAL PERSPECTIVE OF THE CHANGING ROLE OF THE CARE PROVIDER FOR THE AGED IN A CHINESE CONTEXT*
    Lucy C. Yu   205

22. *SOCIAL SUPPORT IN THE ELDERLY: A CROSS-CULTURAL COMPARISON*
    Cynthia L. Frazier and Chavannes Douyon   216

23. *CROSS-CULTURAL COMPARISONS OF DISABILITY AND DEPRESSION AMONG OLDER PERSONS IN FOUR COMMUNITY-BASED PROBABILITY SAMPLES*
    David E. Wilder and Barry J. Gurland   223

24. *THE PLACE OF AGE IN CULTURE: AN APPLICATION OF THE CULTURAL GRID*
    Anne Pedersen and Paul Pedersen   234

25. *WHEN CAN WE SAY MEMORY DIFFERS FROM AGE TO AGE AND/OR CULTURE TO CULTURE?*
    David S. Gorfein and Andrea Spata   247

26. *CROSS-CULTURAL COMPARABILITY*
    Lars H. Ekstrand and Gudrun B. Ekstrand   259

    Index   269

    Contributors   277

Acknowledgments

As the editor of this book, I would like to extend my thanks to each of the other 45 authors without whose contributions this volume would not exist. This book brings together internationally renown cross-cultural scientists from around the world. All of them are active and stimulating people who make the work of the editor much easier. And then my hearty thanks and high regard goes to Praeger Publishers' Editors, whose expertise and calm reassuring manner gave rise to the most pleasant interactions of this endeavor. I am also most indebted to my son, Barry P. Adler, for his readiness to help in many ways, any time, especially to get the manuscript camera-ready; and my sincere appreciation is gratefully extended to my daughter-in-law, Karen Adler, who outdid herself to help in the actual process of the production; she put in many long hours to meet the book's time-table, for which I thank her wholeheartedly. And last, but by no means least, I acknowledge the patience and understanding of my husband, Dr. Helmut E. Adler, which he extended to me during the time-consuming activities that kept me busy and occupied with the manuscript for many months. Before closing, I want to acknowledge the unknown and uncounted readers of this book to whom I wish good reading, increased knowledge to foster understanding and tolerance of persons who live in other cultures and environments; and, most importantly, to help promote harmonious existence with people everywhere.

Foreword

Marshall H. Segall

Cross-cultural psychology is a rapidly growing intellectual enterprise, an interdisciplinary effort involving psychologists and other social scientists who are convinced that human behavior can best be understood if studied from a global perspective. Indeed, they would assert that human behavior is understandable only when viewed in the various sociocultural contexts in which it occurs.

Yet, it is still the case that the study of human behavior is dominated by North Americans. Of course, many psychologists work in Canada and in Europe, and some are not themselves rooted in European culture, but most of them are anglophonic. While psychology is part of the curriculum in universities all over the world, most teachers and students of psychology, including the social and developmental branches, reside in universities in the United States. Most research is done there and most of the publications originate there. Domination by the United States, or by any other part of the world, would be cause for concern. The main point of concern is parochialism per se, not the particular variety of parochialism. By limiting attention to the behaviors of individuals in a single society, whichever one it happens to be, we risk losing sight of culture.

Given the cultural complexities of human life and the importance of cultural variables in shaping human behavior, it is imperative that psychologists test the generality of their putative principles. To do this requires that we employ a cross-cultural perspective.

This book, which is edited by Leonore Loeb Adler from the Institute of Cross-Cultural and Cross-Ethnic Studies at Molloy College, is a welcome addition to the small but growing number of efforts to bring a cross-cultural perspective to psychology. In this instance, the topics to which this perspective is applied are those of developmental psychology. This book consists of some two dozen reports, each of which is cross-cultural either because it compares particular developmental phenomena that are revealed by studying persons from more than one cultural setting, or because it presents phenomena that are studied by psychologists who come from more than one cultural setting.

In some of the reports, both of these conditions exist. Some chapters present the results of a research effort in detail; others are brief reviews. Some of the contributions are by psychologists making their first foray into cross-cultural psychology. They are welcome and encouraged to delve more deeply. Other contributions contain efforts at conceptualizing cultural variables, and still others offer methodological suggestions regarding the study of links between culture and behavior. While most of the papers in this volume present empirical results, all are useful. It is encouraging to see so many psychologists trying to inject a cultural perspective into their work.

We are long past the time when psychology can pretend that ignoring culture doesn't matter. This book is another demonstration of that truth. While some psychologists may still deny it, the next generation of psychologists, trained in the cross-cultural tradition to which this book contributes, will only wonder how it was that so many, for so long, failed to understand the value of this perspective.

Introduction

Leonore Loeb Adler

This book deals with a variety of cross-cultural and cross-ethnic issues, while focusing on a life-span perspective. The chapters -- each like pearls in a necklace -- are threaded together to accomplish a total effect contributed by individual empirical studies and reports, which originated in many different geographical areas. Most of the issues are current, not only in the described environments, but also find application in a cross-cultural or a cross-ethnic context, or both. A diversity of major orientations and schools of thought are represented in one or more chapters that link the chain to make a well-rounded exposition of theory and method. Each of the four sections in this volume contribute to an understanding of behavior in a variety of fields in psychology in general, and focus specifically on distinct age-related issues with regard to life-span development.

Part One, "Focus on Childhood", presents topics such as children's reflections on group values in traditional, as well as modern cultural settings. Another focus is on comparisons of Piagetian testing of the cognitive development of schoolchildren in Third World countries with the responses by children in Western countries. The next chapter deals with the assessment of earlier as well as later developmental stages in young schoolchildren; this report includes the current list of collaborators in 13 countries where the rating scale was adapted. This is followed by a discourse on how to help children who are underachievers by methods of applied behavior analysis; though most of the focus is on Hawaiian schoolteachers, it is an important problem not only cross-culturally, but also cross-ethnically. Then, the discussion centers on a very current topic in all societies, which relates to the impact of father absence, as well as such effects on child development and on single-parent households, which are found all over the Western world.

Part Two, "Focus on Adolescence", deals with the issues pertaining to the effects of children's perceptions of parental behavior on the development of moral reasoning. While the report focuses on Jamaican high school students, the discussion centers on comparisons of the results of previous cross-cultural studies on moral reasoning. Another important area concerns self-actualization in adolescents, though this concept generally is not applied to this age group. The topics of the adjustment and functioning of handicapped or addicted youths throughout the world, encompasses all cultural and ethnic environments. These chapters concentrate on issues that concern the brain-damaged adolescent and discuss the effective functioning of thalidomide adolescents and pre-adolescents. Another topic focuses on the ever-increasing problem faced by the multitude of young drug addicts with regard to their rehabilitation and therapeutic management.

Part Three, "Focus on Adulthood", concerns gender comparisons with issues such as dominance and assertion with different ethnic groups in a multicultural environment. Projected effects of ascribed calm or emotional behaviors by stimulus persons of either high or low status were tested in similar social settings in different cultural environments. The social schemata found agreement in the study presented here with other aspects of interpersonal distance research, as well as with theories of social interaction. Not only people in foreign lands are the focus of research; sometimes groups of immigrants are questioned about their attitudes on various topics. For example, one chapter focuses on filial obligations toward parents and parents-in-law by Chinese immigrants to the United States of America or their descendants. Interestingly, it is the daughter-in-law who feels the greater discomfort about having the "in-laws" living under the same roof. The role of the mother-in-law receives a great deal of attention regardless of culture or ethnic affiliation. Here the spotlight falls on the triad of mother-in-law, son, and daughter-in-law in the Hindu household in India. From there, the focus moves to a Greco-American man who, through psychoanalysis, finds the resolution of the father-son relationship. An important topic is the establishment of developmental stages during adulthood in a cross-ethnic comparison. Next comes the report of a developmental cross-cultural study, which showed that, though the cultural and ethnic backgrounds of the subjects were different, perceptions of age-related periods varied depending on the age of the perceivers. An often-neglected topic is that of religiosity, though it is an important aspect of living in many parts of the world. In this case, it is discussed from a Polish point of view and an interdisciplinary perspective.

Part Four, "Focus on Old Age", presents information using a type of "ethnic" sample, which in this study focuses on a population of elderly religious women living in a residential environment. Other recent research deals with aspects of what being a "best friend" means to individuals of different ethnic groups -- a relationship that gains importance among elderly women. The focus on the elderly deals with a variety of topics, including the changing role of women in China, though most women there still function in the traditional role of careprovider. Since among the most salient research areas on the elderly are those dealing with health -- both mental and physical -- these are discussed from a cross-ethnic and cross-cultural point of view; the problems of dealing with the elderly seem to be universal. In order to provide mental health counselors with guidance for interviews, regardless of their ethnic or cultural environment, the "cultural grid" is presented. In the same vein, a discourse on and review of past studies evaluates a variety of designs for cross-cultural age-related research on memory. Last, but not least, a mainly theoretical discussion focuses on "cross-cultural comparability", which serves as a guideline and has complete applicability to all instances of cross-cultural and cross-ethnic research.

This book on Cross-Cultural and Cross-Ethnic Research in Human Development with its focus on life-span, has two main purposes. First, it focuses on developmental issues in a global approach for an audience with diverse interests. For example, those readers who are familiar with the field will appreciate the broad and expanded scope of the topics presented. On the other hand, the novice will be introduced to the field of developmental research from a cross-cultural and a cross-ethnic approach. Second, the exposition of the theme deals with the awareness that there are parallels and similarities shared by a variety of cultures and a multiplicity of ethnic groups, in all developmental stages throughout the life cycle.

It is not that the world gets smaller -- it just appears that way since radio, television, and the telephone make communication throughout the world almost instantaneous. Whatever happens, either near or far, people in all regions of the world are aware of current events and partake in ongoing situations. It is important to recognize that, on a worldwide basis, there may exist individual as well as group differences when behavior is observed and studied; yet more relevant is the fact that the prevalent attitudes and perceptions of problems faced by people throughout the human life span have many essential similarities in most societies around the globe. This book brings together a diversity of topics with new findings based on empirical studies from a variety of universities by scholars with an expertise in their specialized fields, and by cross-cultural scientists of many different nationalities who often live in multicultural environments.

Among the outstanding features of this book is the approach to age-specific problems. **Part One** deals mainly with school and education-related topics in childhood, as well as the effects of modernization on the child's world. **Part Two** focuses on the adjustment of normal and handicapped adolescents; in addition, it discusses the parental influences on the development of moral values. **Part Three** is concerned with family interactions and their relationships and deals with the perception of age-related stages in adulthood. **Part Four** highlights comparable research in therapy and care of the elderly in a variety of milieus in different cultural or ethnic settings.

Though there are many topics discussed in a well-rounded selection of chapters, the unifying theme is the focus on developmental stages and age-related research, which is applied to studies having both cross-cultural and cross-ethnic perspectives. The common element centers on issues concerning specific developmental stages and problems faced by people in different ecological settings. The life-span developmental aspects featured in these chapters will provide a link for a better understanding of and insight into the concerns of the young and the old, as well as of the manners and customs of people everywhere.

PART ONE: FOCUS ON CHILDHOOD

Photo credit: Maric Productions

Representations of Traditional and Modern Attitudes in Fruit-Tree Drawings by Children From 29 Countries

Leonore Loeb Adler

The study of children's drawings has served as a standard technique and a useful tool in clinical psychology. Analyses of children's drawings of a man or woman, for example, were used by Florence Goodenough (1926) to assess the intelligence level of individuals. Karen Machover (1948), however, used drawings as a basis for her personality assessment of the individual, in both clinical and criminal cases. It was not until Wayne Dennis (1966) interpreted children's drawings in terms of group values or preferences, that social psychologists in particular, and social scientists in general, became aware of the important messages that could be gleaned from the objective analysis of children's graphic representations on paper. *Content only* was analyzed, which was based solely on what the children had drawn.

Dennis (1966) proposed two hypotheses: (1) **The Value Hypothesis,** stated that children draw scenes with themes that, in their culture, have desirable goal qualities and are socially acceptable; and (2) **The Familiarity Hypothesis,** which on the other hand, suggested that children's drawings reflect their environment. In other words, Dennis propounded that group values controlled, to a great degree, what was represented in the pictures. Mostly depicted, however, were those things the children had knowledge of by direct personal or by indirect second-hand experience through books, pictures, photos, video cassette recorders, or movies. Yet only those things that had positive values were drawn. For example, no dentists were represented. Dennis therefore concluded that "in all instances in which the Familiarity Hypothesis and the Value Hypothesis are in conflict, the latter wins" (1966, p. 172).

Not everybody, however, agreed with this conclusion. Leonore Loeb Adler (1981, 1982), suggested that "these two hypotheses cannot be separated and therefore work in harmony at all times" (1982, p. 97). She based her statement on the results of her programmatic study with the Fruit-Tree Test. With this long-term experiment, Adler investigated different sources that exert an influence on children's preferences (in this study, scenes with fruit trees), which they represent in drawings.

THE FRUIT-TREE EXPERIMENT

It is expedient to give a brief history of the Fruit-Tree Experiment here. Years ago, Dr. Lauretta Bender, who was then the chief psychiatrist of the Children's Service at Bellevue Hospital in New York City, observed that the majority of children's drawings pictured apple trees when fruit trees were drawn. (Dr. Pearl Berkowitz, personal communication.) This observation was supported by Adler's studies, which eventually included 29 countries on six continents. Children from the following countries contributed drawings for the Fruit-Tree Study:

- ▸ **Africa:** (1) Angola, (2) Republic of South Africa, (3) Zaire;
- ▸ **Asia:** (4) Hong Kong, (5) India [Bombay: English and Punjab: vernacular], (6) Iran, (7) Israel, (8) Japan, (extra (X) People's Republic of China, collected by Dr. Florence L. Denmark, but not counted), (9) the Philippines, (10) South Korea, (11) Taiwan;
- ▸ **Australia:** (12) Australia [Sydney and Fullabo Nation, and extra (XX) Walbiri Tribe, collected by Dr. John Cawte for another study (Cawte and Kiloh, 1967), but not counted];
- ▸ **Europe:** (13) Denmark, (14) England, (15) France, (16) Germany, (17) Greece, (18) Iceland, (19) Italy, (20) Switzerland, (21) Yugoslavia;
- ▸ **North America:** (22) Canada, (23) Greenland, (24) Netherland Antilles, (25) United States of America;
- ▸ **South America:** (26) Argentina, (27) Brazil, (28) Chile, (29) Peru.

Adler's hypothesis proposed that children from all over the world tended to draw more apple trees than any other fruit tree. Although it had to be partially rejected with qualifications on a regional basis, the hypothesis could be accepted generally. In almost all phases of the Fruit-Tree Experiment, boys and girls between the ages of 5 and 12 years were asked to "draw a picture -- any scene -- with a fruit tree in it" (Adler, 1968). On an overall basis, the apple tree ranked in first place. This category was larger than the next eight fruit-tree varieties combined. All in all, there were 77 different types of fruit trees pictured in the 4,314 children's drawings. This diversity was based on local availability of some of the fruit trees drawn. (For a detailed review of the Fruit-Tree Experiment, see Adler, 1968, 1982; Adler and Adler, 1977.)

Since the children were asked to draw "any scene," the pictures represented several themes; these could be categorized as scenes of a prolific harvest, leisure activities, or undisturbed nature (a landscape), either with or without people and animals. In practically all cases, the Familiarity Hypothesis would apply. Yet the drawings' contents also were representative of and reflected the existing value systems, in agreement with the Value

Hypothesis. In other words, contrary to Dennis (1966), this investigator's inclination was to favor a state of harmony and interdependence between the two hypotheses at all times.

During the process of analyzing the children's drawings, one had to take into consideration the cultural background and the level of modernization of the country where the children lived. A good indicator of the importance of retaining traditional values versus progress in attaining modern goals could be seen in the attire of the persons pictured. Another cue was found in the activities and the equipment pictured. However, boys' pictures generally differed from girls' drawings; not in themes but in content.

ANALYSES OF TRADITIONAL AND MODERN ATTITUDES

Here are some examples of the Value and the Familiarity Hypotheses, which can be identified by the traditional or modern attitudes as seen in the graphic representations. As shown in these figures, both the Value and the Familiarity Hypotheses interact at all times.

Traditional attitudes are quite discernable in the drawings by girls and boys, even when these originated on different continents. (See Figures 1-10. Due to space limitations, only a few pictures can be shown here; and those that are reproduced can be discussed only very briefly.) The first picture, Figure 1.1, was drawn by a 14-year-old girl (and for that reason was not counted in the original Fruit-Tree Study) from Zaire on the African continent. She shows a woman in a traditional dress with a baby strapped to her back, while she performs a household chore. She stands near her thatched-roof hut, which represents the traditional home. This woman is a representation of the traditional function of the woman as a mother and of the desirable goal qualities of being a good provider of food.

Figure 1.2 shows another thatched-roof house, but this time the hut stands on piles in the water. The 10-year-old girl, who produced this picture in pastel paint, came from the Philippines, part of the Pacific islands of Asia. She drew a figure with a traditional hat in the customary boat. This drawing would rank high on artistic ability, but such a skill was not considered important for an objective analysis, which was based entirely on content.

Figure 1.3 clearly represents the social desirability of leisure. From the name of this 10-year-old girl, one sees that she has Danish ancestors. (Danish people are the administrators of this island.) She lived in Dundas, Greenland, part of North America, where no trees grow; this might be the reason why this "orange tree" looks like a pear tree. This is a picture of a blond woman with high-heeled shoes and modern dress reclining on a lawn chair with a tray of fruits and drinks on her lap. The little girl, with a bow in her blond braids, plays with a small dog while she eats a fruit. Both mother and child wear sunglasses. This is a picture that represents traditional values of women's roles in the Western upper middle class.

The next picture, Figure 1.4, was drawn by an 11-year-old girl from Florida (Siracusa), Italy, in southern Europe. The young woman portrayed here wears the traditional costume while she is dancing the ethnic tarantella. A full basket of fruit, showing a prolific harvest, is placed next to a heavily laden tree.

Figure 1.5 is a watercolor painting by a 9-year-old girl from Taiwan, an island in the western Pacific Ocean. Another traditional harvest scene is depicted here. The woman in this picture wears a native outfit of baggy pants, which are gathered together at the ankles, a printed blouse with long sleeves, and a pointed bamboo hat -- all of which complete her traditional work clothes. It is quite common to see women help with the harvest.

The next group of pictures, Figures 1.6-1.10, were contributed by boys from different continents. Figure 1.6 is typical of young boys' interests in a traditional way. In a Freudian analysis, this picture would be interpreted to represent the aggressive tendencies of the child; however, in an objective analysis, the mechanical properties of the large fire truck project positive goal qualities. Here the theme warrants high social approval and civic recognition for the help and rescue by the firemen (who are only stick figures) of the burning house. The orange tree, from which oranges fall to the ground, is barely shown. Obviously, important aspects for this North American 8-year-old boy from New Jersey, the USA, are the fire truck and the water jetting out at the flames.

Figure 1.7 was contributed by a 9-year-old boy from Rennes, France, in Europe. The theme not only represents the age-old stereotypical occupation of "man the hunter," but also in this case depicts the goal qualities of sports and leisure time. The man is well-dressed in a modern hunting suit, hat, boots, shoulder bag, and gun. The bird he shoots is practically out of sight; but it shows the *raison d'être* for the hunt.

The next picture, Figure 1.8, was drawn by a 9-year-old German boy, or a child of German descent, from Argentina, South America. Again we have a traditional sports theme for boys: soccer. He labels the trees in German, although his name, Rodolfo, is Spanish. He also depicts the high mountains in the background, which may represent his environment.

The next two pictures, though quite different, come from Australia, the smallest continent, "down under." In Figure 1.9, one sees an enterprising smiling boy, drawn by an 8-year-old boy from Sydney, New South Wales. He depicts a two-story home with curtained windows and a smoking chimney on the roof. The house is surrounded by fruit trees, which are the basis for the prolific harvest and the (hopefully) profitable produce business. The last drawing in this category, Figure 1.10, comes from an 11-year-old Native Australian Aboriginal boy belonging to the Fullabo Tribe (or Nation) from north Queensland. The theme is a plentiful harvest of coconuts, which is shown in the traditional custom and manner of passing the fruit down the line of the human chain. For good measure, there is also a kangaroo hunt with spears in midair. In the background of this scene, there is a windowless pilehouse at the end of the faint road. In this drawing, as in many children's pictures, the sun has a prominent place in the sky.

Modern attitudes are easily apparent in the next group of pictures. (See Figures 1.11-1.20.) Figure 1.11 was drawn by a 9-year-old North American girl from New Jersey, the USA. In this picture, one sees a big bird flying over the three-story house. Not only the sun smiles, so do the clouds and people. The picture seems to represent a traditional nuclear family in which the father wears a blue (business?) suit and the mother has a short-length dress on. However, the daughter, who sits on the swing with her hair flying, wears a jumpsuit. In the environment of a modern society, such an outfit is considered androgynous. This label conveys a psychological non-sex-sterotypic attitude or orientation. (see Bem, 1974.) It allows for and not only accepts women in "men's jobs," but also -- though it is less frequent because of women's lower status in society -- for "men in women's jobs or roles." In modern societies, women frequently have outside-the-home, money-earning careers in a male-dominated job market, while husbands, after coming home from their jobs, may help with household chores which stereotypically belong to "women's work." In the pictures collected for the Fruit-Tree Study, the investigator found androgynous responses by girls, mainly in technologically advanced countries. The one exception, which may be debatable, is Figure 1.21 in this report.

The next picture, Figure 1.12, was drawn by a 12-year-old European school girl from Denmark. Again there is a harvest scene represented. This time a man, probably the father, stands on a ladder and picks fruits into the big basket. The second theme for this drawing could be leisure time, since the two girls, probably the daughters of the man on the ladder, both relax on the grass in the fenced-in part of the garden, collect, and eat some of the fruits that fall to the ground. These girls with long hair, both wear androgy-nous outfits: shirts and pants. If one could not identify their gender by their hair, this nonsex-stereotypical attire would not offer the slightest cue to the gender of these figures on the grass.

Another European girl, an 11-year-old from West Germany, contributed the next drawing, Figure 1.13. Here the androgynous attitude is very evident. The theme is a rich harvest of fruits, judging by the huge empty basket to be filled, probably by the girl in shorts, knee-high socks, and a long-sleeved shirt, who is carrying a ladder to climb the tree. While her activity is certainly androgynous, wearing lipstick and eye-makeup is absolutely feminine. The girl on the right side also wears androgynous/modern clothes. Only the hair length gives a cue of her gender. (It seems clever and creative to use the picture identification box as a place for the girl on the right to sit on. However, this aspect is not taken into consideration when the attitudes of the schoolchildren are analyzed.)

Figure 1.14, a drawing by a ten-year-old girl from Canada, North America, represents an enterprising girl, who sells lemonade (rather than apple juice!). Typically, this is a boy's job or activity for which she competes. Only the hair is stereotypical for her gender.

Figure 1.15, the last picture in this category, looks at first glance as if it is out of place. Certainly it appears to be typically traditional from a Western point of view (especially when one does not read the caption first). One sees a mother in a garden with flowers (which have prestige value, especially in a hot climate where coconut palms and banana trees grow). In the door of her thatched-roof house stands a little girl. Both mother and child are smiling. Yet the great significance of this picture is the obvious modern attitude it conveys. Both mother and child wear short dresses and both have short haircuts. This is not the usual or traditional attire nor hairstyle for Indian Hindi women, who wear saris that consist of a long piece of material that is draped around the figure from the waist to the ankles and often put over the head, and then thrown over one shoulder; from there it falls softly and flowingly down the back. Another remarkable aspect of this picture by a 9-year-old girl with an Indian name, from Bombay, India in south Asia, is that the child in the drawing is a girl. In India, boys are more desirable and the relationship between mother and son is usually close, whereas that between mother and daughter often lacks closeness and intimacy (Kumar, 1979).

Figures 1.16 to 1.20, the boys' pictures reflect their society's modern attitudes. The first one in this category is Figure 1.16, which was drawn by a 12-year-old boy from Japan, eastern Asia, in the western Pacific Ocean. Inspection of the right side of the drawing shows an elaborate array of modern leisure activities at the seashore. The left side of the picture shows modernization in terms of a skyscraper beside a four-story building, a Buddhist temple, and a Christian church. There is a small house in the foreground, where two old men are talking together nearby.

Figures 1.17 and Figure 1.18 have a great deal in common, though they came from opposite ends of the world. The 12-year-old Native American Eskimo boy from Thule, Greenland (the largest island in North America), depicts a hilly, barren countryside with one tree (no trees grow there). An impressive assembly of mechanical equipment can be seen in this drawing. There is a man handling a machine on a tripod in the foreground. In the air is an impressive show with three helicopters. (The middle one has an identification of "USA" on its tail.) The interpretation of this theme would point to the Familiarity Hypothesis because of the helicopters used to transport goods and also the Value Hypothesis, because of the desirability of technological progress in all areas of the world. Similarly oriented is the picture by the Native Australian Aboriginal boy, a 12-year-old member of the Walbiri Tribe/Nation. He not only draws a truck, an airplane, and a wind-powered well, but also adds a kangaroo and a traditional hunter for good measure. (A kangaroo hunt could represent leisure time and high esteem.) The bush banana trees are indigenous types for that region of Australia.

Figure 1.19 portrays another local tree, the tuna cactus tree of Peru in South America. Again there is an airplane, high up over the peaked mountains. The 9-year-old boy's theme is achievement motivation with the sport of mountain climbing as the focus. Meeting and viewing a llama is the reward for reaching the high goal. The man is fashionably dressed in a Tyrolian hat with a feather, a modern shirt, jeans with many pockets, and spiked shoes for climbing. It appears that the right equipment and accessories are basic to the Value Hypothesis.

Figure 1.20 has a modern, though not realistic, approach. One can see a sports car with skis fastened to the top, which are incongruous, when one sees all the apples on the tree. This picture subtly displays two rare features in children's drawings: (1) the hardly visible driver is a female, identified by her hairstyle; and (2) the tongue-in-cheek humor of the drawing, where the car runs into the tree and has a steaming, smashed-in motor; the heading reads: "The poor apple tree." Such a "sexist attitude" is usually found in men, but not in boys, especially not in young boys who live at home, like this 11-year-old boy from Karlsruhe (near the Black Forest), in the southern part of West Germany in Central Europe.

Next follows a group of pictures, Figures 1.21 to 1.25, which show a concern with social issues. Figure 1.21 was drawn by a 7-year-old North America Canadian boy. He portrays a woman with her hair in a bun, wearing slacks and boots. However, her most decisive features are her smiling mouth with a lot of lipstick on her lips, and her long eyelashes. This picture is the only androgynous drawing by a boy in this series of fruit-tree pictures.

The next two children's drawings have similar, but not identical, themes. Figure 1.22 was contributed by an 11-year-old South American girl from Chile. Not only does she show how she wants to spend her leisure time, but also with whom. This inscription reads "EL Y YO" ("He and I"), and has a bleeding heart painted above the two figures; the girl and boy are holding hands. Such attitudes by an 11-year-old girl may appear to be precocious, or just wishful thinking (prestigious goal qualities). On the other hand, it may be the modern trend of the time. Figure 1.23 seems to be a case for individuality. The 10-year-old European French girl, who drew this picture, placed all the girls in this drawing next to the one apple tree in about the same pose. Yet each girl wears a different traditional outfit, namely a dress or skirt and blouse; each girl in the drawing has another hairstyle and color. While it appears at first glance that these schoolgirls adhere to strict discipline, this drawing is an appeal for girls or women to follow their own individualities and express their own personalities; in other words, it supports the goal qualities of feminist independence.

Figure 1.24 is a picture that was painted by a 9-year-old Asian girl from Japan, in the western Pacific Ocean. She deals with the problem of insecticides and air pollution to secure an abundant harvest of good apples. The gardener in this picture is a man (not a woman, which frequently is the custom), whose nose and mouth are covered with a mask for protection against dangerous fumes.

The last picture of this report, Figure 1.25, was the work of an 11-year-old African boy from Zaire. While no apple trees grow in Zaire's hot climate, the tree in this drawing serves as a background for a boxing match. The remarkable feature here is that the boy draws different skin colors for the two boxers. Such representations are very unusual. Generally, schoolchildren do not fill in the darker skin shades of black individuals, nor do they draw racial features. The impression prevails that the children are oblivious to color or racial differences. This observation was corroborated by Wayne Dennis (1966). He reported that neither his white nor his black subjects drew a black person. Yet one black Sudanese girl pictured a black female (his Figure 106) in the "Draw a Woman Test." -- Perhaps the different shading of the boxers' skin color in this drawing could be either a reflection of any racial upheaval in that country or on that continent, or a representation of a competitive yet harmonious coexistence among different races.

CONCLUDING REMARKS

The present report serves to explain how children's drawings are analyzed in terms of traditional and modern attitudes, which can be interpreted through the Familiarity Hypothesis and the Value Hypothesis. The drawings by children generally reflect the group values of their culture, society, and community, though specifically, boys and girls have different orientations and diverse foci. The cross-cultural themes depicted by schoolchildren in their drawings show socially approved goal orientations and generally accepted attitudes. This graphic method allows for wide applications in many different cultures and with diversified populations, because the representations of prevalent goals do not need to be explicitly nor specifically verbalized. An analysis of the children's drawings, based on content only, provides a reliable measure of social change in both traditional and modern societies. The cues, at times, are subtle, as seen in the androgynous tendencies in some girls' pictures from Europe and North America; recall, for example, the androgynous outfits of the young girls in several pictures from the USA (Figure 1.11), from Denmark (Figure 1.12), and from Germany (Figure 1.13). Cues suggesting the process of modernization,such as the short dresses and short haircuts of mother and daughter in the Indian drawing from Bombay (Figure 1.15), are similarly subtle. Changes in attitudes or in value systems of societies are not easily or quickly achieved; yet they can provide strong motivational orientations and set up powerful goal qualities. Only time will tell which directions social change is taking. Yet on the basis of the children's drawings, one can obtain a glimpse into the future in terms of social values.

REFERENCES

Adler, L. L. (1968). "A Note on the Cross-Cultural Fruit-Tree Study: A Test-Retest Procedure." *Journal of Psychology, 69,* 53-61.

Adler, L. L. (1981). "Analysis of Group Values as Expressed in Children's Drawings." Paper read at the Joint IACCP and ICP Asian Regional Meeting, August 10-11, Taipei, Taiwan.

Adler, L. L. (1982). "Children's Drawings as an Indicator of Individual Preferences Reflecting Group Values: A Programmatic Study." *Cross-Cultural Research at Issue,* edited by L. L. Adler, Chap. 7, 71-98, New York: Academic Press.

Adler, L. L., and Adler, B. S. (1977). "The Fruit-Tree Experiment as a Cross-Cultural Measure of the Variations in Children's Drawings due to Regional Differences." *Issues in Cross-Cultural Research,* edited by L. L. Adler, Vol. 285, 227-281. New York: Annals of the New York Academy of Sciences.

Bem, S. L. (1974). "The Measurement of Psychological Androgyny." *Journal of Consulting and Clinical Psychology, 42,* 155-162.

Cawte, J. E., and Kiloh, L. G. (1967). "Language and Pictorial Representations in Aboriginal Children." *Social Science and Medicine, 1,* 67-76.

Dennis, W. (1966). *Group Values Through Children's Drawings.* New York: John Wiley and Sons.

Goodenough, F. L. (1926). *The Measurement of Intelligence by Drawings.* Yonkers-on-Hudson, NY: World Book Co.

Kumar, U. (1979). "Indian Woman's Quest for Identity." *International Journal of Group Tensions, 9,* (1-4), 149-168.

Machover, K. (1949). *Personality Projection in the Drawing of the Human Figure.* Springfield, IL: C. C. Thomas.

AUTHOR NOTES

The author would like to thank Grace Burke, O.P., Professor in the Media Center of Molloy College, who made the photographs of the children's drawings for this chapter.

Figure 1.1   Zaire, F, 14 yrs.
            Papaya Tree

Figure 1.2   Philippines, F, 10 yrs.
            Coconut Tree

Figure 1.3   Greenland, F, 10 yrs.
            Orange Tree (Pear?)

Figure 1.4   Italy F, 11 yrs.
            Orange Tree

Figure 1.5   Taiwan, F, 9 yrs.
            Banana Tree

Figure 1.6   USA, M, 8 years
             Orange Tree

Figure 1.7   France, M, 9 yrs.
             Apple Tree

Figure 1.8   Argentina, M, 9 yrs.
             Apple and Lemon Trees

Figure 1.9   Australia, M, 8 yrs.
             Lemon and Orange Trees

Figure 1.10 Australia, (Aboriginal)
            M, 11 yrs. Coconut Tree

Figure 1.11 (right) USA, F, 9 yrs.
Apple Tree

Figure 1.12 Denmark, F, 12 yrs.
Plum Tree

Figure 1.13 Germany, F, 11 yrs.
Apple Tree

Figure 1.14 Canada, F, 10 yrs.
Apple Tree

Figure 1.15 (below) India, F, 9 yrs.
Coconut and Banana Trees

14

Figure 1.16 (right) Japan, M, 12 yrs.
Coconut Tree

Figure 1.17 Greenland (Eskimo),
M, 12 yrs. Apple Tree

Figure 1.18 (below) Australia (Aboriginal)
M, 12 yrs. Bush Banana

Figure 1.19 Peru, M, 9 yrs.
Tuna (cactus) Tree

Figure 1.20 Germany, M, 11 yrs.
Apple Tree

Figure 1.21 Canada, M, 7 yrs.
Apple Tree

Figure 1.22 Chile, F, 11 yrs.
Pear Tree

Figure 1.23 France, F, 10 yrs.
Apple Tree

Figure 1.24 Japan, F, 9 yrs.
Apple Tree

Figure 1.25 Zaire, M, 11 yrs.
Apple Tree

2

The Development of Number, Space, Quantity, and Reasoning Concepts in Sudanese Schoolchildren

Ramadan A. Ahmed

This chapter describes an experimental study that was carried out in Khartoum, Sudan, to assess the development of number, space, quantity, and reasoning concepts in Sudanese schoolchildren.

Piaget and his colleagues have studied the formation of the notions of numbers, space, speed-time, quantity, and probabilistic causality from an original point of view. First they analyzed the operations that were fundamental to these concepts. Subsequently, they asked whether the concepts that were acquired resulted only from socially transmitted learning or whether the individual had some active contribution to make in their formation (Inhelder and Matalon, 1970, p. 444).

The basic aim of this research is to explore the development of number, space, quantity, and reasoning concepts in a sample of Sudanese schoolchildren aged 8 to 12 years. Hence, only the concrete operations stage, for which considerable information is available, will be discussed here. In the concrete operational stage the child develops a set of rules that help him to deal with reality and to assimilate and accommodate new events. These rules allow him to conserve mass, weight, volume, and number; to deal with parts and wholes; to serialize; and to understand relational terms.

Ahmed found in 1981 that the concepts of quantity and space developed more readily in his sample of Egyptian schoolchildren than number and reasoning concepts (Ahmed, 1981, e.g., p. 91 ff). One might expect that Sudanese schoolchildren would generally develop quantity and spatial concepts more readily than concepts related to numbers and reasoning ("logico-arithmetical" concepts), because the former are ecologically and culturally more relevant than the latter. For European children this is not the case; the two areas of conceptual development may develop simultaneously during the period of concrete operations. Logico-mathematical concepts may even be acquired earlier than spatial and quantity concepts (Piaget and Inhelder, 1956, e.g., pp. 370 ff and 460 ff).

In general, the main hypotheses for the present study are: (1) the rate of conceptual development in Sudanese schoolchildren is generally slower than in their European counterparts; (2) the rates of cognitive development may vary from one area of conceptual development to another, depending upon the influence of ecological and cultural demands.

The purpose of the research is: (1) to shed light on some developmental aspects of cognition in Sudanese schoolchildren; (2) to assess the effects of social class, father's educational level, and gender on children's performance on cognitive tasks and intelligence tests; and (3) to elucidate the relationships between intellectual performance of children and their performance in cognitive tasks.

METHOD

Subjects

A cross-sectional design was employed with three age and grade-level groups: eight-year-old second graders (mean age = 8.3 years; range = 7.5-9.3 years); 10-year-old fourth graders (mean age = 10.6 years; range = 9-11 years); and 12-year-old sixth graders (mean age = 12.3 years; range = 11-13 years).

Forty-eight children were tested at 8 years of age (24 girls and 24 boys), 50 children at 10 years of age (24 girls and 26 boys), and 48 children at 12 years of age (24 girls and 24 boys). These three age groups corresponded roughly to Piaget's concrete-operational stage, and to the beginning of the formal-operational stage.

The children were chosen from four public primary schools in Khartoum, Sudan, and were randomly selected from school rolls. The children came from skilled and nonskilled working-class and middle-class homes. All participants' native language was Arabic; and all the children were Muslims. Additional information was collected about their family's socioeconomic status and their father's educational level.

Procedures

The children were tested individually at the school. Each was asked all the questions related to the material with which he was tested, that is, each of the 146 subjects took the ten cognitive tasks and the two intelligence tests, but on different days, so as to avoid verbal perseverations.

Materials

Cognitive Tasks. Ten cognitive tasks were used to assess the development of concepts of number, space, quantity, and reasoning in the three age groups of the Sudanese schoolchildren. This was the first time that such tests were given to Sudanese children. The tasks for three of the concepts were based on the work by Piaget and his associates, and the task for the concept of quantity was designed by Anderson and Cuneo (1978). However, they provided no scoring methods or norms, so it was necessary to devise a system for the evaluation of the performances of the children.

1. **Concept of Number:** Three tasks were given to the children to assess the concept of number.
    a. *The Children and the Donkeys:* This task was aimed at assessing a child's comprehension of one-to-one correspondence, and number. It consisted of a picture in which there were eight children (four boys and four girls), each riding a donkey (see Ginsburg and Opper, 1969, e.g., p. 143 ff).
    b. *Continuous Quantities:* The aim of this task was to assess a child's understanding that a quantity of liquid does not change with a change in its shape. This task consisted of two beakers of the same size and shape (A-1 and A-2; 600 ml); two smaller beakers of the same size and shape (B-1 and B-2; 250 ml); four containers (C-1, C-2, C-3, and C-4) that were smaller than the other beakers (50 ml); one tall and narrow cylinder (400 ml); two wide and short containers (D-1 and D-2; 400 ml); and colored water (see Piaget and Szeminska, 1965, e.g., p. 16 ff).
    c. *Number Serialization:* This task was used to assess a child's reasoning about the serialization of numbers. It consisted of a card with 12 different numbers (i.e., 1,327; 2,111; 1,987; 5,000, 234; 4,122; 1,844; 809; 1,896; 7,185; and 3,596), which had to be put in ordered sequences (see Ginsburg and Opper, 1969, e.g., p. 135 ff).

2. **Concept of Space:** Four tasks were used to assess the concept of space in children.
    a. *Relationships of Right and Left:* The purpose of this task was to determine the child's understanding of right-left relationships, which consisted of four different objects: pencil, key, coin, and a piece of paper (see Vernon, 1973, e.g., p. 129 ff and p.140).
    b. *Topological and Euclidean Drawings:* This task focused on determining whether a child viewed space from a topological or Euclidean perspective. It consisted of three topological and five Euclidean drawings, each on a separate card, and several pieces of paper and a pencil or crayon (see Piaget and Inhelder, 1956, e.g., p. 52 ff.)
    c. *Horizontal and Vertical Axes (Tilted Bottles):* This task consisted of two one-quart bottles, one of which was half-full with colored water;

five sheets of paper with a bottle represented in different positions; and a crayon or pencil (see Piaget and Inhelder, 1956, e.g., p, 375 ff).

d. *Changing Perspectives - Mobile and Stationary:* This task was used to assess a child's ability to change perspectives. It consisted of a tower, a house, and a tree made of cardboard so that they could stand upright, and four pictures of four different perspectives (see Piaget and Inhelder, 1956, e.g. p. 210 ff).

3. **Reasoning Concept:** This concept was assessed by the use of two tasks.

a. *Conservation of Volume Solids (blocks):* This task served to assess the child's understanding of solid volumes and the conservation principle that a change in shape does not result in a change in volume. It consisted of 90 one-inch wooden blocks; and three pictures representing the models (see Flavell, 1970, e.g., p. 1,013 ff).

b. *Dissolution of Sugar Weight, Substance, and Volume:* This task consisted of two identical beakers or jars (250 ml) filled to the same level with warm water and several cubes or packets of sugar. It aimed at assessing a child's reasoning about dissolved substances (see Piaget and Inhelder, 1969, e.g., p. 112 ff).

4. **Concept of Quantity:** The concept of quantity was measured by using a task designed by Anderson and Cuneo (1978, p. 335 ff), which was based on the Height-Width Rule in children's judgments of quantity. It consisted of a modified graphic rating scale, which contained a series of 19 white circles, 0.50 centimeters in diameter and spaced 0.50 centimeters apart on a black wooden bar. A white circular schematic face, 8 centimeters in diameter, with a downward curving mouth (a "frowny" face), was mounted on the left end of the bar, and a similar face with an upward curving mouth (a "smiley" face) was mounted on the right end of the bar. The response bar and end-faces were mounted on a black wooden base; this response scale was placed 30 centimeters from the child.

Intellectual Tasks. Intelligence was assessed by using two intelligence tests: *(1) Wechsler's Intelligence Scale for Children (WISC) Subscale "Similarities" Test* as the verbal test for intelligence; and *(2) Raven Progressive Matrices Test* as the nonverbal test for intelligence. The experimenter had to use the regular (noncolored) Raven Progressive Matrices (RPM) Test, not the colored RPM, because the latter was not available.

Socioeconomic Status. Socioeconomic status (SES) was determined by using an index (Abdel Ghafar and Kashkoush, 1978), by which the following categories were measured: (1) mother's and father's occupational level; (2) mother's and father's educational level; and (3) family income.

RESULTS AND DISCUSSION

The results obtained from the present study gave support, in general, to the two hypotheses: (1) the rate of conceptual development in Sudanese schoolchildren was generally slower than that in their European counterparts; and (2) the rates of cognitive development varied from one area of conceptual development to another.

On the whole, the results indicated that the same stages of development could be found in Khartoum as in Geneva. A succession of the conservation of number, space, quantity, and reasoning concepts appeared in the data. The results are shown in Tables 2.1 and 2.2 and Figures 2.1 and 2.2, for children's performances on the cognitive tasks and for their intellectual performances.

The results of the present investigation were compared with the results of a previous study using Egyptian schoolchildren (Ahmed, 1981). The same methodology and tests were employed in the two studies. As may be seen in Table 2.1, Sudanese schoolchildren received higher conservation scores than their Egyptian counterparts on tasks involving the concept of quantity, while the Egyptian children received higher conservation scores than the Sudanese children on tasks involving space and reasoning concepts. Also in Table 2.2, the differences between the two populations on the intelligence tests became apparent. The differences were greater on the Raven Progressive Matrices Test than on the WISC "similarities" test.

On the whole, the obtained results indicated that cognitive abilities and intellectual performances steadily improved with increasing age. These results were in line with Piaget's postulates that children systematically developed their cognitive abilities, and that their mastering of these abilities increased with age. It was noted that the ordering of group differences progressively stabilized. The outcomes were clear-cut, but not unexpected. The three age groups were compared by performing one-way analyses of variance and Scheffe's multiple comparisons method. The results of these comparisons showed that the differences between the three age groups, with respect to all cognitive tasks and intelligence tests, were significant at 0.05, 0.01, and 0.001 levels, respectively. Analyzing the data, it was noted that the boys' scores were higher than those of the girls. However, these differences were not statistically significant. One might interpret those differential responses in terms of sex-stereotyped roles. Sudanese society, like other traditional societies, does not allow females to have the same opportunities as males have.

Examination of the data for all age groups on all cognitive tasks showed that those children who had high scores on the intelligence tests also tended to have high scores on cognitive tasks, especially on tasks involving the concept of space. In other words, the results revealed that the cognitive development in Sudanese schoolchildren was influenced by the factor of intelligence. Yet the father's educational level, the socioeconomic status, and sex differences had only weak and statistically nonsignificant effects upon cognitive development.

In summary, it can be said that the results of this preliminary research must remain incomplete, leaving important questions for further investigations. These questions would concern the differences between literate and illiterate children and adults on cognitive tasks; they would address the different types of socialization practices through which children are socialized with regard to nationality, ethnicity, and culture and the way in which children's backgrounds affect cognitive and intellectual development. In addition, the investigations could deal with the relationship between cognitive development and academic achievement and the standardization of testing tools. A massive task awaits developmental psychologists working in the Sudan in view of these questions. (Ahmed, 1984.)

REFERENCES

Abdel Gafar, A. M., and Kashkoush, I. (1978). "The Index of Social Position." *Journal of Faculty of Education, Ain Shmas University (Egypt), Vol. 1,* September, 1, 1-18 (in Arabic).

Ahmed, R. A. (1981). "Zur Ontogenese der Begriffskompetenz bei ägyptischen Kindern in Abhängigkeit von sozialen und kulturellen Entwicklungsbedingungen." Unpublished Dissertation, Karl Marx Universität, Leipzig, D.D.R. (German Democratic Republic).

Ahmed, R. A. (1984). "The Place of School Psychology in the Sudan at the Turn of the Century." *School Psychology International,* 5(1), 43-46.

Anderson, N .H., and Cueno, D. O. (1978). "The Height and Width Rule in Children: Judgment of Quantity." *Journal of Experimental Psychology: General, 107,* 335-378.

Flavell, J. H. (1970). "Concept Development." *In Carmichael's Manual of Child Psychology,* edited by P. H. Mussen, *Vol. 1,* 983-1059. New York, NY: John Wiley and Sons.

Ginsburg, H., and Opper, S. (1969). *Piaget's Theory of Intellectual Development: An Introduction.* Englewood Cliffs, NJ: Prentice-Hall, Inc.

Inhelder, B., and Matalon, B. (1970). "The Study of Problem Solving and Thinking." In *Handbook of Research Methods in Child Development,* edited by P. H. Mussen, 421-455. New Delhi, India: Wiley Eastern University.

Piaget, J., and Inhelder, B. (1956). *The Child's Conception of Space.* London, GB: Routledge and Kegan Paul.

Piaget, J., and Inhelder, B. (1969). *The Psychology of the Child.* New York, NY: Basic Books, Inc.

Piaget, J., and Szeminska, A. (1965). *Die Entwicklung des Zahlbegriffs beim Kinde*. Stuttgart, B.R.D. (Federal Republic of Germany): Klett.

Vernon, P. E. (1973). *Intelligence and Cultural Environment*. London, GB: Methuen and Co., Ltd.

AUTHOR NOTES

The author is very grateful to many Sudanese schoolchildren who agreed to be subjects in the present study, and also to the Sudanese staff in many primary schools in the city of Khartoum, Sudan, for their help. In addition, the author is very indebted to Dr. Al-Adel Abou-Allam, Department of Psychology, College of Arts, Kuwait University, Kuwait, for his helpful advice for the statistical analyses of the data of the present research.

Figure 2.1: Development of four concepts in Sudanese Children
(Conceptual performance is expressed by operational-
item percentages).

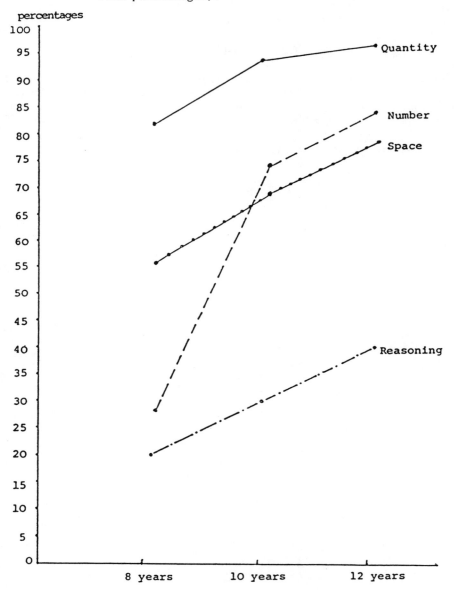

Figure 2.2: Intellectual Performance in Sudanese Children
          (Mean Scores)

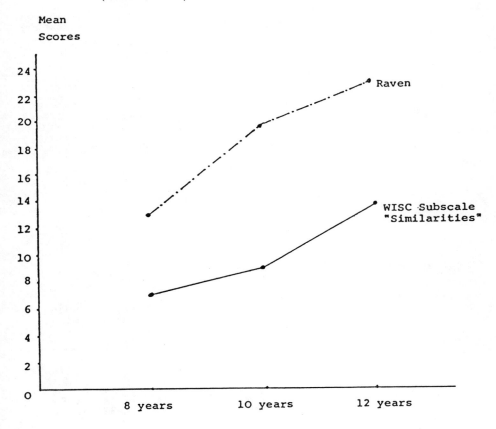

Table 2.1

Comparisions between Egyptian and Sudanese School Children
on Conceptual Performance Tasks

Age	Egypt-Sudan Number		Egypt-Sudan Space (in per cent)		Egypt-Sudan Quantity		Egypt-Sudan Reasoning	
6	06 n=32	- -	27 n=32	- -	38 n=32	- -	0 n=32	- -
8	43 n=32	28.7 n=48	65 n=32	55.6 n=48	62 n=32	82.3 n=48	44 n=32	20 n=48
10	73 n=33	74 n=50	84 n=33	68.1 n=50	87 n=33	94 n=50	58 n=33	30.4 n=50
12	83 n=32	84.9 n=48	85 n=32	78.1 n=48	92 n=32	96 n=48	59 n=32	41.2 n=48

Table 2.2

Comparisions between Egyptian and Sudanese School Children
on Intelligence Tests

Age	Egypt-Sudan Raven (in means)		Egypt-Sudan WISC/Simil.	
6	13.7 n=32	- -	7.24 n=32	- -
8	19.04 n=32	12.92 n=48	10.14 n=32	6.94 n=48
10	26.15 n=33	19.76 n=50	12.06 n=33	8.94 n=50
12	27.99 n=32	22.94 n=48	13.31 n=32	13.56 n=48

3

Application of a Teacher Rating Scale in the Assessment of Early and Later Dates of Development in Young Schoolchildren in Different Cultures

Peter F. Merenda

Sixteen years ago, after seven years of developmental research, the Rhode Island Pupil Identification Scale (RIPIS) was published and made available for operational use (Novack, Bonaventura, and Merenda, 1973). The scale was developed primarily for use by teachers, specialists, and other educators for the early identification of young children with learning problems. Its success as a valid instrument for such purposes is attested to, beyond its applications in the USA, by its adoptions and planned adoptions in a variety of other cultures. The early phases and stages of this cross-cultural research program, which was designed to produce unique forms adapted to different cultures, has been described by Merenda (1982). A complete report on the development of the Chinese form for use in Taiwan (Merenda, Guadagnoli, Miao, and Yu-Wen, 1984) and two reports on the standardization of the Italian form (Merenda, Guadagnoli, and Sparacino, 1983, 1985) have since appeared. Although the primary intent and initial uses of the scale both in the USA and in foreign countries have been to screen young children in normal classrooms at the kindergarten (grade K) level through grade 2, the RIPIS has utility for following and evaluating their scholastic development through those grade levels and beyond. In fact, the original standardization sample subjects of 1969-1970 were followed up four times from 1972 to 1983 when the youngest group of subjects who were in grade K in 1969-1970 graduated from high school.

The first of these follow-up studies was conducted by Bik (1972, 1974) when the original subjects in the standardization sample were still in the early grades. The latter studies were conducted by Bonaventura (1978, 1983) when the subjects were in the last grades in middle school and then close to graduation from high school. The findings were consistent. Students who were identified as possessing learning difficulties initially in grades K, 1 and 2 and who had received no intervention treatments tended, in general, to carry those problems with them throughout their academic history through grade 12. There were, of course, exceptions. Some children who did not receive interventions went on to become successful high school students and some went on to college. However, there were those, in the majority, whose learning problems were identified early and were not ameliorated, or apparently did not vanish for other reasons. For them, the unanswered question remains: had proper and successful intervention techniques been applied early, would their educational progress have been much more favorable than it was? It is the conviction of this author and his colleagues, both domestic and foreign, that it certainly would have been.

Results also revealed that the validities of the scale initially established in terms of academic performance and standardized achievement criteria were upheld at both the middle school and high school levels. Also early pilot studies conducted by the authors prior to the publication and release of the scale, in which monthly progress of the subjects was charted throughout the entire academic year, revealed the following: (1) children in special schools for the seriously disabled, that is, children suffering from organic damage or developmental arrest of the brain or nervous system, or from multiple handicaps, continuously showed elevated profiles -- which are evidence of serious learning problems and difficulties; and (2) many children in normal classrooms, especially the younger ones (ages 4-5 years) who showed elevated profiles in the early months of the academic year, suddenly began to show lowered or even low profiles in the last few months. This latter finding is an indication that some apparent learning problems in young schoolchildren have their source simply or primarily in sheer physiological maturation and developmental factors.

DESCRIPTION OF THE SCALE

Before proceeding further, it is necessary to briefly describe the basic and salient features of the scale.

The RIPIS comprises two parts, or clusters of items. The 21 items in Part I of the scale relate to observable classroom behavior. Part II consists of 19 items relating essentially to written work produced by pupils as part of their classroom work. The items reflect types of learning problems or behaviors that are typical of children who are referred for remedial help or for special placement (see Appendix).

Typical item statements for Part I are:

Has difficulty cutting.

Gives appearance of being tense.

Tends to be discouraged.

Typical item statements for Part II are:

Mirrors and/or reverses letters, numbers, words, or other forms in copying.

Runs words or parts of words together when visual stimulation is provided.

Makes omissions, substitutions, or reversals of letters, numbers, and/or words in reading.

Each of 40 items are evaluated according to a 5-point Likert-type scale ranging from 1 point (never) to 5 points (always), (Merenda, 1982, p. 126).

Reference has been made to elevated and low profiles. These can perhaps be best described by reproducing a page from the RIPIS Manual (see Figure 3.1).

REVIEW OF ORIGINAL AND CROSS-CULTURAL RESULTS

A. Factorial Structure

The initial scale and all subsequent versions developed to date for adaptations to foreign cultures have been factor analyzed. The basic data for these analyses have been those yielded by the administration of experimental forms to large representative samples drawn from those cultures. These experimental forms were developed by both translating the items into the appropriate foreign language and modifying, on the basis of a priori judgments, certain items to adapt to the respective cultures. There is a dual purpose to these replications: (1) to test the hypothesis of factorial invariance; and (2) to modify the scoring and norming of the scale wherever deemed necessary from the replicated factor analysis results.

Inspection of the data revealed that, with the exception of Part II of the Italian version of the RIPIS, which yielded three components, all forms possess a factorial structure composed of nine components: five for Part I and four for Part II. These structures account for between two-thirds and three-fourths of the total variance, and the item clusters are essentially the same across the three cultures. Such results are typically obtained with other forms of the RIPIS, notably the Persian form that was developed for use in Iran and the French form that was developed for use in Haiti, but each research project was suspended due to politics.

It should be noted that for both the North American (USA) and Chinese (Taiwan) forms of the RIPIS, the factor structure is based on orthogonally rotates axes (Varimax), whereas that for the Italian form is based on oblique transformations (Direct oblimin). The reason for this is that the initial reference axes yielded by the Principal Component Analyses for the former were close to being orthogonal, whereas those for the latter were definitely oblique (separated by acute angles). The tables reporting the intercorrelations of the paired components may be found elsewhere (Merenda, Guadagnoli, and Sparacino, 1983).

B.   Internal Consistency and Reliability

For the three-cross-cultural forms, these psychometric properties have been reported by Merenda, Bonaventura, and Novack (1977); D'Amico, Merenda, and Sparacino (1982), in Italian; and Merenda, Guadagnoli, Miao, and Yu-Wen (1984). The internal consistency coefficients are all Cronbach Alphas and they are all consistently high. The coefficients range in the .80s and .90s essentially for subscales, and in the low to upper .90s for total scale scores, both for Part I and Part II.

Reliability has been established for these forms through test-retest procedures, with time interval set at approximately five months between observations. Both linear correlational methods (for total scores) and canonical correlation analyses (for subscale scores) have been applied to the data. Pearson product-moment correlation coefficients are as low as .53 for eighth-month intervals, but as high as .89 for one-month intervals. Redundancy analyses performed on canonical correlational data indicate that the test-retest reliabilities of the profiles described earlier in this paper are in the middle .70s for both Part I and Part II subscales. Most of these results are discussed and summarized in the references cited above with the addition of Novack, Bonaventura, and Merenda (1973).

C.   Validities of the RIPIS

Before a scale or other psychological assessment/measurement instrument or technique is deemed ready for operational use, it must, over and above possessing other psychometric properties, have demonstrated evidence of validities against several pertinent criteria. For the fully operational forms (North American, Chinese, and Italian) this has been done and the results have been reported previously (Novack, Bonaventura, and Merenda, 1973; Merenda, Miao, Guadagnoli, and Yu-Wen, 1984; Merenda, Guadagnoli, and Sparacino, 1985). (Note that the validities of the Chinese form are reported by Merenda, Miao, Guadagnoli, and Yu-Wen, 1984, which was published under a publication grant awarded to Professor Merenda. A copy of this report may be obtained by interested readers by requesting it from the author.) The validities are essentially concurrent and predictive validities. The criteria are scores on aptitude and achievement tests, pupil educational progress and educational outcomes, and independent teacher ratings.

Validity coefficients have ranged from $r = .43$ to $r = .94$. Other validating statistics have been found to be statistically significant at $p = .001$ and to possess substantial power. Hence, *practical* as well as statistical significance has been achieved across these three cultures in terms of the validating criteria. These results have been reported in the three references cited above.

PROJECTIONS FOR FUTURE CROSS-CULTURAL RESEARCH

To review what has already been said: research with the RIPIS in the USA has involved the application of the scale both for the early identification of young schoolchildren with learning problems and for the assessment of physiological and psychological development of these children as they progress through the educational process. In this way, the value of the scale can be recognized as an initial screening device on the one hand, and on the other hand, as a means for evaluating the effects of intervention techniques directed toward amelioration of the problems and/or distinguishing between sources of problems that involve physical maturation rates and levels, and those that relate to fundamental inherent factors. That this dual purpose of research programs has not yet been realized in the cross-cultural studies involving foreign language/culture forms of the RIPIS is understandable. The magnitude of the effort required to produce unique forms of the scale for use in different cultures has been so great that attention has been focused exclusively on the development of well-standardized reliable and valid scales to be applied within individual cultures for the early detection only of learning problems in young children in normal classrooms. However, now at least two fully operational foreign language/culture forms exist after many years of developmental research: Italian (1975-1982) and Chinese (1979-1983). As these become applied in their respective cultures in the detection and diagnosis of learning problems, plans can be formulated for both the application of intervention techniques designed to ameliorate the problems and the follow-up in successive later grades of these children. These two objectives can best be accomplished by the Chinese form used operationally in Taiwan, because of the way in which that form was developed and standardized. Unlike all of the other forms of the RIPIS, the Chinese form is administered in an explicit structured format. The classroom teacher presents the activities involved in each of the 21 items of Part I to the pupils on an individual basis, and either presents or evaluates the academic tasks required in the 19 items of Part II. In the use of the other forms of the RIPIS, the teachers' periodic ratings are essentially impressionistic.

In light of the foregoing points, Taiwan is considered the ideal setting for initiating a program, outside the USA, for installing the operational use of the scale on a longitudinal basis. Implementation would involve the full three phases: (1) identification of children with learning problems; (2) intervention toward amelioration of those problems; and (3) follow-up in later grades for the detection of persistence of those problems. Also, as new cross-cultural research studies are initiated in the future, attempts will be made to incorporate all three phases in the research plan. At the moment, those which appear to present the greatest likelihood of this happening are the ones being planned in Ireland and Japan. A third likely prospect appears to be the Dutch form, which is in the process of being standardized and validated in The Netherlands during the fall of 1986. From September to October, 1986, the author traveled abroad to collaborate, on-site, in Dublin and The Hague, in research for the development of the Irish and Dutch forms. Research on the Japanese form will likely follow later in this decade.

Readers who are interested in the possibility of entering into collaborative cross-cultural research with the RIPIS are encouraged to contact the author of this chapter. A listing of foreign collaborators until 1982 may be found in Merenda (1982). This listing is updated to 1986 in the following section.

Principal Collaborators in Cross-Cultural Research on RIPIS, by Country

- ▶ **Brazil:** Bettina Katzenstein Schoenfeldt, Head, Psychological Institutes, Julio de Mesquita Filho University, São Paulo.
- ▶ **Denmark:** K. Spelling, Dansmarks Laererhojskole, Copenhagen.
- ▶ **Great Britain:** Janice M. Fields and Seamus Heggarty, National Foundation for Educational Research in England and Wales, Windsor, England.
- ▶ **Haiti:** Madeline Bourrelly Laroche, Consulting School Psychologist, Port-au-Prince.
- ▶ **Iran:** Reza Shapurian, Department of Psychology, Shiraz University, Shiraz.
- ▶ **Ireland:** Patricia Fontes and Peter Archer, Educational Research Center, St. Patrick's College, Dublin.
- ▶ **Israel:** Chanan Rapaport, Director, The Henrietta Szold Institute, The National Institute for Research in the Behavioral Sciences, Jerusalem.
- ▶ **Italy:** Guido D'Amico, Didactic Director, Polesine School District; and Rosalia Russello Sparacino, Palermo, Sicily.
- ▶ **Japan:** Seisoh Sulkemune, College of Education, University of Hiroshima.
- ▶ **The Netherlands:** Leny Tabak, Haags Centrum voor Onderwijsbegeleiding, The Hague.
- ▶ **Poland:** Jozef Rembowski, Director, Institute of Psychology, University of Gdaṅsk; and Boleslaw Homowski, Director, Institute of Psychology, Adam Mickiewicz University, Poznan.
- ▶ **Taiwan:** Emily S. C. Miao, Dean of Students, Chinese Culture University, Taipei.
- ▶ **Turkey:** Gunduz Vassaf, Bogazici University, Instanbul, Turkey.

REFERENCES

Bik, E. L. (1972). "Learning Disabilities: A Rose by any other Name?" Mimeographed. Kingston, RI: University of Rhode Island.

Bik, E. L. (1974). "Degree and Nature of Relationships among Readiness, Aptitude and Achievement Measures." Unpublished Ph.D. Research Competency Report, University of Rhode Island, Kingston, RI.

Bonaventura, E. (1978). "A Longitudinal Study of the Differential Prediction by the Rhode Island Pupil Identification Scale of Upper Grade Achievement." Unpublished doctoral dissertation, University of Connecticut, Storrs, CT.

Bonaventura, E. (1983). "Report of Sabbatical Leave Research Project, 1982-1983 Academic Year." Mimeographed. Providence, RI: Rhode Island College.

D'Amico, G., Merenda, P. F., and Sparacino, R. R. (1982). *Rhode Island Pupil Identification Scale (RIPIS)*. Contributi. Palermo, Sicily: Universita degli Studi di Palermo, 133-164.

Merenda, P. F. (1982). "The Rhode Island Pupil Identification Scale (RIPIS) in Cross-Cultural Perspective." In *Cross-Cultural Research at Issue*, edited by L. L. Adler, New York: Academic Press. Ch. 10, 125-136.

Merenda, P. F., Bonaventura, E., and Novack, H. S. (1977). "An Intensive Study of the Reliability of Rhode Island Pupil Identification Scale." *Psychology in the Schools*, *14*, 282-289.

Merenda, P. F., Guadagnoli, E., Miao, E., and Yu-Wen, H. (1984). *The Chinese Form of the Rhode Island Pupil Identification Scale: Standardization and Validation*. Providence, RI: AVA Publications.

Merenda, P. F., Guadagnoli, E., and Sparacino, R. R. (1983). "Standardization of the Italian Form of the Rhode Island Pupil Identification Scale." *School Psychology International*, *4*, 41-46.

Merenda, P. F., Guadagnoli, E., and Sparacino, R. R. (1985). "Validation of the Italian Form of the Rhode Island Pupil Identification Scale." *School Psychology International*, *6*, 244-250.

Novack, H. S., Bonaventura, E., and Merenda, P. F. (1972). *Manual for the Rhode Island Pupil Identification Scale*. Providence, RI: RIPIS.

Novack, H. S., Bonaventura, E., and Merenda, P. F. (1973). "A Scale for the Early Detection of Children with Learning Problems." *Exceptional Children*, *40*, 98-104.

Part Scoring of the RIPIS

For scoring purposes the order of the factors yielded by the factor analysis has been changed.

Part I

Scoring of Part I is accomplished by accumulating the item scale values (omits are assigned the scale value of 1.). The items which are scored within each factor in Part I are:

Body Perception (score range: 2 - 10)

No. 3 Bumps into objects

No. 4 Trips over self

Sensory-motor Coordination (score range 6 - 30)

No. 1 Difficulty cutting

No. 2 Difficulty pasting

No. 5 Difficulty catching a ball

No. 6 Difficulty jumping rope

No. 7 Difficulty tying shoes

No. 8 Difficulty buttoning buttons

Attention (score range: 3 - 15)

No. 9 Difficulty sitting still

No. 10 Difficulty standing still

No. 11 Has short attention span

Self-Concept (score range: 6 - 30)

No. 12 Gives appearance of being tense

No. 15 Cries

No. 16 Fails to take reprimands well

No. 18 Tends to be discouraged

No. 19 Tends to give up

No. 20 Tends to avoid group activity

Memory for Events (score range: 5 - 25)

No. 11 Has short attention span

No. 13 Difficulty remembering what is seen

No. 14 Difficulty remembering what is shown

No. 17 Difficulty understanding directions

No. 21 Difficulty completing assignments in allotted time

Part II

Scoring for Part II is identical to that for Part I except that there are four subscales instead of five. The items which are scored within each factor of Part II are:

Memory for Reproduction of Symbols

(score range: 6 - 30)

No. 22 Difficulty staying within lines

No. 23 Work varies in quality

No. 24 Poor handwriting on papers

No. 25 Erasures on papers

No. 26 Papers are dirty

No. 27 Difficulty writing within lines

Directional or Positional Constancy

(score range: 3 - 15)

No. 28 Starts writing in middle of paper

No. 29 Mirrors/reverses letters, number in copying

No. 30 Mirrors/reverses letters, numbers, words when no visual stimulation is provided

Spatial and Sequential Arrangements of Letters and Symbols

(score range: 5 - 25)

No. 31 Runs words together in copying

No. 32 Runs words together when no visual stimulation is provided

No. 33 Omits or substitutes letters, words, numbers in copying

No. 35 Omits or substitutes letters, words, numbers when no visual stimulation is provided

No. 40 Omits or substitutes or reverses letters, numbers, words in reading

Memory for Symbols for Cognitive Operations

(score range: 5 - 25)

No. 34 Difficulty with names of letters and/or numbers

No. 36 Difficulty completing written work in time allotted

No. 37 Difficulty grasping number concepts

No. 38 Difficulty arranging numbers vertically

No. 39 Difficulty with addition and subtraction

Profiling the RIPIS

Norms have been established for each of the sub-scales of Part I and Part II, based on the original standardization sample. The Sub-scale distributions were normalized and the raw scores were transmuted to T-scores. These standard score distributions permit the construction of a profile on each of the two parts of the RIPIS for each child which is observed. An example of a completed profile card follows:

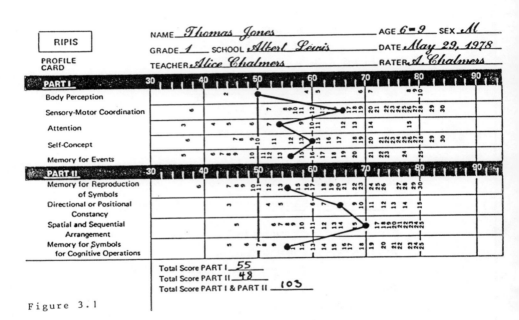

Figure 3.1

There are several points to consider in the interpretation of these two profiles:

(1) Since the distributions have been normalized, the standard scores on the scale (30-90) will yield directly percentiles taken from a table of areas under the normal curve for normal deviates, z. (T = 50 + 10z). For example, in the example above, the subscale, Sensory-Motor Coordination, Part I, placed the individual at the 95th percentile in that problem area (T = 66, z = +1.6).

(2) All but one subscale (Body Perception, Part I) places the individual above average in problem areas (Mean T = 50).

(3) The Part I profile definitely suggests that the individual's major problem areas which might be creating learning problems are low Sensory-Motor Coordination and a poorly-developed or negative self-concept. The Part II profile suggests that the learning problems likely involve Directional and Positional Constancy and Spatial and Sequential Arrangement.

(4) Once the teacher has isolated these facts, he/she is placed in a much better position both to perform further diagnosis and/or to more properly and effectively apply intervention techniques.

36

4

The Cultural Difference Model and Applied Behavior Analysis in the Design of Early Childhood Intervention

Junko Tanaka-Matsumi

In the 1960s, the American public began to pay special attention to the education of minority children in the United States. President Johnson initiated the "War on Poverty" with the purpose of eradicating inequity in children's educational opportunities. Within this political and social climate, early intervention programs such as Project Head Start were initiated in the summer of 1965, with over half a million preschool children as the target population (Zigler and Berman, 1983). These children came from economically deprived homes and frequently were members of ethnic minority groups. It was necessary to investigate effective means of educating these children by using the natural environment as laboratories for research (Campbell, 1969). The purpose of this presentation is to examine the role of the cultural context in developing educational programs for children.

MODELS OF EARLY INTERVENTION

Two competing models of educating "underachieving" minority children have influenced the design of specific program. The first model was the deficit model. According to the deficit model, the culture of the lower socioeconomic classes and minority ethnic groups was assumed to be inferior to that of the white middle class (see, e.g., Jensen, 1969). Achievement was measured in terms of the values associated with the middle-class socioeconomic status (SES). Child development was not viewed in its cultural context, but rather was said to be determined largely by subject variables, such as genetic background, SES, and age. In short, proponents of the deficit model assumed that the culture of lower SES is inferior to that of the white middle class (Zigler and Berman, 1983).

The cultural difference model is an alternative model. Proponents of this model emphasized the importance of accommodating the child's social and cultural context in the design of educational programs by measuring achievement in terms of social competence, rather than IQ per se, and by involving parents for the purpose of bridging the home environment and the school environment (Zigler and Trickett, 1978). The difference model is similar to the "conflict model" (Bond, 1982). These models are similar in that they "assume that the comparatively poor educational performance of minority students results from a learning history which is in direct conflict with effective instruction" (Bond, 1982, p. 108).

The cultural difference model calls for an investigation of the functional relationship between child development and cultural and institutional contexts. The idea that development occurs in the cultural context is well represented in the works of Bronfenbrenner (1979), Kessen (1979), Laboratory of Comparative Human Cognition (1979), and Rogoff, Gauvain, and Ellis (1983). The classroom teaching environment became one of the most important contexts to be considered in developing a program for "underachieving" children. Rather than blaming the child, the difference model supports a cultural relativistic approach that views the child as a product of social construction (Kessen, 1979). It gives more responsibility to the people in charge of developing intervention programs.

EDUCATION AS SOCIAL INFLUENCE

Learning occurs in context (Cole, Gay, Glick, and Sharp, 1971). When context resembles that of the child's natural environment, or when specific efforts are made to bring the ecologically relevant material to the learning situation, effects of schooling may be maximized (Rogoff, 1981). In the late 1960s, in the developing climate of education for the children of the economically disadvantaged, behavioral psychologists began to conduct functional analyses of children's behaviors in the specific classroom environment and demonstrated the importance of training teachers in the use of contingent reinforcement of desirable classroom behaviors (e.g., Hall, Panyan, Rabin, and Broden, 1968; O'Leary and O'Leary, 1972). Teachers became a critical variable in the educational environment of the child and began contributing to the cultural context of education by reinforcing specific behaviors (Buckley and Walker, 1970). Through interaction with the teacher, the child acquired specific learning skills in the classroom; thus the teacher is responsible for arranging effective conditions for learning. Moreover, it is necessary to specify methods to achieve "intended consequences" of educating children, particularly the roles of teachers in achieving the goal (Sarason, 1971). Enhancing the educational achievement of culturally different children must start with teacher training (Jones, 1982).

THE KAMEHAMEHA EARLY EDUCATIONAL PROGRAM (KEEP): TRAINING THE TEACHERS OF HAWAIIAN CHILDREN

The Kamehameha Early Education Program is a research and development program whose purpose is the development, demonstration, and dissemination of methods for improving education of Hawaiian and part-Hawaiian children. There are about 35,000 Hawaiian and part-Hawaiian children in the public schools in the state of Hawaii, and KEEP's mission is to disseminate innovative educational information to the public schools. This project is presented here to illustrate the relationship between culture-specific variables of education and more generalizable principles of learning, both of which comprise an integral part of this educational project. While KEEP has conducted research on various aspects of education, such as the curriculum, this paper focuses on one area of their research, namely, teacher training.

A number of anthropological and psychological studies reported that Hawaiian children are labeled "underachievers," noted for problems of low motivation, behavior management in class, and poor academic performance (MacDonald, 1971). The majority of these Hawaiian and part-Hawaiian children were educated in regular public schools whose structure and teaching style closely resemble those of "formal institutional schooling" of the U.S. Mainland (Jordan and Tharp, 1979). Many of the public schoolteachers in Hawaii are Japanese Americans who have been successful in educating Japanese, Caucasian, and Chinese-American students, but not Hawaiian-American children. Jordan and Tharp (1979) reported that by the time Hawaiian children are in the fourth grade in the public school, they score in the first and lowest stanine of national norms on the Stanford Achievement Test. Similarly, their mean reading achievement score is at about the twenty-seventh percentile on the Gates-MacGinite Test of Reading Achievement. Hawaiian children were not succeeding in the public schools. The researchers and educators at KEEP challenged this situation and embarked on a massive research endeavor to develop a more effective educational environment by operating a demonstration school (Tharp and Gallimore, 1975). The first issue to be addressed was the problem of motivation, namely, how to get the children to work.

When formal schooling is viewed as an influence process in which professional teachers interact with their students in the classroom to impart information (Krasner and Ullmann, 1973), it is necessary to analyze the teaching behavior of the teachers. The triadic model (Tharp, 1975; Tharp and Wetzel, 1969) of teacher training consists of consultants, who train the teachers, trainee teachers, who teach in the classroom, and children. It incorporates the influence of mediators (teachers) who have a continuing relationship with the child. The first goal of KEEP was to develop a system to increase the incentive value of school activities. Increasing motivation of "underachieving" minority students has been a common goal regardless of cultural group, because failure experiences have been found to lead to low motivation for future academic endeavors (Zigler and Trickett, 1978). Success experiences are necessary for the young Hawaiian child, and such experiences must be programmed by training the teachers to attend to the positive acts rather than negative results, such as failure. The KEEP has emphasized positive teacher acts in the classroom (praise, patting, or hugging), and making these acts contingent upon specific and desirable student behaviors (Tanaka-Matsumi and Tharp, 1977).

Training of the KEEP teachers was based on the step-by-step development of the teacher's ability to attend to his/her own behavior in the classroom with the goal of learning that the rate of desirable classroom behaviors can be increased by giving contingent positive praise. A variety of techniques were employed to train the teachers. Instruction, modeling of desirable teacher behaviors, videotape performance feedback, direct coaching in the classroom by the teacher trainers, and goal setting were some of the methods used to train the teachers in the use of contingent praise for appropriate classroom behaviors. Empirical program evaluations have demonstrated the combined effectiveness of these methods (Speidel and Tharp, 1978). In general, there were large individual differences in the responses of the trainee teachers to the training; some teachers increased their rate of praise significantly more than other teachers in training (Tanaka-Matsumi and Tharp, 1977). There was also a significant effect of the increased teacher praise rate on the classroom behavior of the Hawaiian children. These children engaged in on-task behavior between 85 and 96 percent of the time sampled daily in the classroom through a one-way screen (Tanaka-Matsumi, 1976). Jordan and Tharp (1979) reported that the KEEP teachers use up to five times more praise than comparison public school teachers and employ little punishment. Rates of praise are high in kindergarten and gradually become low as the grades go up.

The KEEP demonstration project shows that by designing a classroom context rich in success experiences, Hawaiian children do show motivation to attend to the academic material being taught, disproving the public schoolteachers' belief that the children are being "lazy." The results also demonstrated the generality of the effectiveness of contingent reinforcement, modeling, behavioral rehearsal, and feedback. Most of these techniques used to influence the behavior of other people can be found in other cultures as well, though they may be called by different names (Frank, 1973; Torrey, 1972). These methods are not specific to a particular culture and can be used effectively to influence the behavior of the culturally different individuals so long as values associated with specific target behaviors are salient to the cultural group (Tanaka-Matsumi and Higginbotham, in press).

CULTURAL VARIATIONS IN APPLIED BEHAVIOR ANALYSIS

Although principles of learning, such as reinforcement and modeling, are said to have cross-cultural validity (Bandura, 1969; Skinner, 1971; Staats, 1975), one must take into account cultural contextual factors and learning history of the child in applying such principles to education. The Hawaiian educational experience illustrates the need for a careful assessment of the socialization practices of the Hawaiian-American people.

Ethnographic and experimental psychological studies amply point out that the Hawaiian culture values affiliation and group solidarity rather than individual achievement. For example, MacDonald (1971) conducted extensive classroom observations and found that time spent working for academic rewards increased when Hawaiian-American students were allowed to work as members of teams. In contrast to Anglo-American students, the Hawaiian-American students showed a greater increase in time spent working if the reward was to be shared by the group rather than given to individuals. Kubany and Slogett (1971) obtained a significant increase in the amount of time spent working on a standardized arithmetic test when they provided tangible reinforcement contingent upon correct response. These experimental results are quite consistent with the ethnographic reports of the Hawaiian people. Group contingency may be more culturally salient than individual contingency within the Hawaiian culture.

Gallimore (1974) investigated the question of delay of gratification in Hawaiian high school students as compared with that of Japanese-American students in Hawaii. When the students were each asked, "if someone gave you $1,500, what would you do with it?," the Hawaiian students were more inclined toward the immediate use of the money than the Japanese American students. However, the Hawaiian students more often chose to use the money to help family members, while the Japanese chose to spend the money for education more frequently. Use for personal expenditure was comparable between the two groups, indicating, according to Gallimore (1974), that "Hawaiians are no more likely to seek immediate personal pleasure or 'impulse gratification' than are the Japanese." In a culture that values affiliation and sibling caretaking (Gallimore, Boggs, and Jordan, 1974), windfall receipts that reinforce group membership and social solidarity might be more relevant and appropriate instances of deferred gratification. These differences may also reflect the differences in values attached to education in that Japanese Americans regard education as very important, and they have had a reinforcing history of educational achievement in Hawaii. The Hawaiian Americans as a group have experienced little success in educational achievement. Thus, although the concept of delay of gratification is applicable to the Hawaiian culture, the method of investigation should take into account salient features of the culture of the subjects.

Culturally accommodated schooling for Hawaiian children should emphasize contingent positive consequences for study behavior, which increases motivation, but that consequences would better be arranged for the group than the individual. This would serve to strengthen culturally desired group solidarity and affiliation. Educational instructions should encourage peer interactions and cooperation, and the classroom structure should be planned in such a way to facilitate peer interaction and group performance.

By accommodating these cultural factors unique to the Hawaiian-American culture effects of an educational program based on the cultural difference model can be expected to increase.

EARLY INTERVENTION: TRAINING PARENTS TO ENHANCE EFFECTS OF SCHOOLING

One major question that has plagued the investigators of early intervention is how to maintain the effects of training. Initially, when Project Head Start was evaluated, the Head Start children were found to be significantly better prepared for school than the control children. These early gains were, however, not maintained six to eight months after Head Start children had been placed in normal public schools (Wolff and Stein, 1967). The Westinghouse report pronounced that Head Start was a failure (Zigler and Berman, 1983). These reports do not necessarily weaken the cultural difference model, but they demonstrate clearly that little long-term gains could be evidenced unless the high quality educational environment was maintained. Bronfenbrenner (1974) emphasized the need for involvement of parents in the home as well as in the schools, and the need for continued implementation of programs beyond preschool.

The literature on applied behavior analyses of children sheds some light on the problem of "fade out." Stokes and Baer (1977) reviewed that unless generalization is actively *programmed*, one cannot expect that children continue to exhibit learned behaviors, such as appropriate classroom behavior, in a different situation. Thus theoretically, it is necessary to train multiple "teachers" in the child's natural environment. The results of the Milwaukee Project (Heber and Garber, 1975) showed that the mothers who received training in homemaking, child rearing, and remedial education, significantly changed the manner in which they interacted with their children. They also changed their self-concept and self-confidence to be more positive. The changes were also reflected in the experimental children's performance. On problem-solving tasks, they performed significantly better than the control children, as well as scoring significantly higher on the Stanford-Binet Intelligence Scale. Coleman's report (1966) also found that an increase in the mother's sense of control in life related positively to the child's academic achievement. These examples suggest that the home environment provides informal schooling for the child to acquire and practice learned skills. Cross-cultural research on school readiness showed that the differences in the maternal behavior in children's problem solving in Japan and the United States reflected the respective culture's schooling policies (Hess, et al., 1986). These authors observed that the maternal behavior during the children's preschool years is correlated not only with behaviors indicative of school readiness, but also with school-related performance several years later.

Taken together, the success of early education depends on the extent to which the program incorporates culturally salient features of the child's ecological environment by training multiple "teachers," including the parents

(Weinberg, 1979). Formal and informal schooling should be regarded as a continuum, and efforts should be made to design a program of education that increases chances for success, particularly for children of underachieving cultures.

CONCLUSION

The cultural difference model of education and principles of applied behavior analyses are compatible. In both models, the observation of children in their cultural context is emphasized and education is regarded as the learning of various skills through the influence of teachers to increase social competence. Rather than isolating children from their natural environment and looking for deficits to explain causes of "underachievement," educators should analyze conditions under which children's culturally appropriate and desirable behaviors can be increased. The cultural difference model helps to generate information unique to the culture of the child, so that universal techniques of social influence may be practiced effectively within appropriate contexts.

REFERENCES

Bond, L. (1982). "The IQ Controversy and Academic Performance." *Behavior Modification in Black Populations*, edited by S. M. Turner and R. T. Jones, 95-120. New York: Plenum Press.

Bandura, A. (1969). *Principles of Behavior Modification*. New York: Holt, Rinehart, and Winston.

Bronfenbrenner, U. (1974). "Is Early Intervention Effective?" *Teachers College Record*. 76, 279-303.

Bronfenbrenner, U. (1979). *The Ecology of Human Development*. Cambridge, MA: Harvard University Press.

Buckley, N. K., and Walker, H. M. (1970). *Modifying Classroom Behavior: A Manual of Procedure for Classroom Teachers*. Champaign, IL: Research Press.

Campbell, D. T. (1969). "Reforms as Experiments." *American Psychologist*, 24, 409-429.

Cole, M., Gay J., Glick, J. A., and Sharp, D. W. (1971). *The Cultural Context of Learning and Thinking*. New York: Basic Books.

Coleman, J. S. (1966). *Equality of Educational Opportunity*. Washington, DC: U.S. Department of Health, Education, and Welfare, Office of Education.

Frank, J. C. (1973). *Persuasion and Healing*. 2nd ed., New York: Schoken Books.

Gallimore, R. (1974). "Affiliation Motivation and Hawaiian-American Achievement." *Journal of Cross-Cultural Psychology, 5*, 481-492.

Gallimore, R., Boggs, S., and Jordan, C. (1974). *Culture, Behavior, and Education: A Study of Hawaiian Americans*. Beverly Hills, CA: Sage Publications.

Hall, R. V., Panyan, M., Rabin, D., and Broden, M. (1968). "Instructing Beginning Teachers in Reinforcement Procedures which Improve Classroom Control." *Journal of Applied Behavior Analysis, 1*, 315-322.

Heber, R., and Garber, H. (1975). "The Milwaukee Project: A Study of the Use of Family Intervention to Prevent Cultural-Familial Retardation." In *Exceptional Infant, Vol. 3: Assessment and Intervention*. New York: Brunner/Mazel.

Hess, R., DeVitt, T., Azuma, H., Kashiwagi, K., Nagano, S., Miyake, K., Dickson, W. P., Price, G., and Hatano, G. (1986). "Family Influences on School readiness and Achievement in Japan and the United States: An Overview of a Longitudinal Study." In *Child Development and Education in Japan*, edited by H. Stevenson, H. Azuma, and K. Hakuta, 147-166. New York: W. H. Freeman.

Jensen, A. R. (1969). "How Much Can We Boost IQ and Scholastic Achievement?" *Harvard Educational Review, 31*, 1-123.

Jones, R. T. (1982). "Academic Improvement through Behavioral Modification." In *Behavior Modification in Black Populations*, edited by S. M. Turner and R. T. Jones, 121-149. New York: Plenum Press.

Jordan, C., and Tharp, R. G. (1979). "Culture and Education." *Perspectives on Cross-Cultural Psychology*, edited by A. J. Marsella, R. G. Tharp, and T. J. Cibrowski, 265-285. New York: Academic Press.

Kessen, W. (1979). "The American Child and Other Cultural Inventions." *American Psychologist, 34*, 815-820.

Krasner, L., and Ullmann, L. P. (1973). *Behavior Influence and Personality: The Social Matrix of Human Action*. New York: Holt, Rinehart, and Winston.

Kubany, E. S., and Slogett, B. B. (1971). "The Role of Motivation in Test Performance and Remediation." *Journal of Learning Disabilities, 4,* 426-429.

Laboratory of Comparative Human Cognition (1979). "Cross-Cultural Psychology's Challenges to our ideas of Child and Development." *American Psychologist, 34,* 827-833.

MacDonald, W. S. (1971). *Battles in the Classroom.* Scranton, PA: INTEXT Educational Publishers.

O'Leary, D. K., and O'Leary, S. G., (1972). *Classroom Management.* New York: Pergamon Press.

Rogoff, B., (1981). "Schooling and Development of Cognitive Skills." In *Handbook of Cross-Cultural Psychology, Vol. 4: Developmental Psychology,* edited by H. C. Triandis and A. Heron, 233-294. Boston: Allyn and Bacon.

Rogoff, B., Gauvain, M., and Ellis, S. (1983). "Development Viewed in its Cultural Context." In *Developmental Psychology: An Advanced Textbook,* edited by M. H. Bornstein and M. E. Lamb, 533-571. Hillsdale, NJ: Lawrence Earlbaum.

Sarason, S. B. (1971). *The Culture of the School and the Problem of Change.* Boston: Allyn and Bacon.

Skinner, B. F. (1971). *Beyond Freedom and Dignity.* New York: Bantam/-Vintage Books.

Speidel, G. E., and Tharp, R. G. (1978). "Teacher Training Workshop Strategy: Instructions, Discrimination Training, Modeling, Guided Practice, and Videotape Feedback." *Behavior Therapy, 9,* 735-739.

Staats, A. W. (1975). *Social Behaviorism.* Homewood, IL: Dorsey Press.

Stokes, T. F., and Baer, D. M. (1977). "An Implicit Technology of Generalization." *Journal of Applied Behavior Analysis, 10,* 349-367.

Tanaka-Matsumi, J. (1976). "KEEP Consultation Research Strategies: 1971-1975." *Technical Report No. 58.* Honolulu: The Kamehameha Schools. The Kamehameha Early Education Program.

Tanaka-Matsumi, J., and Higginbotham, H. N. (in press). "Behavioral approaches to Cross-Cultural Counseling." In *Counseling across Cultures,* edited by P. P. Pedersen, J. G. Draguns, W. J. Lonner, and J. E. Trimble, 3rd ed. Honolulu: University Press of Hawaii.

Tanaka-Matsumi, J., and Tharp, R. G. (1977). "Teaching the Teachers of Hawaiian Children: Training and Consultation Strategies." *Topics in Culture Learning*, 5, 92-106.

Tharp, R. G. (1975). "The Triadic Model of Consultation: Current Considerations." In *Psychological Consultation: Helping teachers Meet Special Needs*, edited by C. A. Parker, Minneapolis, MN. Minnesota University Leadership Training Institute, Special Education.

Tharp, R. G., and Gallimore, R. (1975). "A Proposal to Build an Education and Research Program: A Kamehameha Early Education Project Proposal." *Technical Report No. 3*. Honolulu: The Kamehameha Schools. Kamehameha Early Education Program.

Tharp, R. G., and Wetzel, R. H. (1969). *Behavior Modification in the Natural Environment*. New York: Academic Press.

Torrey, E. F. (1972). *The Mind Game: Witchcraft and Psychiatrists*. New York: Bantam Books.

Weinberg, R. H. (1979). "Early Childhood Education and Intervention: Establishing an American Tradition." *American Psychologist, 34*, 912-916.

Wolff, M., and Stein, A. (1967). "Head Start Six Months Later." *Phi Delta Kappan*.

Zigler, E., and Berman, W. (1983). "Discerning the Future of Early Intervention." *American Psychologist, 38, 394-906*.

Zigler E., and Trickett, P. (1978). "I.Q., Social Competence, and Evaluation of Early Childhood Intervention Programs." *American Psychologist, 33*, 789-798.

5

The Consequences of Father Absence:
A Cross-Cultural Perspective

Mitchell W. Robin and Regina C. Spires

> "Dad left when I was such a baby
> and I never had a chance to talk to
> him and I still feel - kind of
> temporary about myself." Willy
> Loman in Arthur Miller's *Death of
> a Salesman.*

During the past decade a great deal of research has been published concerning the influence that living in a single-parent father-absent home has upon the psychological development of the child. This research is of particular importance considering the fact that approximately 8 million children under the age of 18 years (approximately 12 percent of the children in the United States today) are currently living in father-absent homes, and their numbers are increasing yearly. Various factors contribute to the increasing numbers of fatherless homes: (1) the increasing divorce rates (roughly 50 percent of first marriages end in divorce); (2) the increasing desire and ability of single individuals, especially women, to adopt children; and (3) the increasing ability of single women to support and care for their biological children born out of wedlock.

In our previous reviews of the literature, we focused attention on the more or less global impact that father absence has upon a child's social, emotional, cognitive, and academic behaviors (Robin, 1979); we also examined whether or not this impact was the same cross-culturally (Spires and Robin, 1982).

In this current chapter we will take a more narrow, albeit still cross-cultural, view. We will examine the cross-cultural literature on the clinical consequences of living in a father-absent home. Specifically, we will examine the cross-cultural research on the impact that Father Absence has upon personality development, sex-role development, delinquency and other antisocial behaviors. For the purposes of this chapter, we will only examine that literature which investigates the impact of father's absence upon children who had previously lived in father-present conditions. We will exclude from our present survey the small but growing body of literature that examines the developmental impact of living in a mother-only (by choice) household. In an effort to update our last review, we will also examine, but in a briefer and less systematic fashion, the literature concerning the impact of father absences upon their children's cognitive development and school performance.

STRESS: THE IMMEDIATE CONSEQUENCE OF FATHER ABSENCE

When the traditional dyadic family relationship disintegrates, or is routinely and repeatedly disrupted, a number of consequences occur regardless of the cause of that disintegration. The most obvious and omnipresent result is stress for the remaining family members, which has been documented in numerous reports, (Colletta, 1983; Colletta, 1979; Luepnitz, 1978; McCarthy, et al., 1982; Parish, Kappes, and Bruno, 1980; McLanahan, 1983; Gongla, 1982; Bradley, et al., 1984; Gullotta and Donoghue, 1983; and Rembowski, 1981). The stress comes from a variety of sources: emotional, social, economic, and in at least two reported cases "political," (Benchekroun, et al., 1982; and Haffani, et al., 1982). It is this all-pervasive stress which seems to encumber the family and, if not handled effectively, interferes with "normal" development.

One of the major stressors of divorce, as Colletta (1983, 1979) and McLanahan (1983) have pointed out, is the crippling loss of income that the typical family suffers as a consequence of even an amicable divorce. This loss of income severely and negatively affects the ability of the woman to care for her children, and generally results in her becoming more demanding and restrictive and less affectionate than she had been previously. This was especially true for women whose family income was already low prior to the divorce. It was also discovered that the women studied suffered losses of significant psychological support as a consequence of the divorce proceedings, and this loss interfered with her ability to provide psychological support for her children, which in turn had an impact on their development (Bradley, et al., 1984; and Gongla, 1982).

Divorce and the consequent economic disruption is not the only source of stress in father-absent homes. Another source of family stress appears to be the mother's increased feeling of psychic deprivation, which can be communicated to her children (Maijer and Himmelfarb, 1984, for an Israeli sample; Boss, 1980; Stern, 1980; Wojciechowska, 1981, for a Polish sample; Vincelet, 1982, for a French sample). In cultures, such as the ones cited, where fathers are perceived as being more important than mothers, the loss of a father may very well be viewed as a catastrophic deprivation. This perception may lead the caretaking mother and her children to increase the frequency and intensity of their negative interactions. This is especially true if the mother feels that mothering during this time of "crisis" of necessity must be comprised of caring for the child's biological needs rather than social and emotional needs. This negative effect is further aggravated if the mother feels that her own social and emotional needs and deprivations are more important than those of her child, and therefore centers all her attention upon herself. This self-centered attitude in effect places the child in a state of double jeopardy: living in a household where the father is physically absent and where the mother may be emotionally absent.

While most of the literature examines father absence due to death, divorce, or abandonment there are many households whose members live under conditions of periodic father absence who also experience this stress. Gullotta and Donoghue (1983) report on the impact of fathers absence due to corporate relocation. Their findings replicate earlier studies on military families and document the greater incidence of feelings of alienation and rootlessness that these families experience. This alienation is compounded by the stress produced by the father's leaving and reentering the home, and is linked to the fact that children in these families experience greater dependency needs, and greater academic problems than children from more typically intact families. Similar findings were obtained by Rembowski (1981) using a sample of 139 two-child families of Polish sailors. In fact, Haffani, et al. (1982) report that in societies where the culture enhances males superiority, as in the case of Tunisia, the loss of a father has a devastating impact leading to a wide variety of psychiatric and social disturbances. This was especially true for fathers who had to leave the village to seek work in other communities, which served to lower the status of the remaining family members in the eyes of the villagers.

Another example of the variety of stresses that women and remaining family members experience when families disintegrate is reported by Huttunen and Niskanen (1979), who investigated the long-term consequences of the death of the husband/father during prenatal development of the child. In this retrospective epidemiological study in Finland, it was discovered that the stress of losing a husband while pregnant (especially during the second and last trimester) was more highly correlated with incidences of schizophrenia, delinquency, and alcoholism than for a sample of children whose father died during their first year of life.

CLINICAL CONSEQUENCES OF FATHER ABSENCE

Psychiatric Disturbances

A large number of studies have reported the psychological impact of living in a father-absent home. The results suggest that father absence (and its resultant maternal and family stress) is implicated in a wide variety of psychological problems ranging in severity from diminished self-esteem, (Miller, 1984; Wiehe, 1984; and Slater, Stewart, and Linn, 1983), lowered ego development, (Grossman, Shea, and Adams, 1980; Bannon and Southern, 1980; and Tietjen, 1982), and school adjustment problems, (Smilansky, 1982; and Levy-Shiff, 1982; both using Israeli samples) to problems in sex-role identity and sexuality, (Covell and Turnbull, 1982; Shill, 1981a, 1981b; Gispert, et al., 1984; and Eberhardt and Schill, 1984), to more severe cases of depression, (Deaton, 1979), death fantasy, (Oshman and Manosevitz, 1978), encopresis, (Benchekroun, et al., 1982), and schizophrenia, (Huttunen and Niskanen, 1979).

Case histories from both the past (Freud, 1910/1947 and 1912/1962) and the present (Benchekroun, et al., 1982; Deaton, 1979) provide suggestive data that father absence is implicated as a source of psychiatric problems. However, it is from the large sample surveys that the most telling results are obtained, despite some controversies as to who is the most severely affected: males or females. Generally, research is supportive of the hypothesis that early father absence (prior to the age of six years) has a more detrimental effect than later father absence (after the age of six years), and that males are typically more negatively influenced than females. In only three of the studies reviewed in this area (Oshman and Manosevitz, 1978; Slater, Stewart, and Lynn, 1983; Grossman, Shea, and Adams, 1980) were males "benefitted" as a consequence of father absence; that is, the boys had few death fantasies in the former study and greater ego-identity in the latter two. These were atypical results not only in the area of psychiatric disorders but tended to be atypical throughout the other areas as well. Cross-cultural studies from Canada, (Tietjen, 1982), Finland, (Huttunen and Niskanen, 1979), and Tunisia, (Haffani, Attia, Douki, and Amman, 1982) again tend to support the results reported by U.S. researchers.

Antisocial Behavior

Fathers absence is also reported to have a negative impact upon conduct disorders, (Goldstein, 1984; Montare and Boone, 1980; using a Puerto Rican sample), males' juvenile delinquency, (Bourdin, Henggeler, Hanson, and Pruitt, 1985; Renner, 1984, using an Austrian sample; Daum, and Bieliauskas, 1983; Horne, 1981), and substance abuse, (Brook, Whiteman, and Gordon, 1985; Stern, Northman, and Van Slyck, 1984; Sullivan and Fleshman, 1975).

Generally, research supports the hypotheses that father absence, especially when interacting with low or lowered SES, is implicated in increases in antisocial, aggressive, and abusive behaviors in children. This result might be because of less mature moral judgment on the part of the father-absent subjects, compared with father-present subjects. Daum, and Bieliauskas (1983), Schenenga (1983), and Parish (1980) all report results that support the notion that level of moral reasoning is related to father presence or absence; the father-present males usually score higher levels of moral reasoning than the father-absent males. In fact, Daum, and Bieliauskas (1983) report that juvenile delinquents whose fathers were present attained higher levels of moral reasoning than delinquents whose fathers were absent. As we had noted in previous publications, (Spires and Robin, 1982; Robin, 1979), father's presence appears to be related to cognitive behavior generally.

Cognitive Behavior and Academic Performance

Shinn (1979), in a review of the literature on the effects of father absence upon cognitive development, summarized the generally detrimental effects associated with father absence. The studies reviewed at that time suggested that there were differential effects based upon differences in the reason for the absence (death, divorce, or abandonment), as well as the onset and duration of the absence (early absences were more detrimental than later absences, and longer absences were more detrimental than those that were shorter). More recent studies report similar results (Roach, 1980, 1979 for a Jamaican, West Indies sample; Bain, Boersma, and Chapman, 1983 for a Canadian sample; Parish, 1982; Goldstein, 1983 and 1982; Svanum, Bringle, and McLaughlin, 1982; Belz and Geary, 1984; the last three studies cited all examine racial or ethnic differences).

In studies of field dependence versus independence and locus of control, it was reported that father-absent subjects tended to be more field dependent and externalizing than did father-present subjects (Roach, 1980 and 1979; Bain, Boersman, and Chapman, 1983; Parish, 1982). These results are typical of previous research, as are the data suggesting that father-absent boys do less well on tests of academic performance than father-present boys. However, the current studies, unlike previous research, tend to show that, in the area of academic performance, father-absent subjects may do as well as father-present subjects if the confounding variables of SES and parents' education and occupation are controlled for, (Bain, et al., 1983; Goldstein, 1983, 1982; Svanum, Bringle, and McLaughlin, 1982; and Belz, and Geary, 1984). In the studies cited, white subjects were reported to be slightly less affected than nonwhite subjects.

THE CONSEQUENCE OF FATHER ABSENCE IN THE "NEW FAMILY"

While the literature reported earlier has generally supported the belief that living in a father-absent home can have a negative impact upon the individual's mental health, the evidence is far from clear that it is specifically the lack of fathering that is the culprit. As was seen, the most significant problem was not merely the father's absence but the increase in psychic, social, and economic stress upon the remaining family members. If the father-absent situation can be nonstressful, it is possible that the reported effects would be different. In fact, as was reported by Agbayewa (1984), Maruani (1982), and Chiland (1982), the increasing numbers of women who are choosing to have children out of wedlock and raise them either alone or with another woman may provide a living laboratory to test such hypotheses.

REFERENCES

Agbayewa, M. O. (1984). "Fathers in the Newer Family Forms: Male or Female?" *Canadian Journal of Psychiatry* 29(5), 402- 406.

Bain, H. C., Boersma, F. J., and Chapman, J. W. (1983). "Academic Achievement and Locus of Control in Father-Absent Elementary Schoolchildren." *School Psychology International* 4(2), 69-78.

Bannon, J. A., and Southern, M. L. (1980). "Father-Absent Women: Self-Concept and Modes of Relating to Men." *Sex Roles.* 6(1), 75-84.

Belz, H. F., and Geary, D. C. (1984). "Father's Occupation and Social Background: Relation to SAT Scores." *American Educational Research Journal.* 21(2), 473-478.

Benchekroun, M. F., et al. (1982). "Pere et Fils dans la Migration ou Reflexion a propos des Enfants d'Immigres Restes au Pays" (Father and Son in a Migratory Situation or some Reflections about Immigrant Children who Remain at Home.) *Annales Medico-Psychologiques.* 140(6), 606-609.

Boss, P. G. (1980). "The Relationship of Psychological Father Presence, Wife's Personal Qualities, and Wife/Family Dysfunction in Families of Missing Fathers." *Journal of Marriage and the Family* 42(3), 541-549.

Bourdin, C. M., Henggeler, S. W., Hanson, C. L., and Pruitt, J. A. (1985). "Verbal Problem Solving in Families of Father-Absent and Father-Present Boys." *Child and Family Behavior Therapy.* 7(2), 51-63.

Bradley, R. H., Elardo, R., Rosenthal, D., and Friend, J. H. (1984). "A Comparative Study of the Home Environments of Infants from Single-Parent and Two-Parent Black Families." *Acta Paedologica, 1*(1), 33-46.

Brook, J. S., Whiteman, M., and Gordon, A. S. (1985). "Father Absence, Perceived Family Characteristics and Stage of Drug Use in Adolescence." *British Journal of Developmental Psychology, 3*(1), 87-94.

Chiland, C. (1982). "A New Look at Fathers." *Psychanalytic Study of the Child, 37,* 367-379.

Colletta, N. D. (1979). "The Impact of Divorce: Father Absence or Poverty?" *Journal of Divorce, 3*(1), 27-35.

Colletta, N. D. (1983). "Stressful Lives: The Situation of Divorced Mothers and Their Children." *Journal of Divorce, 6*(3), 19-31.

Covell, K., and Turnbull, W. (1982). "The Long-Term Effects of Father Absence in Childhood on Male University Students' Sex-Role Identity and Personal Adjustment." *Journal of Genetic Psychology, 141*(2), 271-276.

Daum, J. M., and Bieliauskas, V. J. (1983). "Fathers' Absence and Moral Development of Male Delinquents." *Psychological Reports, 53*(1), 223-228.

Deaton, H. S. (1979). "An Analytic Intervention in the Life of a Girl Growing Up in a Chaotic Environment: 'Why are my glasses so hot?'" *Journal of Child Psychotherapy, 5,* 69-87.

Eberhardt, C. A., and Schill, T. (1984). "Differences in Sexual Attitudes and Likeliness of Sexual Behaviors of Black Lower-Socioeconomic Father-Present vs. Father-Absent Female Adolescents." *Adolescence, 19*(73), 99-105.

Freud, S. (1947). *Leonardo da Vinci: A Study in Psychosexuality.* New York: Random House. (Originally published in 1910.)

Freud, S. (1962). *Three Contributions to the Theory of Sex.* 2nd ed. New York: E. Dutton and Co. (Originally published in 1912.)

Gispert, M., Brinich, P., Wheeler, K., and Kreiger, L. (1984). "Predictors of Repeat Pregnancies among Low Income Adolescents." *Hospital and Community Psychiatry, 35*(7), 719-723.

Goldstein, H. S. (1982). "Fathers' Absence and Cognitive Development of 12-to 17-Year-Olds." *Psychological Reports, 51*(3 pt.1), 843-848.

Goldstein, H. S. (1983). "Fathers' Absence and Cognitive Development of Children Over a 3- to 5-Year Period." *Psychological Reports, 52*(3), 971-976.

Goldstein, H. S. (1984). "Parental Composition, Supervision, and Conduct Problems in Youths 12 to 17 Years Old." *Journal of the American Academy of Child Psychiatry, 23*(6), 679-684.

Gongla, P. A. (1982). "Single Parent Families: A Look at Families of Mothers and Children." *Marriage and Family Review, 5*(2), 5-27.

Gullotta, T. P., and Donoghue, K. C. (1983). "Families, Relocation and the Corporation." *New Directions for Mental Health Services, 20,* 15-24.

Grossman, S. M., Shea, J. A., and Adams, G. R. (1980). "Effects of Parental Divorce during Early Childhood on Ego Development and Identity Formation of College Students." *Journal of Divorce, 3*(3), 263-272.

Haffani, F., Attia, S., Douki, S., and Amman, S. (1982). "Le Prix de l'Absence ou la 'Mission Impossible' du Migrant." (The Price of Absence or the "Mission Impossible" for the Migrant.) *Annales Medico-Psychologiques, 140*(6), 672-676.

Horne, A. M. (1981). "Aggressive Behavior in Normal and Deviant Members of Intact vs. Mother-Only Families". *Journal of Abnormal Child Psychology, 9*(2), 293 290.

Huttunen, M. O., and Niskanen, P. (1979). "Prenatal Loss of Father and Psychiatric Disorders." *Annual Progress in Child Psychiatry and Child Development.* 331-338.

Levy-Shiff, R. (1982). "The Effects of Father Absence on Young Children in Mother-Headed Families." *Child Development. 53*(5), 1400-1405.

Luepnitz, D. A. (1978). "Children of Divorce: A Review of the Psychological Literature." *Law and Human Behavior, 2*(2), 167-179.

Maruani, G. (1982). "Californie: Les Enfants de l'Electronique et du Matriarcat" (California: Children of the Electronic Matriarchal Age). *Genitif, 4*(5-6), 63-69.

McCarthy, E., Doyle, A., et al. (1982). "The Behavioral Effects of Father Absence on Children and Their Mothers." *Social Behavior and Personality, 10*(1), 11-23.

McLanahan, S. S. (1983). "Family Structure and Stress: A Longitudinal Comparison of Two-Parent and Female-Headed Families." *Journal of Marriage and the Family, 45*(2), 347- 357.

Maijer, A., and Himmelfarb, S. (1984). "Fatherless Adolescents' Feelings about Their Mothers: A Pilot Study." *Adolescence, 19*(73), 207-212.

Miller, T. W. (1984). "Paternal Absence and its Effect on Adolescent Self-Esteem." *International Journal of Social Psychiatry, 30*(4), 293-296.

Montare, A., and Boone, S. L. (1980). "Aggression and Paternal Absence: Racial Ethnic Differences among Inner-City Boys." *Journal of Genetic Psychology, 137*(2), 223-232.

Oshman, H. P., and Manosevitz, M. (1978). "Death Fantasies of Father-Absent and Father-Present Late Adolescents." *Journal of Youth and Adolescence, 7*(1), 41-48.

Parish, T. S. (1980). "The Relationship between Factors Associated with Father Loss and the Individuals' Level of Moral Judgment." *Adolescence, 15*(59), 535-541.

Parish, T. S., Kappes, B. M., and Bruno. (1980). "Impact of Father Loss on the Family." *Social Behavior and Personality, 8*(1), 107-112.

Parish, T. S. (1982). "Locus of Control as a Function of Father Loss and the Presence of Stepfathers." *Journal of Genetic Psychology, 140*(2), 321-322.

Rembowski, J. (1981). "Father Absence in Sailor Families with Two Children." *Polish Psychological Bulletin, 12*(4), 233-239.

Renner, W. (1984). "Juvenile Delinquency in an Austrian Sample of Foster Children without a Father Substitute: Review of the Literature and Some Findings." *Personality and Individual Differences, 5*(5), 587-589.

Roach, D. A. (1979). "Effects of Some Social Variables on Field Dependence." *Perceptual and Motor Skills, 48*(2), 559-562.

Roach, D. A. (1980). "Some Social Variables in Conceptual Style Preference." *Perceptual and Motor Skills, 50*(2), 452-454.

Robin, M. W. (1979). "Life Without Father: A Review of the Literature." *International Journal of Group Tensions, 9*(1-4), 169-194.

Schenenga, K. (1983). "Father Absence, the Ego Ideal and Moral Development." *Smith College Studies in Social Work, 53*(2), 103-114.

Shill, M. (1981a). "TAT Measures of Gender Identity (Castration Anxiety) in Father-Absent Males." *Journal of Personality Assessment, 54*(2), 136-146.

Shill, M. (1981b). "Castration Fantasies and Assertiveness in Father-Absent Males." *Psychiatry, 44*(3) 262-272.

Shinn, M. (1979). "Father Absence and Children's Cognitive Development." *Annual Progress in Child Psychiatry and Child Development,* 293-330.

Slater, E. J., Stewart, K. J., and Linn, M. W. (1983). "The Effects of Family Disruption on Adolescent Males and Females." *Adolescence, 72,* 931-942.

Smilansky, S. (1982). "The Adjustment in Elementary School of Children Orphaned from Their Fathers." *Series in Clinical and Community Psychology: Stress and Anxiety, 8,* 249-253.

Spires, R. C., and Robin, M. W. (1982). "Father Absence Cross-Culturally: A Review of the Literature." In *Cross-Cultural Research at Issue,* edited by L. L. Adler, 99-109. New York: Academic Press.

Stern, E. E. (1980). "Single Mothers' Perceptions of the Father Role and the Effects of Father Absence on Boys." *Journal of Divorce, 4*(2), 77-84.

Stern, M., Northman, J. E., and Van Slyck, M. R. (1984). "Father Absence and Adolescent Problem Behaviors: Alcohol Consumption, Drug Use and Sexual Activity" *Adolescence. 19*(74), 301-312.

Sullivan, N. D., and Fleshman, R. P. (1975-1976). "Paternal Deprivation in Male Heroin Addicts." *Drug Forum. 5*(1), 75 79.

Svanum, S., Bringle, R. G., and McLaughlin, J. E. (1982). "Father Absence and Cognitive Performance in a Large Sample of Six-to Eleven-Year-Old Children." *Child Development, 53*(1), 136-143.

Tietjen, A. M. (1982). "The Social Networks of Pre-Adolescent Children in Sweden." *International Journal of Behavioral Development, 5*(1).

Vincelet, P. (1982). "Reconstitution dans la Vie de l'Enfant de l'Histoire du Pere Absent." (Reconstitution in the Child's Life of the Absent Father's History.) *Neuropsychiatrie de l'Enfance et de l'Adolescence. 30*(12), 715-719.

Wiehe, V. R. (1984). "Self-Esteem, Attitude Toward Parents, and Locus of Control in Children of Divorced and Non-Divorced Families." *Journal of Social Service Research, 8*(1), 17-28.

Wojciechowska, L. (1981). "Maternal Rearing and Social Adaptation of Children from Broken Homes." *Polish Psychological Bulletin, 12*(4), 213-218.

PART TWO: FOCUS ON ADOLESCENCE

Photo credit: Maric Productions

6

Perceptions of Parental Behavior and the Development of Moral Reasoning in Jamaican Students

Uwe P. Gielen, Claudette Reid, and Joseph Avellani

The purpose of this study was to investigate the relationship between parental behaviors and the development of moral reasoning in children. More specifically, this study examined the effects of the child-rearing practices of Jamaican parents, as perceived by their children, upon the moral judgment development of those children. A limited amount of research on moral judgment development has been conducted with subjects from Caribbean countries (e.g., Beddoe, 1980; Gielen, et al., 1986; White, 1986), but no published studies of moral judgment development in Jamaican students could be located.

Kohlberg's (1984) and Rest's (1979a) cognitive-developmental stage theories of moral judgment development provided the theoretical framework for this research. In recent years, these theories have dominated the study of morality in North American (Kohlberg, 1984; Rest, 1983) and cross-cultural psychology (Moon, 1986; Snarey, 1985).

The cross-cultural empirical validation of Kohlberg's and Rest's theories has slowly progressed in recent years. Snarey (1985) recently surveyed 45 studies in the Americas, Asia, Africa, Europe, and Oceania that together give considerable support to Kohlberg's theory at least for his first three to four stages of moral reasoning. The cross-cultural evidence for post-conventional moral reasoning is much weaker, because few or none of the subjects in cross-cultural investigations spontaneously produce arguments at the highest stages of moral judgment (i.e., principled moral thought). At the same time, subjects in cross-cultural studies commonly prefer or endorse principled moral arguments when those arguments are presented to them by the experimenter (Moon, 1986). However, in spite of differing methodologies, most cross-sectional and longitudinal studies support Kohlberg's proposal that moral maturity steadily increases throughout childhood and adolescence.

According to Kohlberg (1984) and Rest (1979a), as a person matures, he or she transverses a series of increasingly abstract moral philosophies or schemes of cooperation. These cognitive schemes arise out of the interaction between developmental tendencies inherent in the person and role-taking opportunities provided by various formal and informal institutions of society, such as families, schools, peer groups, voluntary associations, etc. A number of factors influence the rate of moral development, including education, age, experience in leadership positions, exposure to cognitive conflicts, and involvement in complex social situations. Thus, Kohlberg considers the family to be only one among many institutions that may influence the moral development of children and adolescents. He does not hypothesize strong or very consistent relationships between patterns of parental child-rearing practices and structural indices of moral development. However, recent research inside and outside the United States suggests that Kohlberg may have underestimated the importance of family factors (Parikh, 1975; Speicher-Dubin, 1982). In light of this recent research, the following hypotheses guided the present study.

The first research hypothesis was that parental warmth contributes to the growth of moral reasoning in children, because children who feel accepted rather than neglected by their parents are more responsive to parental influence. Since parents usually reason in more complex ways than their children, acceptance supports the development of increasingly complex forms of moral reasoning in children, while parental neglect or rejection interferes with the moral development of children.

The second research hypothesis in this study was that strong conflict between parents interferes with the development of role-taking abilities, since it leads to emotional and cognitive confusion in children and adolescents. Children have difficulty taking the perspective of parents who argue with each other constantly, since the parents themselves are unable to do so. At the same time, complex schemes of cooperation do not develop in children whose parents demonstrate an unwillingness to cooperate in a reasonable way on a daily basis.

The third research hypothesis in this study suggested that adolescent children develop autonomous, principled moral reasoning if their parents encourage them to behave autonomously and responsibly. In other words, parents who adopt democratic strategies of child rearing (e.g., share decision making with their adolescent children; emphasize equality; and respond to children's viewpoints) further the development in their children of more equilibrated forms of thinking.

METHOD

Setting

Jamaica is the third largest of the West Indian islands with a population estimated at about 2.4 million. Jamaica became an independent nation in the British Commonwealth of Nations in 1962. The population of Jamaica consists mainly of African and Mulatto descendants of slaves, East Indians, and a small minority of Whites. In recent years, there has been a considerable amount of intermarriage and mixing between the various ethnic groups. Jamaica shares with other English-speaking Caribbean nations, such as Trinidad-Tobago and Belize, a number of common cultural influences. Among these are the English language, including frequently spoken Creole dialects; English educational and political institutions; intense exposure to recent North American cultural influences; multiracial and multiethnic populations, including a majority of inhabitants from African and Mulatto backgrounds; and strong African cultural influences.

The research was conducted at Glenmuir High School, a grammar or academic school located in May Pen, Jamaica. Subjects taught at the school include sciences, languages, history, religious studies, and others. Before being admitted to Glenmuir High School, students must pass a nationwide entrance examination. Students attending the school come from a wide variety of ethnic and socioeconomic backgrounds.

Subjects

The sample consisted of 79 female and 32 male students. Their ages ranged from 11 to 18 years, with a mean age of 14 years and 10 months, and 88.3 percent of the students fell into the 13 to 17-year-old age range. While 88 percent of the students identified themselves as Protestant, 12 percent indicated other religious denominations. Ethnic backgrounds included 77.5 percent Black, 4.5 percent Indian and 18 percent mixed or occasionally white backgrounds. When asked about the occupation of their fathers, 28 percent of the respondents did not answer this question because they had only limited or no contact with their fathers. Among the fathers of the remaining students, 59 percent held blue-collar jobs, 34 percent held lower white-collar jobs and 7 percent fell into upper-middle or upper white-collar categories.

Questionnaire

The questionnaire consisted of background questions and five separate scales: (1) "Parents and Children" scale; (2) "Mother" scale; (3) "Father" scale; (5) "Parental Conflict" scale; and (5) "Defining Issues Test" (DIT), an objectively scored moral judgment questionnaire. The "Parents and Children" scale contained 24 items about perceptions of child-related parental behavior. These items were adapted from a longer scale by Coopersmith (1967) and used a four-item Likert answering format, ranging from "Always True" to "Never True." The 24 items were scored individually, and in addition, various items were combined to form subscales measuring perceived "Acceptance," "Autonomy," and "Democracy." These three subscales combined to form an overall measure of perceived parental "Child-Rearing Quality."

The "Mother" and "Father' scales each contained 31 items describing perceived maternal and paternal behavior. The items were selected and adapted from longer scales provided by Rohner (1980). All items used a Likert answering format and were scored individually. Following Rohner, items were also combined to form subscales for perceived "Warmth," "Aggression," "Indifference-Neglect," and "Rejection" on the part of a mother and father. In addition, all 31 items were combined to create an overall "Parental Acceptance Rejection" (PARQ) index separately for mothers and fathers.

The "Parental Conflict" scale contained 24 items concerning parental conflicts about "Finances," joint "Family Activities" and "Child-Rearing Practices." These items were adapted from a more extensive scale by Schwarz and Gettner (1980). The 24 items were combined to form the overall measure of "Parental Conflict."

Moral judgment was measured by Rest's (1979b) Defining Issues Test (DIT). Studies of moral reasoning have either used production measures employing semiopen-ended interviews (Kohlberg, 1984) or, more recently, recognition-preference measures (Rest, 1979a). The DIT is the most frequently employed, objective recognition measure of moral reasoning. The test contained the following moral dilemmas:

1. Should a poor husband steal a drug in order to save the life of his very sick wife if he cannot get the drug any other way?
2. A man escapes from prison and subsequently leads a model life. Should a neighbor who years later recognizes him report him to the police?
3. A woman is in terrible pain and is dying of cancer. She asks the doctor to kill her in order to end her suffering. Should the doctor do this?
4. Should the owner of a gas station hire a highly qualified foreigner as his mechanic, when he is afraid that many of his prejudiced customers will take their business elsewhere?
5. Should a high school principal stop the publication of a highly controversial student newspaper?
6. Should students occupy a university building in order to express their opposition to military training programs at their university?

Following each dilemma, 12 arguments were provided that could be used to solve the conflict. The arguments reflected different moral stages. Respondents were asked to rank the importance of each argument. In addition, the subjects were asked to select the four most important arguments.

The DIT was objectively scored following procedures recommended by Rest (1979b). The test provided moral stage scores for stages 2, 3, 4, $4\frac{1}{2}$ (A-score), 5A, 5B, and 6. Preferences for principled thinking stages (5A, 5B, and 6 combined) were expressed by the P%-Score. The P%-Score indicated the percentage of a respondent's rankings that fell in the principled range. In addition, an overall weighted indicator of moral judgment development was available in the D-Score. The D-Score reflected a person's relative preference for principled reasoning (stages 5A, 5B, and 6) over conventional reasoning (stages 3 and 4) and preconventional reasoning (stage 2). The D-Score was based upon a complex mathematical formula that weighed a subject's ratings of the 72 moral arguments provided by the DIT. All students included in the present study passed a standard consistency check proposed by Rest (1979b), indicating that the students understood the nature of the task provided by the test.

RESULTS

Distribution of Moral Stage Scores

Table 6.1 contains the distribution of moral stage scores for the Jamaican subjects in this study. For comparison purposes, the moral stage scores of 118 high school students from Belize (formerly British Honduras) and 147 high school students from Trinidad-Tobago were also included in the table. The stage scores for Belize and Trinidad have been taken from Gielen, et al. (1986). Both Belize and Trinidad-Tobago are English-speaking Caribbean countries that are culturally similar to Jamaica.

The results for the Jamaican students indicated that they strongly preferred conventional moral arguments (stages 3 and 4 = 58.6 percent) over principled arguments (stages 5A, 5B, 6 = 21.8 percent) and preconventional arguments (stage 2 = 10.3 percent). It should be noted, however, that the DIT contains more conventional than principled or preconventional arguments. The obtained results, therefore, reflect in part the overall construction of the DIT. The overall distributions of moral stage scores for the three Caribbean countries -- Jamaica, Belize, and Trinidad-Tobago -- were fairly similar to each other. Jamaican students preferred stage 3 arguments over stage 4 arguments, while Belizean and Trinidadian students reversed this order. The important P%-Scores for the three countries were highly similar. Students from Trinidad-Tobago received slightly higher D-Scores than did the students from Jamaica and Belize.

Comparison of Moral Stage Scores between Jamaica and the USA

In past studies, North American samples with age and educational levels similar to the present Jamaican sample typically have received higher P%-Scores and D-Scores than were found in the present study. Table 6.2 presents a comparison between Jamaican data and data obtained in a previous study conducted in the USA (Gielen, et al., 1986).

It should be noted that the average age for the North American sample is one year and four months higher than for the Jamaican sample.

Statistical comparisons between the moral stage scores of the Jamaican and North American students revealed many highly significant differences. The Jamaican students received significantly lower P%-Scores and D-Scores than the students from the USA, indicating lower overall moral judgment levels for the Caribbean sample. Mean moral judgment scores for stages 4,

5A, and 5B were lower for the Jamaican sample. The mean score for meaningless items (a validity check) was significantly lower for the Jamaican sample than for the North American sample, indicating that the Jamaican students must have ranked the moral arguments in the DIT with considerable care.

Correlations of Moral Stage Scores with Age

The DIT purports to measure the development of moral understanding. To investigate this claim, the moral stage scores of male and female Jamaican students were correlated with their ages. With one exception, all of the correlations were statistically insignificant, giving very little support to the developmental claims underlying the DIT. For male students, stage 4 scores were negatively correlated with age ($r(32) = -.34$; $p < .03$). The correlation between age and P%-Score was $r(32) = -.05$; n.s. for male students, and $r(79) = +.01$; n.s. for female students. The correlation between age and D-Score was $r(32) = +.14$; n.s. for male students; and $r(79) = +.01$; n.s. for female students.

Correlation Between Perceived Parental Behavior and the Weighted Judgment Score (D-Score)

In order to establish possible connections between perceived parental behavior and moral judgment development, Pearson product-moment correlation coefficients between parental behavior scales and the overall weighted D-Score were computed separately for female and male students. They are reported in Table 6.3.

One-tailed probability estimates were used, since the direction of the association between parental behavior and moral judgment score was predicted for all parental behavior scales. For female students, moderate support was found for some of the theoretical predictions. Mother's warmth and father's warmth were both positively correlated with the daughter's moral judgment development, while father's aggression was negatively related to the daughter's moral judgment development. Overall acceptance by fathers (PARQ) was positively related to the daughter's moral judgment score, but for mother's overall acceptance, the correlation was not significant. Indifference and rejection by either mother or father were not related to the daughters' moral judgment score. Parental conflicts, and specifically parental conflicts about child-rearing, were associated with lower moral judgement development in female students. Scales measuring the combined child-rearing practices of both parents (Parents - Child-Rearing Quality and associated subscales) were not significantly associated with the moral judgement scores of female students. For male students, associations between parental behavior and moral judgment scores were generally statistically insignificant. Theoretical predictions for male students were borne out only for the scales measuring overall parental conflict and parental conflicts concerning finances.

Both scales were negatively correlated with the moral judgment development of male students.

DISCUSSION

In our discussion, we will first focus on the moral reasoning scores obtained with the DIT. Subsequently, the discussion will shift to a consideration of the linkages between perceptions of parental behavior and moral reasoning scores.

The overall distribution of moral reasoning scores for the Jamaican students resembles rather closely the distribution of moral reasoning scores previously found for high school students from Belize and Trinidad. This is especially true for the important P%-Scores and D-Scores that Rest considers to be among the best overall indicators of moral reasoning development. At the same time, the moral reasoning scores for the three Caribbean countries are significantly lower than those obtained in some other cross-cultural studies. Ma (1980) reported an average P%-Score of 27.9 percent for 17-year-old Chinese students from Hong Kong. Hau (1983) also tested Chinese students from Hong Kong and reported a mean P%-Score of 25.2 percent for a combined sample of seventh and eighth graders. Park and Johnson (1984) reported average P%-Scores of 25.0 percent and 30.2 percent for South Korean sixth and eighth graders, respectively. These and other results summarized by Rest (1979a, 1979b) and Moon (1986) suggest that students from the Far East, North America, and Australia typically received higher overall moral judgment scores on the DIT than students from Jamaica and some other Caribbean countries.

Several previous studies using either Kohlberg's interview method or Rest's recognition-preference measure in Caribbean societies have reported results that lend support to this generalization. White (1986) summarized several of his studies that investigated the moral development of Bahamian schoolchildren using Kohlberg's interview procedure. In two studies, the moral reasoning protocols of children were predominantly rated at stages 1 and 2. More recently, White (1986) has found in a small sample of older Bahamians a strong preponderance of stage 2 scores. Gorsuch and Barnes (1973) interviewed 10-to-16-year-old "Black Caribs" from British Honduras (now Belize). With one exception, all interviewees received stage 1 and 2 ratings. Beddoe (1980) gave a short version of the DIT to 210 students from Trinidad-Tobago that attended four teacher's colleges. The students varied in age from 20 to 39 years. Mean P%-Scores at three of the four colleges varied from 25 to 26.7 percent, while students from the fourth college received a mean P%-Score of 35.1 percent. These scores, especially from the three colleges in the 25-26.7 P%-Score range, are lower than those typically reported for North American and Far Eastern college students (Rest, 1979a; Moon, 1986).

The present study, then, agrees with previous research conducted in Caribbean societies by showing relatively depressed moral reasoning scores for students from an English-speaking Caribbean society. One may explain these findings by arguing that they reflect the inappropriate use of a culture-alien measure of moral reasoning skills. Such a possible explanation is weakened by the findings of several studies conducted in Far Eastern societies. These studies find moral reasoning scores that typically fall in the same range as those reported for North American students (Snarey, 1985; Moon, 1986). Why should Kohlbergian moral reasoning measures be inappropriate for English-speaking Caribbean cultures, but appropriate for Chinese, Japanese or Korean students from the Far East?

In the present study, no significant correlations were obtained between age and P%-Scores or D-Scores. This is an unusual finding undermining the developmental status of the DIT for high school students from Jamaica. In a previous study (Gielen, et al., 1986), modest, but statistically significant, positive correlations between age and both P%-Scores and D-Scores were obtained in Trinidad-Tobago. For students from Belize, a statistically significant correlation between P%-Scores and age was obtained, but the correlation between D-Scores and age was not found to be significant. Thus, the correlations between age and moral judgment scores are inconsistent for the three Caribbean countries, suggesting a need for further research. Such further research should include students and adults from varied social and educational backgrounds.

The obtained correlations between perceived parental behavior and the weighted moral judgment score (D-Score) provided only modest confirmation for some of our experimental hypotheses. For female students, parental conflicts about child-rearing were clearly connected to inhibited moral judgment development. Aggressive fathers appeared to interfere with the development of moral reasoning skills of their daughters. Mothers and fathers judged to be warm by their daughters had a positive influence upon the development of moral reasoning skills in their daughters. Mothers and fathers appeared to have quite limited effects upon the development of moral judgments skills in their sons, at least as these were measured in the present study. However, parental conflicts appeared to interfere with the development of moral reasoning skills in male students.

The results concerning perceptions of parental behavior and the development of moral reasoning skills in Jamaican students partially replicate a similar study previously conducted in the USA (Gielen, et al. (1987). However, the North American study provided much more consistent support for the experimenters' hypotheses than the present Jamaican study. We can only speculate why this should be so. The DIT appears to have measured the development of moral reasoning skills in Jamaican adolescents only to a quite limited extent, since P%-Scores and D-Scores did not correlate with age. However, the perceptual measures of parental behavior employed in the present research showed considerable promise within a Jamaican cultural context. We are now engaged in follow-up studies in Jamaica and Belize that hopefully will throw further light on perceptions of parental behavior and developing moral reasoning skills in adolescents from English-speaking Caribbean countries.

REFERENCES

Beddoe, I. B. (1980). "Assessing Principled Moral Thinking among Student Teachers in Trinidad and Tobago." Unpublished manuscript, University of the West Indies, Trinidad and Tobago.

Coopersmith, S. (1967). *The Antecedents of Self-Esteem*. San Francisco: W. H. Freeman.

Gielen, U., Cruickshank, H., Johnston. A., Swanzey, B., and Avellani, J. (1986). "The Development of Moral Reasoning in Belize, Trinidad-Tobago and the USA." *Behavior Science Research*. 20(1-4), 178-207.

Gielen, U., Swanzey, B., Avellani, J., and Kramer, J. (1987). "Moral Judgment and Parental Behavior." Unpublished manuscript, Brooklyn: St. Francis College.

Gorsuch, R. L., and Barnes, M. L. (1983). "Stages of Ethical Reasoning and Moral Norms of Carib Youths." *Journal of Cross-Cultural Psychology, 4*, 283-301.

Hau, K. T. (1983). "A Cross-Cultural Study of a Moral Judgment Test (DIT)." Unpublished master's thesis, The Chinese University of Hong Kong, Shatin, N. T., Hong Kong.

Kohlberg, L. (1984). *The Psychology of Moral Development*. San Francisco: Harper and Row.

Ma, H. K. (1980). "A Study of the Moral Development of Adolescents." Unpublished master's thesis, University of London, London, United Kingdom.

Moon, Y. L. (1986). "A Review of Cross-Cultural Studies on Moral Judgment Development using the Defining Issues Test." *Behavior Science Research, 20*(1-4), 147-177.

Parikh, B. S. (1975). "Moral Judgment Development and Its Relation to Family Environmental Factors in Indian and American Upper-Middle-Class Families." Unpublished doctoral dissertation, Boston University, Boston, MA.

Park, J. Y., and Johnson, R. C. (1984). "Moral Development in Rural and Urban Korea." *Journal of Cross-Cultural Psychology, 15*(1), 35-46.

Rest, J. (1979a). *Development in Judging Moral Issues*. Minneapolis, MN: University of Minnesota Press.

Rest, J. (1979b). *Revised Manual for the Defining Issues Test: An Objective Test of Moral Judgment Development*. Minneapolis, MN: Moral Research Projects.

Rest, J. (1983). "Morality." In *Handbook of Child Psychology*, edited by P. Mussen, Vol. 4, 556-629. New York: Wiley and Sons.

Rohner, R. (1980). *Handbook for the Study of Parental Acceptance and Rejection*. Storrs, CT: University of Connecticut.

Schwarz, J. C., and Gettner, H. (1980). "Parental Conflict and Dominance in Late Adolescent Maladjustment: A Triple Interaction Model." *Journal of Abnormal Psychology, 89,* 573-580.

Snarey, J. (1985). "Cross-Cultural Universality of Social-Moral Development: A Critical Review of Kohlbergian Research." *Psychological Bulletin, 97,* 202-232.

Speicher-Dubin, B. (1982). Relationships Between Parent Moral Judgment and Family Interaction: A Correlational Study." Unpublished doctoral dissertation, Harvard University, Cambridge, MA.

White, C. B. (1986). "Moral Reasoning in Bahamian and United States Adults and Children: A Cross-Cultural Investigation of Kohlberg's Stages." *Behavior Science Research, 20*(1-4), 47-70.

AUTHOR NOTES

The authors are grateful to the students of Glenmuir High School, Clarendon, Jamaica, who so patiently filled out a lengthy and difficult questionnaire. The research reported in this paper was supported by much appreciated research grants from the H. F. Guggenheim Foundation and St. Francis College to the first author.

Table 6.1

Moral Stage Scores in Three Caribbean Countries

	Country		
Stage Scores	Jamaica (N=111) Mean	Belize (N=118) Mean	Trinidad (N=147) Mean
Stage 2	10.27%	10.1%	9.7%
Stage 3	33.62%	28.4%	22.7%
Stage 4	24.95%	32.4%	37.1%
Stage 4½ (A)	6.43%	3.6%	3.7%
Stage 5A	11.97%	13.2%	14.4%
Stage 5B	3.13%	3.6%	3.8%
Stage 6	6.08%	3.7%	3.7%
Meaningless	2.98%	4.9%	4.8%
P-Percent	21.17%	20.5%	21.9%
D-Score	11.73	11.0	13.7
Average Age	14 years 10 months	15 years 3 months	15 years 3 months

Note: Only respondents having passed the standard DIT consistency check
        are included in this table. With the exception of D-Scores, moral
        judgment scores are expressed in percentages. Data from Belize
        and Trinidad are taken from Gielen, et al. (1986) and are included
        for comparison purposes.

Table 6.2

Comparison of Moral Stage Scores between Jamaica and the USA

	Country		
Stage Scores	Jamaica (N=111) Mean	USA (N=106) Mean	T-Tests (two-tailed)
Stage 2	10.27%	10.45%	$t(215)= .82$;n.s.
Stage 3	33.62%	20.72%	$t(215)= 9.85$;p$<$.001
Stage 4	24.95%	34.59%	$t(215)=-7.69$;p$<$.001
Stage 4½(A)	6.43%	3.22%	$t(200)= 5.08$;p$<$.001
Stage 5 A	11.97%	17.82%	$t(215)=-5.80$;p$<$.001
Stage 5 B	3.13%	6.24%	$t(188)=-4.97$;p$<$.001
Stage 6	6.08%	2.50%	$t(193)= 6.16$;p$<$.001
Meaningless	2.98%	4.44%	$t(215)=-3.09$;p$=$.002
P-Percent	21.17%	26.53%	$t(201)=-3.79$;p$<$.001
D-Score	11.73	18.75	$t(203)=-9.40$;p$<$.001

Note: Only respondents having passed the standard DIT consistency check are
        included in this table. With the exception of D-Scores, moral
        judgment scores are expressed in percentages. Degrees of freedom for
        the t-tests are adjusted to separate or pooled variance estimates
        depending on the homogeneity of variance in the two countries. Data
        for the U.S.A. are taken from Gielen, et al , (1986). The mean ages for
        the two samples are 14.8 years for Jamaica and 16.2 years for the USA.

Table 6.3

Correlations Between Perceived Parental Behavior and Weighted Moral Judgment Score

Parental Behavior	Females		Males	
	Correlation with D-Score	Probability (One-tailed)	Correlation with D-Score	Probability (One-tailed)
Composite Scales				
Mother – PARQ	+.12	.08	–.03	n.s.
Mother – Warmth	+.21	.017	+.13	n.s.
Mother – Aggression	.01	n.s.	+.14	n.s.
Mother – Indifference	–.04	n.s.	–.11	n.s.
Mother – Rejection	–.08	n.s.	+.03	n.s.
Father – PARQ	+.18	.04	–.04	n.s.
Father – Warmth	+.22	.019	–.08	n.s.
Father – Aggression	–.22	.017	–.04	n.s.
Father – Indifference	–.01	n.s.	.03	n.s.
Father – Rejection	–.08	n.s.	–.10	n.s.
Parents – Child Rearing Quality	+.01	n.s.	–.07	n.s.
Parents – Democracy	+.09	n.s.	+.07	n.s.
Parents – Autonomy	.00	n.s.	+.05	n.s.
Parents – Acceptance	–.04	n.s.	–.14	n.s.
Parental Conflict	–.24	.022	–.29	.04
Par. Conflict – Child Rearing	–.28	.008	–.17	.10
Par. Conflict – Finances	–.12	.10	–.24	.06
Par. Conflict – Fam. Activities	–.15	.07	–.08	n.s.

Note: Df = 27-32 for Males and DF = 53-78 for Females. High scores on the "Warmth" scale indicate a high degree of parental warmth. High scores on the "Aggression" scale indicate a high degree of parental aggression, etc.

7

Some Thoughts on Self-Actualization in Adolescents

Machiko Fukuhara

Recently in Japan, along with issues of educational reform, behavioral problems of early and late adolescents were the focus of great concern. Included among these behavioral problems (for both individuals and groups) were those of school phobia, apathy, and violence for early adolescents, and apathy for late adolescents (college age).

The number of adolescents between the ages of 10 and 24 years in Japan is 36,890,000. The breakdown is as follows: 10,020,000 (ages 10-14 years), 18,830,000 (ages 15-19 years), and 8,031,000 (ages 20-24 years).[1] These age groups will be influential in supporting the nation during the twenty-first century, with its anticipated population explosion, rapid changes in the social system with the help of technological development, etc. These conditions are expected to create serious problems intranationally as well as internationally. Therefore, the self-actualization of these age groups is especially important at this stage in terms of their healthy development.

Self-actualization, which has been defined in humanistic (psychological) terms by Maslow,[2] though there may be several different connotations, means the state in which one can develop positive assets for further development and satisfaction.

Among the many factors affecting adolescents' behavior (challenges for self-realization), the conflicts that adolescents experience, especially with regard to decision making, are important and overt. In this chapter, I would like to discuss these issues from this viewpoint.

I will first look at the cause of conflicts with regard to decision making and then add some thoughts from the standpoint of an educator-counselor. Decision making here is divided into two types: (1) decision making for education (for both high school and college students); and (2) for choosing a career (especially for college students).

CAUSES OF NEGATIVE SELF-CONCEPTS BY STUDENTS

Nature of Negative Self-Concepts by Students

Japanese students seem to be concerned with their personal problems (ability and personality) as well as educational-vocational problems. Research by the Association of Private Colleges and Universities in Japan found that a large number of students (about 30 percent) have personal problems related to their perception of their ability, personality, etc. This percentage is as high as that of educational-vocational problems as indicated by a 1979-1980 survey.[3] A similar tendency was also found in a survey done by the Institute for the Study of Students about 20 years ago.[4] The students indicated that they were concerned about their ability. This tendency was found to be particularly strong when students were faced with decision making about their future.

A similar tendency by students was also found in research conducted by this author, as well as in practice, based on her counseling experience at the University Counseling Center in Tokyo.[5] This tendency seems to be consistent in Japanese adolescents.

In addition, Japanese students tend to devaluate their competence, ability, aptitude, and/or personality. A survey conducted by the Prime Minister's Office, reported that only 36 percent of Japanese children between the ages of ten and 15 years, compared with 92.7 percent of their USA counterparts, showed that they have confidence in their ability to do well in school.[6] This is interpreted as meaning that Japanese children are forced to evaluate themselves according to their school grades; thus they fail to see themselves and their abilities from different angles. Therefore, they tend to form inappropriate self-concepts. This tendency seems to be found among college students, too.

Parent-Child Relationships as Exerting an Influence in Students' Self-Concept

Japanese children are accustomed to maintaining strong ties with their parents. This parent-child relationship, which is typical of the Japanese family system, seems to foster in children a dependent attitude, known as *Amae*. In this kind of relationship, children's achievements are likely to be reinforced by their parents rather than by themselves. On the other hand, achievement motives of Japanese children,[7] by their very nature, appear to be self-rewarding instead of being socially reinforced. This means that children give self-rewards for their achievements based on norms that are actually decided by their parents. Consequently, the feeling of uncertainty and failure follows; they are likely to aim for unattainable goals. Again, this might affect their self-image.

Education in Terms of Affecting Students' Own Decision Making

The high competition to pass entrance examinations exacerbates the previously mentioned tendency. Students are forced to apply to different schools depending on their grades. Therefore, parents and teachers reinforce their children/students, respectively, to attain a higher level of achievement, so that they can obtain admission to highly ranked educational institutions that will guarantee their future success. This is especially true with junior high school children. Many are forced to enter schools that are not their first choice. Thus, they must aim for unattainable goals, which might arouse frustrations and consequently result in dropping out, refusal to go to school (phobia), and violence.

Social Factors that Affect Decision Making for Education and/or Career

The Japanese society is called a "vertical society," well-known as *Tateshakai*, which is hierarchical in nature. A Japanese psychologist once compared it with birth order; just as the order of birth within a family can never be changed, it is likely that the relative ranks of educational institutions in Japan cannot be changed either. This order affects students' choice of educational institutions. They tend to choose schools that are ranked high in the hierarchy rather than those reflecting their own preferences. Naturally this creates greater competition for students who enter schools, which becomes increasingly true with regard to colleges. Then again, they are forced to go to schools that do not necessarily meet their needs.

With regard to the labor market, according to a general survey made in 1985, almost 100 percent of college graduates could get jobs if they were not so concerned with the hierarchical order in ranking businesses. It should be added, however, that for female students, it is still hard to find career satisfaction, compared with male students.

Summary

The problems of self-actualization of Japanese adolescents seem to be closely related to conflicts of decision making, in which a negative self-image plays an important role. In turn, negative self-image is likely to be affected by the family, education, and the social system. That is, there is a possible conflict between genuine individual needs and needs affected by the other factors.

SOME THOUGHTS ON PRECEDING SITUATIONS
IN A CROSS-CULTURAL PERSPECTIVE

Factors affecting the self-actualization of adolescents might be different depending on the society and/or culture in which they grow up. The needs of the individual, as indicated in the foregoing presentation, must be understood. The educator/counselor should be aware of these facts. Therefore, what he/she is to deal with first, is probably universal to individuals living in different societies and cultures. It is hypothesized that we might see different types of conflicts among adolescents living in different societies and cultures. For instance, in a "horizontal society," such as the USA, where people are accustomed to experience different relationships (individual interactions with educational institutions, the business world, etc.) without giving any priority to hierarchical order, adolescents might face different kinds of conflicts. Naturally, the style and type of self-actualization might be different. Even in Japan, because of the social change, a little change has appeared recently in the phenomena mentioned earlier. Therefore, when we deal with the issue of self-actualization in adolescents, it might have to be looked at from phenomenological, longitudinal, and horizontal perspectives. I am interested in the universal aspects of the individuals, as well as in the differences. I believe that in order to deal with adolescents for their own welfare, we have to be fully aware of both similarities and differences.

NOTES

1. Statistical Handbook of Japan, 1985.
2. A. H. Maslow, 1954. *Motivation and Personality*. New York: Harper and Row, Inc.
3. Committee on Student Personnel, 1979-1980. "Survey on Student Life." Nihon Shiritsu Daigaku Renmei (Association of Privately Supported Universities in Japan).
4. Gakusei Mondai Kenkyusho (Institute for Study of Student), 1960. *A Survey of Student Anxiety*. Tokyo: University of Tokyo.
5. Chuo University.
6. The Youth Development Headquarters, 1981. *International Comparison of Japanese Children and their Mothers -- Findings of a Survey Conducted in Commemoration of the International Year of the Child*. Tokyo: Prime Minister's Office of Japan.
7. M. Fukuhara, 1981. "Factors Affecting Student Counseling Services; a Study of the EPPS Needs." Doctoral dissertation, University of Tokyo. In Fukuhara, M., 1986. *Factors Affecting Student Counseling: From the Viewpoint of Counseling Psychology*. Tokyo: Kasama Shobo (In Japanese).
8. M. Sera. Invited Lecture, Counseling Seminar, Chuo University, Tokyo, Japan.

Understanding the Brain-Damaged Adolescent: Behavior and Treatment

Manny Sternlicht

Brain damage is a very complicated and complex phenomenon because we really do not know as much about the central nervous system as we need to. What are the causes of brain damage? By the way, brain damage is brain damage; there is nothing unique about brain damage in adolescence, with the possible exception that the adolescents' normative stage of developmental maturation must be taken into account. Likewise, the only cultural differences that we find in brain damage is that it occurs more frequently among the lower socioeconomic groups. This has been hypothesized as being due to poorer prenatal care and to the generally poorer quality of postnatal living; for example, the presence of lead in the paint in a low-rent housing residence. If this variable of low socioeconomic status is factored out, however, then there are no apparent differences either in the quantity or quality of brain damage on any ethnic, religious, or racial basis.

Sometimes brain damage is the consequence of traumatic events, such as a person being smashed on the head or being involved in a skiing or automobile accident. With regard to auto accidents, adolescents, particularly white middle-class adolescents, frequently are involved in these, often because of developmental phenomena. Adolescents frequently are prone to view the world through rose-colored lenses (i.e., responding to a dare and believing that they are invincible).

At any rate, there are two diagnostic types, which sound like the regular broadcasting networks: ABS, or acute brain syndrome, and CBS, or chronic brain syndrome. By the way, once there is brain damage, there is no way currently known to repair it. It is permanent in the person, and that is why some of the science fiction stories like "Donovan's Brain" cannot be true; one cannot transplant a brain because the neurons will not regenerate. Once they are cut, they are dead. At this point, you can have all kinds of transplants, but you cannot have a successful brain transplant.

There are also various kinds of (and these are the majority) so-called "congenital" causes of brain damage, which just mean that damage occurs at or around birth. Of course, some of the more common congenital causes include micro- or macroencephaly, any kind of rare inherited disorder that causes brain damage, and difficulties caused as a consequence of the delivery process itself. If the delivery is at all difficult, there is always the chance of asphyxiation occurring. Prematurity, especially in lower-income minority groups, also can present a problem, because about 5 percent of all prematurely born children are born with brain damage. In fact, one piece of advice that is given to young women who are becoming mothers is to get the best obstetrician they can to ensure not only that they will be as healthy as possible but also that the newborn infant will be healthy.

A delivery goes well in 95 percent of the cases. In the other 5 percent of the cases, however, the person assisting the delivery could make a crucial difference. Let us say, you have a really difficult delivery and you have to get the neonate's head out. As soon as you go in with any kind of surgical instrumentation you have no feeling. You have to go in on the basis of experience: you must know how deep can you clamp and pull out without doing damage. Of course, it is preferable to perform this procedure with your hands because you get immediate feedback about what you are doing and whether or not there is likelihood of brain damage to the child. That is when you really need the skills of a truly competent and experienced obstetrician.

Next, what are some of the more common symptoms of brain damage? The symptoms that are most common are hyperactivity and impulsive behavior. Most brain-damaged individuals are always in a constant state of activity. The reason why is difficult to illustrate, but here is an example. You are all familiar with the knee reflex, where a person puts one leg over the other, and you give a little tap on the knee and it will shoot out with a great deal of force. You are going to have a magnified intensive reaction. Let us pretend that there are ten different nerves going to the knee. The sole purpose of nervous tissue is to carry nervous energy. Let us arbitrarily say that there are 100 units of energy that have to be carried. If we have 10 individual nerve cells and 100 units, then each nerve cell is going to carry 10 units. Now let us suppose that 5 of these nerve cells have been damaged and are no longer functioning, which means that each of the remaining 5 are now carrying 20 units of energy, and therefore you get an exaggeration of the response. That is what happens with brain damage. The more brain tissue is destroyed, the more energy becomes available, and therefore the more active the individual is going to become. So that is why you see a great deal of hyperactivity and impulsivity. Further, there is no way that a typical brain-damaged individual can really delay his need for gratification. That is where the impulsive behavior comes from.

Then you also have real deficits in attention and concentration. Almost anything that takes place in the environment is going to distract the brain-damaged individual. This is why, to some extent, the best therapy room or classroom for a brain-damaged individual is one that is totally barren, without pictures on the walls or anything else, so that there are no distractions for the individual. Although the brain-damaged person has a poor attention span and limited concentration, he or she can focus on one topic or one area for a short length of time, perhaps 5, 10, or 15 minutes at a maximum. Then they have to move on to another area. They can always come back to the original topic later on, as if it were a new area, but they cannot concentrate, for example, on one task during a one-hour period. It just does not work.

Another difficulty that brain-damaged persons have is interpreting figure-ground relationships; that is, the ability to distinguish the foreground from the background. The armed forces have been very interested in figure-ground relationships to develop effective camouflage which represents a perfect figure-ground relationship, when you cannot tell the figure from the background or the point at which the figure just blends right in. Brain-damaged individuals are also very susceptible to illusions, sometimes called "erroneous perceptions." They respond very intensely to these illusions, which are an interesting phenomenon. Individuals who are brain-damaged see "reality" more objectively than we do. That is the case in another situation too. For instance, if you were to stare at a light bulb for about a minute and then look away at a blank wall, you would see a blob of light on the wall. The blob is an afterimage because there is actually nothing on the wall. Now a brain-damaged individual looking at the light for a minute and then looking at the wall will not see the blob of light at all. So who really sees reality objectively: the brain-damaged individual or the nonbrain-damaged individual? This is one of the peculiarities that we have with brain-damaged individuals. They see reality very objectively, but by that token we know that there is some degree of abnormality in these individuals.

Another symptom is that there is invariably a great deal of perseverance. Once brain-impaired individuals start something, they will just continue doing it *ad infinitum* unless they are stopped. Another difficulty is that, invariably, as a consequence of the brain damage, there is some deficit in memory, which tends to be much poorer than it would be in an equivalent nondamaged individual. This includes memory for recent events as well as memory for remote events. Testing memory deficits is one of the ways to determine brain damage and to differentiate between the congenital kind and the kind that can be responsible for psychosis. In brain damage affiliated with psychosis, the process for remote memory (memory of something that may have happened 20 years ago) is very good, but recent memory (memory of what happened this morning or yesterday) is virtually nil. Brain-damaged persons just do not remember what happened several hours ago.

There is also some degree of brain damage responsible for learning disabilities. Humans have to learn with the brain. So if the brain is damaged, or in any way immature, there may be problems with an individual's ability to learn. This is not to say that every brain-damaged individual is learning disabled or has a low IQ, because there are people who are learning disabled with some brain damage, but who have superior IQs. Therefore a brain-damaged person does not necessarily have difficulties with learning. However, brain damage is one of the contributing factors to learning disabilities.

Then, too, the brain-damaged person has a great deal of difficulty with abstractions, and they have a concrete orientation toward the world. They live in the "here-and-now" and do not conceptualize events in the future. Very often, in this regard, they share similarities with young children. For example, if you have a young child who wants to go outside, you might say, "Okay, we'll go out in ten minutes, I just have to do something." Then maybe a minute later, that child is going to come over and start crying to go out. The same thing happens with brain-damaged individuals. They have the same kind of inability to conceptualize what a ten-minute time span actually is.

Finally, one of the major symptoms (there are many others to be sure), is that brain-damaged persons have a great deal of difficulty in planning and anticipating the consequences of their actions. This is also a part of the impulsive symptom. They just go ahead and usually don't take into account the end result of their actions.

The next area of concern centers on the diagnosis, whether or not an individual in fact has brain damage. The answer is that it is not at all easy, because there are subtle and sophisticated types of brain damage. One of the procedures that is available is the neurological workup, which basically consists of two procedures. One is laboratory procedures, such as a computerized axial tomography (CAT Scan), or an electromyography (EMG), a magnetic resonance imaging (MRI Scan), and also an EEG or electro-encephalogram recording. An EEG is simply a measure of the electrical potential of the brain. Two electrodes are set up on opposite sides of the cerebrum and then the brain pattern between the two electrodes is analyzed. The normal pattern is an alpha or beta wave, which is about roughly six to 12 cycles per second. When there is brain damage, the brain-wave patterns are like those of a person who is sleeping but not dreaming. This pattern is called the delta pattern, which is much slower than the alpha or beta pattern, and is between three and six cycles per second. Then the electrodes are rotated so that you can identify where the damage is located. In other words, certain areas may have normal patterns while others may disclose abnormal patterns. Unfortunately, EEG data are not always definitive, because there are nearly 20 percent false positives and 20 percent false negatives with EEG readings. This means the results of an EEG can never be taken in isolation; they must always be utilized as part of a total neurological workup.

The second type of procedure performed during neurological examination is an evaluation of reflexes, which is conducted by a neurologist. If all of the reflexes are normal, then presumably the individual does not have brain damage. If any of the reflexes are deviant, then there is a likelihood of brain damage. The previous example of tapping the knee was used to check a reflex. If there is an exaggerated response with that reflex, there is brain damage. If the response is normal, it is unlikely that there is damage. Another common reflex is the Babinski reflex, which occurs on the sole of the foot. Interestingly, the Babinski reflex normally is found in all infants less than nine months of age, indicating not that there is brain damage, but that there is a brain immaturity. Then after nine months of age, the reflex no longer occurs. Another familiar reflex is the pupillary reflex: when light is shined next to the eye, the pupil will constrict; on the other hand, when the light is removed, the pupil will dilate or expand.

In addition to neurological examinations, there are psychological evaluations, which some experts think are superior to any other diagnostic tool available for determining brain damage. However, there is one test which is pathognomic for brain damage. In other words, when the results of this test are positive, then one can say with 100 percent accuracy that the person is brain damaged. The procedure is called the Spiral Aftereffect Test, or SAET, and was originally called the Archimedes Spiral Aftereffect Test, because Archimedes was the first person to elucidate the principle involved. The testing procedure is as follows: after a disc with the design of a spiral is rotated for about 30 seconds, it is stopped. The brain-damaged person reports that the spiral does not move. However, the normal individual sees the spiral move in the opposite direction.

There are a number of other tests that are especially good at indicating brain damage, and these may include all or nearly all of the projective techniques available. With various drawing tests -- the Bender-Gestalt, the Benton Visual Retention Test, and the Rorschach -- you can determine the brain damage often with relative ease and certainty. Another point is, obviously, you have to be reasonable proficient with the instruments. By the way, on the Figure Drawing Test, there is one pathognomic indicator of brain damage: when the drawing has a continuous, heavy line pressure.

There is also a whole series of tests for brain damage. The Halsted Reitan Tests, for example, evaluate brain damage on the basis of the physiological underpinnings of behavior. This is as much a physiological test as it is a psychological test.

There is also an educational evaluation possible, which is based on the individual's achievements and the way he or she learns, as well as the kind of behavior that the individual engages in. Essentially, with the more common types of symptoms of brain damage that were mentioned above, one can detect the brain-damaged adolescent in a classroom because that individual is going to behave very differently from the other students in the class.

One of the great difficulties in the diagnostic arena is that it is sometimes exceedingly difficult to differentiate between brain damage, mental retardation, and mental illness. Sometimes the same types of symptoms are going to be found in all three groups. It is advisable to give as many tests as is feasible while taking into account whatever behavior the individual shows. Interviewing the significant other people in the patient's life, is standard procedure. Often, it is not fully clear just what is the primary diagnosis. In addition, it is not just a question of semantics, because the primary diagnosis determines the kind of treatment program and rehabilitation program that will be developed for this individual.

Finally, to round the discussion out, let us talk about what can be done in terms of treatment and rehabilitation. One method of treatment for brain damage is the use of appropriate medication, or drugs. These drugs tend to be used in a number of different ways. However, the important thing to remember about drugs is that for different individuals, the reaction may not be the same. For example, a prescription that is intended to reduce hyperactivity may actually increase the symptom. Any time that medication is given, the physician must have some degree of feedback from the parent, or whoever else is around the individual, regarding the effects of the medication. The basic purpose of drugs that are given to the brain-damaged individual is essentially to reduce hyperactivity, thereby getting the patient to pay more attention to what is going on and to have a longer attention span and better concentration. For example, it is "utter death" for any brain-damaged individual to be placed in a workshop setting that has only one kind of contract, or regimen of treatment. That is why, particularly for brain-damaged individuals, it is much more advisable to place them in a shop that has eight to ten different contracts at the same time. The person stays with one contract for awhile, but can then move to another, which presents an entirely new task at that point.

Another treatment modality is that of psychological intervention, primarily through behavior modification. As with the retarded person, the brain-damaged individual also profits greatly from this routine of repetition and reinforcement. You must repeat things again and again until the brain-damaged individual understands what is required and can continue to carry out that requirement. These programs are relatively easy to design, but very difficult to implement and maintain because they involve constant repetition and supervision.

Finally, there is the area of education, which is broadly defined as the environment in which a brain-damaged individual can function reasonably well. It is accepted that the individual is not going to change physiologically. There is nothing one can do about the brain damage per se: the damage is there and is irreversible. Therefore, the next best thing to do is to try to create a relatively prosthetic environment using all possible aids, within which the individual operates, so that the consequences of the brain damage are minimized. As mentioned before, there are generally a great many distractions. One thing that might be done is to create a nondistracting room where a brain-damaged adolescent may work or study. The room should have blank walls, shades drawn over windows, and carpets or rugs on the floor to deaden any intrusive sounds. Thus, you create the kind of environment where the brain-damaged individual, regardless of age, socioeconomic, or ethnic status, can operate most effectively. Since with brain damage, there is usually some difficulty with fine motor control, you would also want to have just very large objects for the individual to deal with, so that he or she principally uses gross motor movements rather than fine motor movements. Again, the more prosthetic an environment you can create, the better. In addition, it may be good to be aware that some brain-damaged individuals have difficulties operating under fluorescent lights, since lighting conditions have an important effect upon functioning. Thus the "plain old" light bulb may be much better in the work setting for this kind of population.

To conclude, the brain-damaged adolescent can be diagnosed with reasonable accuracy and can benefit from a remedial, ameliorative assistance program. Nor are they any cross-cultural or cross-ethnic issues involved: whatever can be said about an American brain-damaged adolescent, generally holds equally true for a brain-damaged adolescent living in any European, African, or Asian country.

9

Thalidomide Adolescents and Preadolescents in Brazil

Jefferson M. Fish, Saulo Monte Serrat, and Maria Emilia Tormena Elias

In 1954 a German laboratory produced a synthetic tranquilizer and sedative, to be used especially for its combined properties by people who were anxious and had difficulty sleeping. The drug was called Thalidomide and its brand name in Brazil was Contergan. Following two years of satisfactory studies on its effects, it went into wide usage in Germany, throughout Europe, and subsequently in North America, Australia, and South America (Coriandoli, 1963). As is generally the case with new drugs in the Third World, Thalidomide was first used in Brazil somewhat later than elsewhere, and its usage also ceased somewhat later.

Beginning in 1959, a disturbing increase was noted in many countries in the incidence of congenitally malformed babies. This increase reached a peak in 1961, and in November, 1961, the hypothesis was first raised that Thalidomide was responsible for the deformities (Soules, 1966; Coriandoli, 1963). These deformities mainly affected the four limbs. Arms, hands, legs, and feet were either not present at all (amelia) or were present in greatly atrophied form. Sometimes they would just emerge from the trunk; for example, a few fingers or flipper-like hand appendages would extend from each shoulder. The latter condition was named phocomelia, derived from the Latin word for seal. There were also other kinds of disfigurement, including facial abnormalities and eye problems.

Germany itself provides a clear example of the dramatic increase in these deformities. Between 1930 and 1958, from a total of 200,000 newborns in Hamburg, only one case was found with malformations similar to those due to Thalidomide. By contrast, in August, 1962, there were between 1,500 and 2,000 children with such malformations born in the territory of Westphalia. So this phenomenon was a serious problem, raising worldwide concern.

Unfortunately, when doing research in a third world country such as Brazil, a great deal of information is unavailable that could be obtained in a developed country. For example, we could neither find out the date when

Thalidomide was first used in Brazil nor when it was stopped. All we know is that the pre-adolescents and adolescents in our study were born in a period from 1959 to 1965. That is, they ranged in age from 10.4 to 16.9 years when they were tested in 1975-1976 (M = 13.6 years; SD = 1.5 years).

This research was undertaken in part as the result of a movement that was under way in the state of São Paulo, to form an organization of parents to obtain reparations from the drug company that produced Thalidomide. Despite the lack of means available in Brazil for the identification of specialized populations, the organization was able to find 32 cases. The Ministry of Health assisted them in identifying another 38 cases in the state. A similar association formed in 1973 in Pôrto Alegre, capital of the southern-most state of Rio Grande do Sul, identified 63 cases there. In Belo Horizonte, a group identified 52 cases in the State of Minas Gerais. These are the only data we could find regarding the dimensions of the problem in Brazil. We know that there were many more cases. In addition, these figures omit the cases of children who died earlier, in infancy, or were stillborn.

Given the existence of this unusual population, we decided to evaluate their psychological development in comparison with a group of physically normal control subjects. The appropriateness of a matching design was immediately apparent. The reason for this choice is that each Thalidomide-affected subject was truly unique. They varied from one subject, who was missing all four limbs and had problems with both her eyes, along with other malformations, to a subject who was missing one finger and had some deformation of a second finger, both on his right hand. This variability meant that, on any given task, an unpredictable number of subjects would be unable to be tested. We felt that the most reasonable strategy was to identify control subjects who were as similar as possible to the experimental (Thalido-mide) ones, but were otherwise physically normal. Then, whenever a Thalidomide-engendered handicap kept an experimental subject from being tested, the pair of subjects would be removed from that statistical analysis.

With regard to evaluating the intellectual performance of our subjects, some further points need to be made. The Wechsler IQ tests (Wechsler, 1964) used in Brazil have not been standardized in the American sense. Brazil is a huge country with great socioeconomic and educational variation from one region to another, and with major problems of illiteracy. The tests have been translated into Portuguese, and some studies have been done with local populations to modify items and adapt them to Brazilian culture. For example, one can translate an item that asks how many states are in the United States, or how many stars are on the American flag into one that asks how many states are in Brazil or stars are on the Brazilian flag. Since the corresponding item might be relatively easier or more difficult than the English version, local studies can help in rearranging the ranking of translated items. Still, since Brazil is so diverse and the people in the north are so different from the people in the south, it is difficult to know how far the validity of the revised ranking extends.

Other items, such as "Why is it better to build a house of brick than of wood?" must be discarded as culturally inaccurate (there is no need for better protection against the cold in a tropical country). As a result, alternative items had to be developed. For reasons similar to those already mentioned, the authors of the Brazilian version of the tests cautioned against the use of the vocabulary subtest, and we decided to follow their advice.

The IQs that resulted from our testing should, therefore, be viewed with some suspicion. One of the benefits of a matched subject design is that regardless of whether the test produces overestimates or underestimates, both members of a pair of subjects are affected equally, so their performance relative to each other can be evaluated.

Testing took place on two mornings, and consisted of the Rorschach, a standardized interview regarding the subjects' present life and life history, Raven's Progressive Matrices, the Brazilian WAIS or WISC (depending on their ages), and a very thorough examination of their motor behavior. While the subjects were undergoing the motor examination, their mothers participated in a standardized interview regarding all aspects of their development from conception to the present, including physical, emotional, social, educational, familial and other factors as well as issues related to their handicap (in the experimental group).

Pairs of subjects in the two groups were matched according to sex, age, socioeconomic level (which varies very greatly in Brazil, particularly at the lower end of the scale, in comparison with that in the United States), and residence (urban, suburban, and rural). Once again, the terms "suburban," and particularly "rural" in Brazil, given the severe problems of poverty and illiteracy, are quite different from the corresponding terms in the United States. When there was more than one control person that fit all of these criteria (though frequently there was only one), we used the one with the closest birth date to our experimental subject. The matching of subjects was done quite carefully, with the cooperation of three schools in Campinas and two others (suburban and rural) outside the city. In the end, we wound up with 22 pairs of subjects, 14 male and 8 female.

The participants in both groups were slightly ahead of their age mates in school, and the Thalidomide group did somewhat better than the control group (55 percent no failures versus 32 percent no failures). This latter result was qualified by the fact that two of the Thalidomide-affected subjects had (understandably) dropped out of school, while none of the controls had.

The performance of both groups on measures of intelligence is briefly summarized in Table 9.1. As can be seen, the full scale IQs on the Wechsler Tests and the scores on Raven's Progressive Matrices were virtually identical for the two groups. One interesting difference was that the Thalidomide subjects scored higher than the controls on the Wechsler Verbal IQ, and scored lower on the Performance IQ, so that the gap between the Verbal and the Performance IQ was significantly different for the two groups. For the control subjects, the gap was only 4.32 IQ points whereas for the Thalidomide subjects, it was 12.86 IQ points ($t = 2.28$; $p < .05$). While the verbal-performance difference is sometimes taken as evidence of cerebral disfunction, we do not think that this was the case here. Instead, we believe that the Thalidomide subjects showed a slight increase in their verbal performance because school is the only significant social environment many of them have, so that they work very hard. Similarly, we believe that they were somewhat handicapped on the performance tests because of their physical condition. Interestingly, though, their decrement was not the result of slower performance on timed tasks. For example, the Thalidomide group did slightly (but not significantly) better than the control group on the coding test, even though some subjects had to hold the pencil with their toes or in their mouth (Monte Serrat, 1976).

Angelini, Rosamilha, and Almeida (1966) have published norms for Raven's Progressive Matrices for the central-south region of Brazil where we did our work. Eleven of the experimental subjects and 12 of the controls scored above the fiftieth percentile, while only two experimental and three control subjects scored below the fiftieth percentile. These results, along with our subjects' somewhat elevated socioeconomic status (as is to be expected of people who have access to a tranquilizer) suggest that the Wechsler IQs they obtained are an underestimate of their ability compared with their Brazilian age mates.

We also examined the correlation between severity of lesion and IQ. This could be done because the wide range of lesions allowed them to be easily ranked. A psychologist and an orthopedist ranked the 22 subjects based on written descriptions of their lesions and agreed in every case except for the relative severity of the sixteenth and seventeenth most affected. The correlation between severity of lesion and IQ is .07, confirming again, (this time in the experimental group) that the effects of Thalidomide could not be seen as limiting intellectual development. This is consistent with the conclusions of Décarie and O'Neill (1973-1974).

This lack of difference is quite interesting from a Piagetian point of view. Piaget's theory is that intelligence develops through a process of assimilation and accommodation, which unfolds through the child's manipulation of the world (Piaget, 1975). This process takes place initially through sensorimotor schemas and coordination of sensorimotor schemas (resulting, e.g., from the coordination of grasping and sucking). It would seem that a child born without arms, or even without arms and legs, would be severely limited in its ability to manipulate the world, implying that his or her intelligence would not develop normally. However, Décarie (1969) suggests that alternative paths such as toes-mouth, eyes-toes, or shoulder-chin-eyes (to pick up an object between the shoulder and chin) can serve the same purpose. Sinclair (1971) goes so far as to indicate that even in the extreme case, where a paralyzed infant can only move its eyes and see objects change their position as a result, the feedback resulting from coordinated ocular movements would be sufficient for intellectual development.

There is a great interest in psychomotor development and training in Brazil, influenced by the French psychologists Souberain and Mazo (1971). All subjects underwent a very thorough motor examination, following their work, and an elaborate protocol was developed so that each subject could go through the identical examination in the same order. In addition, a simple scoring system (present, absent, or untestable because of Thalidomide-induced handicap) was developed for many of the tested items. In this way, pairs of experimental and control subjects could be compared on the proportion of items passed, or for certain tasks, on how well they performed.

The motor examination included testing of coordination, equilibrium, body image (evaluated by figure drawings), spatial orientation, temporal orientation, language (oral and written; receptive and expressive, including an analysis of educationally relevant aspects, such as letter reversals), visual and auditory perception, the presence of involuntary associated movements during testing (e.g., facial grimaces or making a movement bilaterally when the experimenter requested a unilateral performance), tension, and lateral dominance. In all, 164 scorable items were included in the examination of the ten areas mentioned (Tormena, 1976). Unfortunately, space limitations prevent a more thorough description of the procedure.

Before describing the results of the motor examination, some mention should be made of the physical condition of the Thalidomide subjects. The age at which they began to walk and the number of surgical operations they underwent provide useful illustrative background.

Subject 1 walked at one year but only on his knees, because he was missing his lower legs. Subsequently, he received mechanical leg prostheses. Subject 5 walked at six years after a mechanical left leg was attached at the thigh level. Subject 8 walked at one year and ten months, after surgery on the toes of both feet. Subject 10, who walked at two years and six months, had been in a cast from his feet to his hips until he was five months old. In addition, there was a seven-centimeter difference between the length of his legs. Subject 15 was able to move around in a seated position from the age of a year and a half, since he didn't have legs. Subject 16, who walked at three years, had a reduction in the size of his legs. Subject 17 walked at two and a half years because, according to his mother, "he had a big head" and his trunk wasn't strong enough to hold it up (though, when tested, this subject showed no signs of macrocephaly). As to surgical operations, 11 subjects had no operations, one subject had two operations, one had three operations, two had eight operations and one had 15 operations; additional operations were anticipated for some of the subjects. The personal stories that emerged were often quite moving. For example, one subject, who had a deformed foot removed from a partial leg so that a mechanical prosthesis could be attached, said to the psychologist, "I really liked my little foot." In another case, a woman who gave birth to a child who was missing all four limbs dedicated herself to raising the infant, even though it involved carrying an ever larger child on her back from place to place to do so.

The results obtained by comparing the two groups on their motor performance in the preceding ten areas revealed no statistically significant differences in five of them: coordination, body image, spatial orientation, involuntary associated movements, and lateral dominance. In the other five areas, there were significant differences found, but these were of small magnitude, and of little relevance for the adaption of the Thalidomide adolescents to society. Rather, they would seem to reflect the sensitivity of the t-test for related measures, since the psychologist testing the subjects had not been clinically aware of any performance deficit in the experimental group.

One qualitative recommendation that did emerge from the motor examination was that some of the subjects, who had gotten by quite well without prostheses or other mechanical aids through childhood, might well be able to profit from them in adolescence. For example, an adolescent who has hands coming out of his shoulders can't take down his pants to go the bathroom. Even a device as simple as a pole with hooks on it, which could be manipulated to lower and raise his pants, could prove very helpful to his independence and self image.

The Rorschach Examination, which was evaluated by a Brazilian scoring system, indicated that the two groups' responses were generally not significantly different from each other, although there were a few differences of small magnitude that reached statistical significance (Lopes Carvalho, 1976). Once again, the striking finding was of how similar the two groups were psychologically, despite their dramatic physical differences.

If the big message of our study was that the Thalidomide subjects were not psychologically different, one might ask why this is so. We are inclined to believe, paradoxically, that one important reason is the relative lack of special facilities available for these children in Brazil. On the negative side, it may well be that a larger proportion of the severely affected infants may have died there, so that the Brazilian Thalidomide survivors may be a more robust group than those in highly industrialized countries. On the positive side, Pringle and Fiddes (1970) found that British Thalidomide children who attended normal classes performed better on psychological and educational tests than those in special classes. Both they and Kirchoff (1972) in Germany recommended that, wherever possible, the children should live at home and attend normal classes. Thus, it may well be that the lack of special facilities in Brazil forced the Thalidomide-affected children to adapt as best they could, using the bodies they found themselves with to the fullest. One might speculate that a child with a few fingers emerging from each shoulder will develop greater dexterity with them if left on his or her own, than if prematurely fitted with prostheses. Possibilities such as this suggest once again the surprising insights that arise when psychological issues are investigated in a cross-cultural context.

REFERENCES

Angelini, A. L., Rosamilha, N. and Almeida, R. M. (1966). "Normas Brasilairas do Teste de Matrizes Progessivas. " *Ciencia e Cultura 3*(2), 113-114.

Coriandoli, E. (1963). "Il Problema della Talidomide." *Bolletino Chimico Farmaceutico, 5,* 289-296.

Décarie, T. G. (1969). "A Study of the Mental and Emotional Development of the Thalidomide Child." In *Determinants of Infant Behaviour*, edited by B. M. Foss. London: Methuen.

Décarie, T. G., and O'Neill, M. (1973-1974). "Quelques Aspects du Development Cognitif d'Enfants Souffrant de Malformations dues a la Thalidomide." *Bulletin de Psychologie*, 5-9, 286-299.

Lopes Carvalho, R.M.L. (1976). "Psicodiagnostico de Rorschach em Pre-Adolescentes e Adolescentes Vitimas da Thalidomida." Master's thesis, Pontificia Universidade Catolica de Campinas, Brazil.

Monte Serrat, S. (1976). "Aspectos Cognitivos e Educationais de Crinca e Adolescentes Vitimas da Talidomida." Master's thesis, Pontificia Universidade Catolica de Campinas, Brazil.

Piaget, J. (1975). *O Nascimento da Inteligencia na Crianca*, translated by Alvaro Cabral. Rio de Janeiro: Zahar.

Sinclair, H. (1971). "Sensorimotor Action Patterns as a Condition for the Acquisition of Syntax." In *Language Acquisition: Models and Methods*, edited by R. Huxley and E. Ingram. London: Academic Press.

Soubiran, G. B., and Mazo, P. (1971). *La Readaptation Scolaire des Enfants Intelligents par la Rééducation Psychomotrice*. Paris: Doin.

Soules, B. J. (1966). "Thalidomide Victims in a Rehabilitation Center." *American Journal of Nursing*, 66, 2023-2026.

Tormena, M. E. (1976). "Desenvolvimento motor en Pre-Adolescentes e Adolescentes Vitimas da Talidomida." Master's thesis, Pontificia Universidade Catolica de Campinas, Brazil.

Wechsler, D. (1964). *Escala de Inteligencia Wechsler para Criances*, translated by Ana Maria Poppovic. Rio de Janeiro: CEPA.

Authors Notes

This chapter is based on masters theses in clinical psychology at the Pontificia Universidade Catolica de Campinas in Brazil, completed by the second and third authors under the direction of the first author. A third masters thesis, by Regina Maria Leme Lopes Carvalho, was also directed by the first author. While the results of this thesis are only alluded to in passing, all three authors wish to acknowledge Lopes Carvalho's work with the research project. This chapter was written by the first author.

TABLE 9.1

Mean Scores on Intelligence Measures by Thalidomide Affected and Normal Control Subjects

	Wechsler Verbal	Wechsler Performance	Wechsler V-P	Wechsler Full Scale	Raven
Thalidomide	93.59	80.73	12.86	86.23	36.00
Control	90.09	85.77	4.32	86.86	36.05

Therapeutic Management of Socioeconomic Conflict in a Suburban Culture: Developmental Stages in Addiction Epidemiology

Justin P. Carey and Alice T. Carey

Before the Vietnam War ended, the President of the United States declared another war -- not against Communism, but against heroin addiction. The first war was lost, and the second has clearly not been won.

While top-level federal management fiddled with national policy and strategic planning for the new war, heroin-based socioeconomic conflict at the tactical level was figuratively burning down the suburbs by a literal destruction of their citizens' personal property and cultural values.

To provide a developmental perspective, we must realize that poppy juice from *Papaver somniferum* has been available for at least 10,000 years, providing opium for rest, relaxation, and recreation to the Sumerians, Assyrians, Egyptians, Greeks, Romans, Indians and Chinese, among others. For cross-cultural appeal, this product is a marketing manager's dream come true.

To continue the marketing analogy, less than 200 years ago, the "new and improved" version of the product became available when the main active alkaloid of opium was isolated by a German pharmacist (Friedrich Serturner, in 1806) and named morphine, for Morpheus, the god of sleep in Greek myth.

Although the real and potential damage from opium addiction had by then been recognized, with the introduction of morphine we see the clear evidence of a cyclical phenomenon in the recreational drug field: the mechanism of denial -- denial of danger -- very similar to Kübler-Ross' first stage attitude toward death and dying.

Dying patients at first deny their mortality, in effect believing that life is a "free lunch," a benefit without a cost. If they survive long enough, progress is made to the eventual development of Kübler-Ross' fifth stage attitude: acceptance that the benefit of living must be paid by the cost of dying. The cultural lag which occurred before society's attitude toward morphine evolved to air acceptance of its addictive potential as the cost of admitted benefits, was far longer -- almost a century.

By then, it was time for the cycle to repeat, starting with another "free lunch" -- heroin -- followed by denial and ending with acceptance. The cultural lag for social values to be changed this time was somewhat shorter, catalyzed by the politicizing of federal policy on heroin control.

The social cycle for heroin began less than 100 years ago, in 1898, when the chemists of the Bayer Company of Germany developed the new narcotic as a derivative from morphine by treating the morphine with acetic anhydride to make diacetylmorphine -- marketed as heroin. Not surprisingly, according to our cyclical theory of social attitude formation, heroin was advertised as having all the benefits of morphine, but to a greater degree, for example, as a more powerful analgesic. In addition, this "new and improved" product was promoted as being nonaddictive and as being the treatment of choice for morphine addiction!

Let us now move the time frame for our developmental perspective forward to 1986 and the development of the latest new and improved product: not an opium derivative, but a fully synthetic relative of heroin, 3-methyl-fentanyl, made in the USA by a 33-year-old chemist employed by the DuPont Corporation of Wilmington, Delaware.

The synthetic heroin was made in the DuPont laboratories with DuPont chemicals, but without the Company's knowledge, and it continues to be produced elsewhere. It has a potency factor of 1,000 times that of the diacetylmorphine heroin. It would be almost impossible to use the pure form in a small enough dose to prevent lethal overdose, thus its potential for dilution with lactose or quinine is tremendous. One ounce is reportedly mixed with a ton of lactose before being marketed on the street to the final consumer. Two ounces of the pure synthetic is valued at $1 million. Compare this with the value of $500,000 for a kilogram (2.2 lbs) of regular heroin. The economic leverage is obvious, matched by ease of concealment and transportation to distribution points of the synthetic substance before dilution.

The synthetic heroin was developed illegally for sale to heroin addicts, thus bypassing the social cycle of attitude development described earlier. Another example, known to us all, has developed in relatively recent time and does fit the cyclic theory: cocaine, the main psychoactive ingredient obtained from the leaves of the coca plant, and the most potent nonsynthetic CNS (central nervous system) stimulant found so far.

The addictive potential of cocaine was denied until the last few years. Acceptance of its dangers is still growing, and there is still much to be learned about this substance and about treatment for cocaine dependency.

Although cheaper by weight than heroin -- about $2,000 for an ounce of cocaine -- much more is consumed. In 1985, for example, this resulted in a higher gross for cocaine than even for heroin: $80 billion compared to about $60 billion.

It is interesting to note the sociopolitical stimulus for the growth of today's cocaine industry. When the federal government initiated a massive and successful campaign in 1965 to inhibit the production, distribution, and use of amphetamines, illegal drug entrepreneurs seized the opportunity to fill the gap with increased production of another CNS stimulant, cocaine, with socioeconomic repercussions far outstripping the former cultural impact of recreational amphetamine use.

In 1984, a "new and improved," more than 90 percent pure, smokable, faster-acting form of cocaine known as "crack" surfaced in New York City. It became a best seller and within two years was the focus of a major widespread social problem. The euphoric "high" of crack, compared with earlier versions of cocaine, has a tremendous intensity with faster onset (4-6 seconds). The sequel is deep depression, stimulating serial use (addiction).

It is important to note that, although media attention has been almost totally diverted to cocaine and its related social and cultural aspects, heroin addiction has not diminished, but is still increasing by about 1 percent a year. Cocaine has given us a second drug-abusing population on top of the probable one million heroin addicts in America.

The socioeconomic conflict generated by each of these two categories of drug-dependent persons is not the same, although both have an average $100-a-day habit. One generalization (based on the different CNS action of the drugs) is that the cocaine user is earning the needed money, while the heroin addict obtains it by stealing the earnings of others. In both cases, of course, it is lost to the community and becomes untaxed revenue for the illegal drug industry.

Returning to the cyclical theory, we see research and treatment for cocaine use following the same track as that followed initially for heroin addiction: total abstinence, drug-free therapy supported by multiple psychosocial modalities, and long-term success only for the extraordinarily motivated patient, while relapse was the rule for others.

Our prediction is that compulsive cocaine users will typically relapse until a chemical control for cocaine use is found that is comparable to methadone for heroin addiction. Keeping this hypothetical analog in mind for its theoretical applicability to the development of broad-scale treatment for cocaine addiction, let us look at the nature of heroin addiction and its therapeutic management in relation to an example of socioeconomic conflict well along the road to destroying a community and its culture.

NATURE OF ADDICTION

The nature of addiction defines the cultural impact generated by a growing population of addicted substance abusers; it also determines the specifications for successful treatment efforts to control the consequences of addiction. To understand the changes brought to a culture by the behavior of members of an addiction subculture, we must first understand the nature of addiction, to heroin, for example. Heroin addiction manifests the four classical components of addiction:

1. A compulsive need or *dependence*, both physiological and psychological, on maintaining a homeostasis that includes heroin as the essential ingredient. Heroin avoids or relieves the tension and pain that follow abstinence, and, initially, it produces euphoria.
2. *Tolerance*, which requires increasing amounts of the drug to maintain a constant physiological and psychological effect.
3. The *withdrawal* syndrome of disturbances resulting from loss of heroin homeostasis within the autonomic and central nervous systems.
4. A *relapse* and return to heroin usage after withdrawal.

Physiological dependence on heroin is a function of time and dosage variables, operating relatively independently of the person involved. Biochemical cellular changes are involved whose nature is not yet fully understood. Psychological dependence is much more individualized as a function of the subject's personality and the perceived value of the heroin experience in relieving tension and pain and providing euphoria.

The homeostatic element in dependence may be seen as analogous to the drive to maintain equilibrium manifested by a group confronted with change, as postulated in 1951 by Kurt Lewin in his field theory model of the dynamics of group behavior.

There is no single solution to drug abuse, just as the term *drug abuse* should not imply a single problem; nor should a single authority or profession hold dictatorial or monopolistic control over the entire field. A rational approach calls for polyprofessional coordination and cooperation, including the disciplines of education, medicine and nursing, psychiatry and psychology, social work, and the developing ancillary areas of the paraprofessions, in addition to law enforcement, political science, and international relations. Research input from the basic sciences of neurophysiology, biophysics, and electrochemistry -- themselves the creation of interdisciplinary input -- is vital to complete our understanding of drug action at the cellular and molecular levels, which will lead to effective output from the applied sciences in operating effective and efficient programs of abuse prevention and addiction treatment.

The concept of multimodal solutions to the problem of drug abuse, however, does not mean that all approaches are equally valid. Once the nature and dimensions of a specific problem area are adequately identified and defined, and the characteristics of the particular drug-abuse situation in the context of a specified subject population are isolated and held reasonably constant, the principles of traditional scientific method may be applied. We can thus determine which of the competing proposals for treatment is most effective and, therefore, deserving of continued support -- which brings us back to the nature of heroin addiction and the dimensions of its treatment.

During the past three decades, numerous approaches to the cure of heroin addiction have been tried. Let us look at one of the best of the early programs: the first "total-push" inpatient treatment center to be established in New York City. In the early 1950s, in response to newspaper coverage of teenage heroin addiction, a hospital was opened on a small island (North

Brother Island) just offshore from Manhattan and the Bronx. The treatment included individual psychotherapy, group therapy, psychological testing, teaching, tutoring, remedial reading, social work aid, and health care.

A follow-up study of 250 patients was made three years after discharge.

The results were:

Dead from heroin overdose	11
Currently using heroin	231
Not using heroin	8

It should be noted that each of those eight nonusers claimed that, at the time they were remanded to the hospital, they were guilty of possessing heroin, but had not been addicted. On this basis, the bottom line is:

Cured of heroin addiction	0

The ethnic and cultural diversity of the study sample was representative of the composition of the patient population in the full program. As is apparent from the results, there was no significant difference regarding response to treatment between ethnic or cultural groups or subgroups in this urban-focused study.

Since the time of the aforementioned study, other groups have used various types and combinations of psychological and psychiatric therapy in attempting to "cure" the addict. All have met with minimal success, again with no significant difference in response to treatment between programs that drew their clients from an urban or a suburban culture, or a predominantly Black, White, or Hispanic population group. Even one of the oldest institutions for the treatment of heroin addiction, the U.S. Public Health Service Hospital at Lexington, Kentucky, was able to point to only a possible 2 to 5 percent cure rate.

Neither psychology, psychiatry, incarceration in jail, nor all the good intentions in the world will cause any appreciable number of addicts to cease using heroin. The addiction is a physiological phenomenon that must be dealt with in a biochemical fashion. Once the acquired chemical imbalance is neutralized, then the other modalities of treatment have a chance to work to rehabilitate the patient. Otherwise, back on the street, the addict returns to the readily available heroin.

The real -- but unrealistic -- solution is, of course, an internationally successful elimination of illegal heroin. Ironically, partial victories at this level serve only to inflate heroin prices for the addict, resulting in even greater cultural disorganization for society, but no loss in untaxed profits for the criminal heroin cartels.

Meanwhile, since its introduction in 1965 by Dole and Nyswander at Rockefeller University, the most effective element of treatment for heroin addiction is an appropriately prescribed daily dose by mouth of methadone hydrochloride. With methadone maintenance as the keystone of an interdisciplinary treatment program, a real -- and realistic -- solution is possible.

Comprehensive psychosocial services and health care can then fulfill their proper professional goals of lasting rehabilitation for each patient.

NATURE OF BEHAVIOR DURING ADDICTION

In the suburban New York addiction treatment program that provided the subjects for this study, 106 patients were asked to cooperate in a confidential survey of their criminal activities during the years prior to joining the methadone maintenance program; 98 actually completed the entire study. It is a tribute to the quality of rapport that existed between the patients and the staff of this clinic at that time, that such a high percentage of responses was obtained, considering the high personal risk involved in divulging information of this nature.

Fifteen categories of crime were described as commonly practiced by the cohorts. These included burglary, assault with a weapon, prostitution, shoplifting, forgery, mugging, pimping, pickpocketing, etc., in addition to selling drugs. The actual amount of money realized by these addicts averaged $39,697 per week, or $405 per addict for his or her heroin habit.

Separating the money realized by stealing tangible goods from that obtained directly in cash, we find weekly totals of $14,630 and $25,067, respectively. However, when we apply the typical factor of 20 percent for conversion of stolen property into cash, we see that $73,150 worth of goods had to be stolen to realize the $14,630. This means that the community lost $98,217 to these addicts each week of the year, or over $52,000 per addict per year.

These are the direct, measurable costs of addiction. To this total should be added the cost of addiction-related law enforcement operations, including courts and prisons, as well as personal and public health expenses. There is no comparable measure that can be placed upon the cost in pain and suffering, in lost emotional security, and psychological trauma experienced by the victims of addiction: residents of the community, parents, spouses, children and other family members and friends of the addict, and the addict himself or herself.

NATURE OF BEHAVIOR DURING TREATMENT

The subjects of this study were initially classified according to ethnic group, among other variables. The current epidemiology of addiction, however, emphasizes a finding of more significance than a report that a particular ethnic group has a higher percentage than another group. Addiction today is truly cross-ethnic and cross-cultural, rather than cultural and/or ethnic regarding its victims. Its nature is epidemic, moving across both geographical and socioeconomic boundaries; there is no "safe harbor" -- cultural, ethnic, or economic -- beyond an effective treatment program.

Although there was a consistently higher percentage of Black males to White males in the program's patient population, this ratio was reversed consistently regarding Black females and White females. A complex of independent variables beyond the scope of the present study is related to this finding, and we present it as a stimulus to future cross-ethnic and cross-sexual research in this field. Similar percentage comparisons for Asiatic, Hispanic, and Amerindic patients were not significant for differences.

The respondents to the survey also volunteered information on their criminal activities, if any, during treatment. Most were completely out of crime, and the average weekly total amount for cohorts came to $2,115, or $109,980 per year -- a decrease of 95 percent from the pretreatment period. Almost exactly 50 percent of this current amount was derived from the usually and relatively victimless crime of prostitution, which was by far the most resistant to elimination of the 15 categories of illegal activity. The pretreatment and in-treatment findings of this study relate to a suburban subculture. It is significant to note the consistency of these findings with the established impact of addiction upon the urban subculture. There is no qualitative difference; the difference is only quantitative since the suburbs, the numbers are smaller.

As former addicts migrate from the heroin subculture to mainstream society, in addition to the immediate and obvious cash benefits to the parent culture, there are other socioeconomic and psychosocial benefits, many of a value beyond price:

- The medical complications from addiction do not occur.
- Death from overdose no longer threatens the patient and his or her family.
- Pushing of heroin by the addict and creation of new addicts stops.
- Arrests decrease.
- Time spent in jail decreases.
- Families are reunited.
- Mothers begin again to take responsibility for the care of their children and home.
- Patients begin to work.
- An upward mobility in vocation can occur.
- Patients become self-supporting, leave the welfare roll and start paying taxes.

NATURE OF THE TREATMENT PROGRAM

To actually terminate the heroin (and cocaine) addiction epidemic, a massive international four-phased effort is essential, combining treatment, research, education, and enforcement. At risk is the cultural stability of the affected nations. Yet neither addicts nor community can wait for the all-out global victory drive against addiction. Hence, the value and necessity of pharmaceutical treatment programs such as those described earlier continue.

This creates the foundation to support effective utilization of the other vital services:

- ▸ Comprehensive medical and health care.
- ▸ Psychosocial counseling and psychotherapy.
- ▸ Marriage and family counseling.
- ▸ Vocational and educational rehabilitation.

When measured by relapse rate, even the most comprehensive of nonchemical rehabilitation programs have produced little or no success (0-5 percent). In contrast, the comprehensive methadone-based rehabilitation program for narcotic addiction has a patient-retention rate of 87 percent and, in the suburban program studied, a gainful occupation rate after five months of participation, of 92 percent (81 percent working, 6 percent in school, and 5 percent mothers caring for young children).

The methadone works because it ceases the craving for heroin and, if necessary, blocks the effect of heroin, all without increasing tolerance for methadone; other rehabilitative services may then succeed. The constructive psychosocial, economic, and other status changes in the life of the former addict are reflected in correlated cultural benefits of saved human resources measured in lives and saved material resources measured in money. This is the model that we propose also for cocaine addiction while urging biochemical research for a pharmaceutical solution (and hoping for a dose of serendipity as accelerating catalyst).

To add one more dimension to the cross-cultural and developmental perspectives we started with, the last word goes to Edmund Burke, as he wrote it in 1791:

> Men are qualified for civil liberty in exact proportion to their disposition to put moral chains upon their own appetites.... Society cannot exist unless a controlling power upon will and appetite be placed somewhere, and the less of it there is within, the more there must be without. It is ordained in the eternal constitution of things, that men of intemperate minds cannot be free. Their passions forge their fetters.

PART THREE: FOCUS ON ADULTHOOD

Photo credit: Maric Productions

11

Ethnic and Gender Comparisons in Dominance and Assertion

Florence L. Denmark and Elaine C. Bow

The formulation of and the belief in stereotypes regarding the various ethnic minorities is an area in which social psychology has traditionally been active. A great deal has been written about stereotypical beliefs in the United States. Curiously, however, stereotypes concerning our Asian population have not been adequately addressed in the research literature. As the United States and large urban cities, in particular, become more ethnically diverse, the need for accurate information concerning the interpersonal styles of the different societal members grows in importance.

Among the most insidious stereotypes that exist about Asian Americans: they are blind followers, unwilling to stand up for their rights, and are inscrutable. Of course, as with all stereotypes, these can be viewed as just one side of the coin. Unwillingness to assert one's rights is another view of cooperativeness. Conformity and following rituals are other ways to speak of loyalty and patriotism. What is inscrutability to one is cleverness to another.

In their 1983 article, Sue, Ino, and Sue reviewed an impressive array of literature to serve as a buttress to the widely held belief that Asians are not assertive.

There is also a considerable body of literature concerning gender-role stereotypes; a few examples include the following. A classic paper by Viola Klein (1950) notes the absence of both aggressiveness and dominance as part of the stereotype of femininity. Rosenkrantz, et al. (1968) similarly note that "not at all aggressive" and "very submissive" persons are stereotypically feminine. In her 1974 paper on androgyny, Bem includes "aggressive" and "dominant" as masculine items in the BSRI.

Deaux (1976) has advanced the point of view that it is behavioral, not physiological factors that account for the discrepant ways in which women and men act on an aggressive impulse. Baron and Byrne (1981) state that aggression is actively discouraged in females through cognitive training, denial of affection, and/or punishment. It was further theorized that this leads to a greater feeling of anxiety regarding the acting-out of aggression, and the subsequent displacement of aggressive impulses (Baron and Byrne, 1981).

Golub and Canty (1982) found that when a personal interaction exists, no sex-related difference in dominance was demonstrated as measured by the California Personality Inventory.

It was in order to empirically investigate the degree to which ethnic and gender differences exist in aggression and dominance that we undertook to do this study. We additionally sought to investigate whether Asian Americans do in fact behave in a manner that is consistent with these stereotypes. It is difficult to function as a political or social agent of change without being able to assert one's rights and point of view, particularly as a minority group. It is important that the Asian-American community and society at large have a proper knowledge of the degree to which Asians exercise these two traits.

In a previous study, Bow and Rabinowitz (1982) found that Asians' mean scores on Levenson's and Gottman's Dating and Assertion Scale (1978) were lower than their Black and White counterparts. However, caution must be exercised in the interpretation of those men's scores as no further statistical analyses were performed.

Support for the Bow and Rabinowitz pilot study may be found in an article by Sue, Ino, and Sue (1983). A difference between Asians and Whites existed such that Asians obtained lower dominance and aggression scores, while scoring higher than Whites on introversion, self-restraint, and passivity.

The authors decided to more fully explore the impact of ethnicity, as well as gender, as they related to dominance and aggression. Items from the Edwards Personal Preference Schedule (EPPS) were used in conjunction with items from the Personality Research Form-E in order to more fully explore the attributes of aggression and dominance. Both tests are considered to be reliable and valid measures of these attributes.

It was hypothesized that the levels of both aggression and dominance, as measured by the EPPS and the PRF-E, would prove to be lower for the Asian group than for the remaining three ethnic groups. It was further hypothesized that all women would score lower than all men, with the Asian women obtaining the lowest scores on all tests. The independent variables were ethnicity and gender; the dependent variables were aggression and dominance scores (four in total) on two tests.

METHODS

Subjects

A total of 400 undergraduate students at Hunter College of The City University of New York voluntarily agreed to participate in a study on interpersonal style. All subjects were fluent in the English language.

The respondents were divided into four ethnic groups: Asian, Black, Hispanic, and White. Each of the four groups consisted of 100 respondents, 50 males and 50 females. The overall mean age of the 400 respondents was 22.14 Years with a range of 17 to 38 years. There were no significant differences in age between the four, ethnic groups, nor between the males and females.

Procedure

A questionnaire consisting of items from the Edwards Personal Preference Schedule and the Personality Research Form-E was administered to each of the 400 respondents. The questionnaire also contained demographic questions pertaining to as sex, age, and income level. Instructions were given both orally and in writing to the respondents.

In accordance with American Psychological Association (APA) ethical standard, each respondent was required to read and sign a consent slip prior to participation in the study. Each respondent was given a full explanation of any risks/benefits associated with participation in the study. All respondents in the study were assured that any information obtained would be used for statistical purposes only and would be held in the strictest confidence, thereby ensuring their anonymity. In addition, it was made plain that any person wishing to withdraw from the study was free to do so at any time.

No attempt was made to obtain representative samples of the four ethnic groups due to problems of availability of respondents.

RESULTS

The means obtained by each group of participants on the four subtests (EPPS-A, EPPS-D, PRF-A, PRF-D) are shown in Table 11.1. Multiple 2 x 2 (race of subject by sex of subject) two-way analyses of variance (ANOVAs) were carried out for each group of items contained in the questionnaire in order to uncover any main effects or interactions that may have existed between the dependent variables. When the results of the ANOVAs were found to be statistically significant, appropriate t-tests were computed.

For the EPPS-A, EPPS-D, and the PRF-D the ANOVAs revealed a significant main effect for sex at the .001 level (F (1,392) = 12.19). A main effect for race significant at the .001 level (F (3,393) = 6.12) was found on the PRF-D. There were no interactions for race of subject by sex of subject on any of the ANOVAs. Neither main effects nor interactions were obtained from analysis of the PRF-A, so no further statistical manipulations were performed.

t-tests for race and for sex were performed on the statistically significant F-scores described above. For race, significant F-test results were obtained on the PRF-D exclusively. The significance occurred only when the Asians were paired with one of the three other ethnic groups. Thus, when Asians were compared with Blacks, the t-value was significant at the .001 level; when Asians were compared with Hispanics; the t-value was significant at the .01 level; and when Asians were compared with Whites, the t-value was significant at the .001 level (see Table 11.2). There were eight significant t-tests for sex (see Table 11.3). The t-tests showed that the Asian males were significantly more aggressive than the Asian females on the EPPS-A and scored higher on the dominance on both the EPPS and the PRF. The same was true for Hispanic males on all three subtests. Black males did not differ significantly from Black females in scores on aggression, but they did score higher on both the EPPS and PRF dominance measures. White males and females did not differ significantly on any of the measures. The scores for each ethnic group on the EPPS-A and D were similar, but somewhat lower than the mean scores presented by Murgatroyd, et al. (1975) for a 1975 urban college sample.

DISCUSSION

The results of the statistical analyses yielded partial support for our hypotheses. Gender was a significant factor in the aggression and dominance scores obtained on the EPPS aggression, the EPPS dominance, and the PRF dominance scales. On these subtests, the females obtained lower scores than did the males. However, no significant effects for gender were found on the PRF aggression scale.

It is not clear why the PRF aggression scale did not yield the same results as did the EPPS aggression scale. The items on the two subtests seem quite similar, and as noted earlier, both tests possess high validity. Further investigation is needed to determine why these two scales, each measuring aggression, yielded such different results.

A main effect for ethnicity was obtained on the PRF-D. Surprisingly, there was no effect for ethnicity on either of the aggression subtests. Not only did the Asian males *not* obtain lower aggression scores, but the mean score of 13.3 on the EPPS was higher than that of any other group. The Asian females' mean score on this measure of aggression was 11.00, identical to that of Hispanic females, and nearly the same as White females (11.04). These results may indicate that Asians, male and female, are not less aggressive than the other three ethnic groups tested in this study. Indeed, Asian males may be more aggressive than the other three ethnic groups tested. However, this aggression may not appear in overt behavior, because outward displays of aggression may be culturally inappropriate. Instead, the aggression is contained and not acted out; perhaps it appears as a personality characteristic. This aggression, which is not acted out, may even be turned against the self. This contention would find some support in applications of Freudian and Eriksonian developmental concepts. It is also possible that Asian Americans in a large urban center such as New York City may be more aggressive than

Asian Americans from less populated areas, as was true of some of the samples from other studies cited by Sue, Ino, and Sue (1983).

Sue, et al., in their 1983 study, reported that a sample of Asian males did not differ in assertiveness from a White sample of a self-report measure of aggression. Perhaps their measure of assertiveness is similar to the measure of aggression used in this study, which could account for the similarity of the findings.

In terms of dominance, other than the aforementioned main effects for gender and ethnicity, the most interesting findings were the low dominance scores obtained by Asian females compared with Asian males on both tests, but particularly on the PRF.

Equally noteworthy were the high dominance scores of White females on the EPPS. Perhaps when it is reported that Asian women are much less assertive than White women, the issue is really one of dominance rather than aggression.

This study has yielded some interesting findings on gender and ethnic differences in both aggressiveness and dominance. It has also raised certain issues, particularly when comparing Asians with other groups, which are not answered by this data. The scope of the project was not sufficient to address all relevant questions. Further investigation and research on this topic should be conducted. A second focus of interest is the development of a scale that is sensitive enough to adequately measure the traits of interest in minority populations (e.g., assertion), specifically Asians. Asians are accorded primary concern because they have only of late presented themselves in large numbers and thus may have been inadequately represented in the validation of most commonly used measures. Finally, research efforts should be directed toward further exploration and delineation of the degree to which Asians are stereotyped, and the degree to which they do in fact behave in accordance with such stereotypes.

REFERENCES

Baron, R. Y., and Byrne, D., (1981). *Social Psychology: Understanding Human Interaction.* 3rd ed. Boston, MA: Allyn and Bacon.

Bem, S. L. (1974). "The Measurement of Psychological Androgyny." *Journal of Consulting and Clinical Psychology. 42.* 155-162.

Bow, E. C., and Rabinowitz, V.C., (1982). "Self Reports of Assertiveness in Asian, Black and White Respondents." Unpublished study.

Deaux, K. (1976). *The Behavior of Women and Men.* Monterey, CA: Brooks/ Cole.

Golub, S., and Canty, E M. (1982). "Sex Role Expectation and the Assumption of Leader by College Women." *Journal of Social Psychology, 16,* 83-90.

Klein, V. (1950). "The Stereotype of Femininity." *Journal of Social Issues, 6,* 3-12.

Levenson, R. W., and Gottman, J. M. (1978). "Toward the Assessment of Social Competence." *Journal of Consulting and Clinical Psychology, 46,* 453-462.

Murgatroyd, D., and Gavurin, E. I. (1975). "Comparison of Edwards Personal Preference Schedule Norms with Recent College Samples." *The Journal of Psychology, 91,* 71-76.

Rosenkrantz, P., Vogel, S., Bee, H., Braverman, I., and Braverman, D. (1968) " Sex-Role Stereotypes and Self-Concepts in College Students." *Journal of Consulting and Clinical Psychology, 32,* 287-295.

Sue, D., Ino, S., and Sue, D.M. (1983). "Nonassertiveness of Asian Americans: An Inaccurate Assumption?" *Journal of Counseling Psychology, 30,* 581-588.

AUTHORS' NOTE

The authors gratefully acknowledge the assistance of Joyce Mak and Linda Fernandez.

TABLE 11.1

ETHNIC AND GENDER COMPARISONS IN DOMINANCE AND AGGRESSION

TEST-ITEM MEAN SCORES

Group	EPPS A	EPPS D	PRF A	PRF D
Hispanic Females	11.00	9.92	8.68	8.16
Hispanic Males	12.70	12.94	8.60	11.16
Black Females	12.26	9.72	9.18	9.32
Black Males	12.56	12.38	7.66	11.84
White Females	11.04	11.08	9.28	9.08
White Males	12.30	12.26	9.18	10.48
Asian Females	11.00	9.12	7.98	6.46
Asian Males	13.30	12.90	8.72	10.10

TABLE 11.2

t-TESTS FOR GENDER DIFFERENCES

	EPPS-A	EPPS-D	PRF-D
Asian males compared to Asian females	.01	.001	.001
Black males compared to Black females	NS	.001	.001
Hispanic males compared to Hispanic females	.05	.001	.001
White males compared to White females	NS	NS	NS

TABLE 11.3

t-TEST COMPARISONS FOR ASIANS

AND OTHER ETHNIC GROUPS

Asians compared with	B	H	W	
	.001	.01	.001	PRF D
	NS	NS	NS	EPPS D
	NS	NS	NS	EPPS A

B = Black; H = Hispanic; W = White

12

Comparison of Projected Social Distances to Stimuli with Ascribed Calm and Emotional Behavior with Either English or Hindi Instructions

Nihar R. Mrinal, Leonore Loeb Adler, Gwendolyn Stevens, Usha Kumar, and Jean G. Graubert

It has long been established that interpersonal distance could serve as a measure of attitudes in interpersonal relationships. For example, stimuli arousing negative affect elicited larger social spacing, while the reverse was true for positive attitudes that elicited closer spacing (Adler and Iverson, 1974). Physical interpersonal distance was found to be systematically related to a number of variables, such as: eye contact between dyads of the same or of the opposite sex (Argyle and Dean, 1965); different seating arrangements (Sommer, 1959); and situations of receiving appropriate (e.g., valid) praise from partners of the same sex, which promoted closer distances than did inappropriate (e.g., invalid) praise, comprising flattery. This effect was more marked when the partners were of lower rather than higher status (Adler and Iverson, 1974.) Another technique, that was used to measure either positive or negative attitudes, was the Figure-Placement Test. In this procedure projective measures of interpersonal spacing were obtained by the use of symbols, which were manipulated by the subjects. This technique measured attitudes in a way that did not need to be articulated or even recognized by the subjects and could therefore tap attitudes at variance with the subject's verbally expressed beliefs. A series of research studies investigated whether the results of the Figure-Placement Tests were in agreement with the physical distances observed in the laboratory. The outcomes of these studies have documented the correspondence of the schemata with both procedures (Kleck, Buck, Goller, London, Pfeiffer, and Vukcevic, 1968; Adler and Iverson, 1975).

The present investigation served to examine schemata relating to the ascribed calm and emotional behavior of the stimulus persons. Previously, Adler (1978a, 1978b) studied the ascribed demeanor, positive and negative, with populations of monolingual and bilingual subjects. Good (positive) demeanor according to Goffman's (1956) definition, comprised behavior in which one indicated that one was dependable for maintaining a positive relationship with another person. Bad (negative) demeanor consisted of behavior that communicated that one was an unreliable party to social interaction and was possibly harmful to others if engaged in a relationship. This then was the explanation for the social spacing found in Adler's (1978a, 1978b) research. For example, behavior of another person, who "remained calm when other people lose control over their emotions" conveyed positive demeanor and resulted in significantly smaller distances than behavior by another individual, which conveyed negative demeanor, such as "losing control over one's emotions when other people remain calm."

In a parallel study, Graubert and Adler (1982) explained that "interpersonal distance may have been seen as having had two components: (1) the fundamental schemata, which were representative of large social entities; and (2) an overlay of the individual subjects' idiosyncratic responses. The objective of all interpersonal distance research was to locate significant schemata and to determine the degree of their generality in the social world." (Graubert and Adler, 1982, p. 336). The findings of research on interpersonal distance were analyzed in terms of social schemata, which were the results of social interaction shared by many people in a variety of environments. Persistent agreement with their findings included the following situations:

1. Closer social spacing was due to the stimulus objects having favorable characteristics rather than unfavorable characteristics, that yielded larger interpersonal distances (Tolor and Salafia, 1971).
2. Good or positive demeanor versus negative or bad demeanor resulted in near social spacing for the former and far social spacings for the latter situation (Adler and Iverson, 1975; Adler, 1978a, 1978b).
3. Responses to stigma-free stimulus persons resulted in nearness between interactants, while individuals representing a stigmatized population elicited farther distances (Graubert and Adler, 1982).

While the subjects of the studies by Adler (1978a, 1978b), and Graubert and Adler (1982) were in general agreement on an overall evaluation, there were some minor idiosyncratic or transitory fluctuations noticeable between populations. However, the robustness of the spatial schemata could not be shaken. Such results left open the answer as to the cause, or causes, of those phenomena. It seemed plausible to speculate that perhaps the language of instructions was a contributor to the similarity of the results, since the participating college students came from countries with different histories and backgrounds, as well as a variety of cultural environments. Some subjects were monolingual while others were bilingual. However, the instructions were always given in English, regardless of the countries in which the students resided. The students, both men and women, who contributed data to these studies came from (in alphabetical order): Australia, Canada, Great Britain, Hong Kong, Israel, the Philippines, South Africa, and the United States of America.

In order to evaluate the impact of instructions in different languages, it was decided to use the Figure-Placement Task (a projective test), to tap the attitudes of the respondents. Previously this type of test had been used in a variety of studies, among others, by Kleck and associates (1968), Iverson and Adler (1971), then modified by Graubert and Adler (1972) and reported in detail by Adler and Graubert (1975), and then used by Adler (1978a, 1978b). The present study was a continuation and an extension of the previous research. It took place in Kanpur, India, with college men and women, native to India. Since all previous instructions for the Figure-Placement Task were given in the English language, the instructions in the present investigation were given both in English as well as in Hindi.

Based on the results of the previous research, the following hypotheses were advanced:

H1. The Indian college students would place themselves at greater projected distances from stimulus persons with the ascription of uncontrolled emotional behavior, compared with individuals who acted calmly.

H2. The ascriptions of status -- either high or low -- of the stimulus person would be responded to with different projected spacings, respectively.

H3. Differences in projected social distances would be a function of the ascribed sex -- male or female -- of the stimulus person.

H4 The language -- either Hindi or English -- in which the instructions were given would influence the responses of the Indian college students.

METHOD

Subjects

The data were obtained from 100 college students, who were selected from English and Hindi medium colleges of Kanpur City, namely, Christ Church College and P.P.N. College. Fifty men and 50 women participated in this research. Their ages ranged from 17 to 22 years with a mean age of 19 years. Both men and women were divided into two groups, so that 25 men and 25 women received English instructions, and conversely, 25 men and 25 women followed Hindi instructions. All participants received one test booklet with either English or Hindi instructions, though all were bilingual.

One of the principal investigators, Nihar R. Mrinal explained the difference between the two college populations as follows: the students from P.P.N. College were from Hindi background. The medium of instructions in the college as well as writing of examinations, was Hindi. For them English was really a foreign language. During high school or intermediate school they might have studied English, but it was just to pass the language tests. They were sons and daughters of the "common people" of Kanpur. On the other hand, the students of Christ Church College had English as the medium of instruction in the college, and they preferred English when writing their examination. Their family background was different. They were from the rich and affluent class. They belonged mostly to a high socioeconomic status. They had their schooling in convent schools. From early childhood they were taught in English. They were given "large doses" of Western culture, and while pursuing their education, they became highly cultured and sophisticated. Their parents were civil servants, doctors, engineers, and lawyers, etc. They could speak Hindi, but they were not encouraged to use the language of the common or lower-class people.

Task and Procedure

A Figure-Placement Task, modeled after Adler (1978a, 1978b) was used to measure projected social distances in millimeters. Colored round stickers, 19 mm (3/4 in.) in diameter, were placed in the center of 21.6 x 28 cm (8½ x 11 in.) pages of white paper. At the top of the page, a brief sentence identified the sticker, for example, "The sticker below represents a female who remains calm when other persons lose control of their emotions." All subjects were given a test booklet of 25 items and an instruction face sheet. Eight experimental items were selected to be reported here. In order to test the effects of the same and the opposite sex on the subjects' responses, "male" and "female" identifications were used to ascribe the sex of the stimulus person. (See Appendix for list of items.)

Attached to each booklet was a card containing 25 removable stickers of the same color, size (3/4 in.), and shape (round), which were identified in the instructions as "Your Self." Subjects were instructed to place the "self" sticker "anywhere on the page." Except for the first sample item ("your bed"), all items were randomized for order in the test booklets. Subjects were instructed not to leaf back nor to change their answers. The Figure-Placement Task was given to the classes as a group, though at times the task was administered individually without resulting in any noticeable differences in the responses. The task took about ten to 15 minutes to complete.

The construction of the Hindi test booklets involved the translation from the English instructions and then the back-translation, from the Hindi to English again.

RESULTS AND DISCUSSION

For the analyses, each page in the test-booklet was measured for the projected social distance. The shortest distance, from the edge of one sticker to the edge of the other sticker, was recorded in mm for each item. The data were categorized by (1) language of instruction: Hindi and English; (2) for gender: men and women college students; (3) the ascribed sex of the stimulus person: male and female: and (4) type of demeanor: either calm or emotional behavior. Analyses of variance (2 x 2 x 2 x 2) (SPSS, Inc., 1983) and the Duncan Multiple Range Test (DMRT) (Kirk, 1978) were performed. As hypothesized in H1, the Indian college students placed "themselves" at significantly greater projected social distances from stimulus persons with the ascription of negative demeanor, that is, uncontrolled emotional behavior, compared with individuals with positive demeanor who acted calmly. (See Table 12.1.) Therefore Hypothesis 1 could be accepted.

However the three other Hypotheses had to be rejected. Testing Hypothesis 2, no significant differences were found between the ascriptions of high and low status. The same was true for Hypothesis 3 with regard to the ascriptions of sex (male and female), which did not yield any significant differences. The same also held for the results for Hypothesis 4, the comparisons of language of instructions. (See Table 12.1.)

In summary, it would be stated that similar to the results of the parallel study with regard to attitudes towards mental patients by Stevens, Adler, Kumar, Graubert, and Mrinal (1985), an individuals attitudes toward another person who was displaying either calm or unwarranted emotional behavior, seemed to be translated schematically in terms of distance as the choice point from which one chose to carry on an interaction. It appeared that the aversive effect to the ascription of an unpredictable behavior resulted in responses of larger projected social distances; however, this was in contrast to the effect of the person, who was ascribed calm behavior, which conveyed and transmitted confidence and dependability, and consequently resulted in closer projected interpersonal spacing.

These schemata were shown to be reliable and consistent, transcending differences of language and culture:

"...cross-cultural research recognizes that while the discovery of differences may be significant, the finding of similarities may provide even more meaningful information..." (Adler, 1977).

REFERENCES

Adler, L. L. (1977). "A Plea for Interdisciplinary Cross-Cultural Research: Some Introductory Remarks." In *Issues in Cross-Cultural Research*, edited by L. L. Adler, Vol. 285, 1. New York: Annals of the New York Academy of Sciences,

Adler, L. L. (1978a). "The Effect of Calm and Emotional Behavior on Projected Social Distances: A Cross-National Comparison." Paper read at the Conference on Silent Communication: Language without Speech and Nonverbal Interaction. The New York Academy of Sciences, New York, NY, March.

Adler, L. L. (1978b). "The Effects of Calm and Emotional Behavior on Projected-Social Distances: A Cross-Cultural Comparison." *International Journal of Group Tensions, 8*(1 and 2), 49-63.

Adler, L. L., and Graubert, J. G. (1975). "Projected Social Distances from Mental Patient-Related Items by Male and Female Volunteers and Nonvolunteers." *Psychological Reports, 37,* 515-521.

Adler, L. L., and Iverson, M. A. (1974). "Interpersonal Distance as a Function of Task Difficulty, Praise, Status Orientation, and Sex of Partner." *Perceptual and Motor Skills, 39,* 683-692.

Adler, L. L., and Iverson, M. A. (1975). "Projected Social Distance as a Function of Praise Conditions and Status Orientation: A Comparison with Physical Interpersonal Spacing in the Laboratory." *Perceptual and Motor Skills, 41,* 659-664.

Argyle, M., and Dean, J. (1965). "Eye-Contact, Distance and Affiliation." *Sociometry, 28,* 239-304.

Goffman, E. (1956). "The Nature of Deference and Demeanor." *American Anthropologist, 58,* 473-502.

Graubert, J. G., and Adler, L. L. (1972). "Comparison between Volunteers and Nonvolunteers of Projected Social Distances from Mental Patient-Related Stimuli." *Proceedings of the 80th Annual Convention in Honolulu, HA, of the American Psychological Association, 8,* 209-210.

Graubert, J. G., and Adler, L. L. (1982). "Attitudes toward Stigma-Related and Stigma-Free Stimuli: A Cross-National Perspective." In *Cross-Cultural Research at Issue,* edited by L. L. Adler. Ch. 27, 335-347. New York: Academic Press.

Iverson, M. A., and Adler, L. L. (1971). "The Effect of Demeanor and Status on Interpersonal Distance and Schema." Paper read at the 42d Annual Meeting of the Eastern Psychological Association, at New York, NY, April.

Kirk, R. E. (1968). *Experimental Design.* Belmont, CA: Brooks/Cole.

Kleck, R., Buck, P. L., Goller, W. L., London, R. S., Pfeiffer, J. R., and Vukcevic, D. P. (1968). "Effect of Stigmatizing Conditions on the Use of Personal Space." *Psychological Reports, 23,* 111-118.

Sommer, R. (1959). "Studies in Personal Space." *Sociometry, 22,* 347-360.

SPSS, Inc. (1983). *SPSSX, User's Guide.* New York: NY: McGraw Hill.

Stevens, G., Adler, L. L., Kumar, U., Graubert, J. G., and Mrinal, N. R. (1985). "The Influence of Language on Projected Social Distances from Mental Patient-Related Items." Paper presented at the 14th Annual Convention of the Society for Cross-Cultural Research, at Isla Verde, Puerto Rico, February.

Tolor, A., and Salafia, W. R. (1971). "The Social Schemata Technique as a Projective Device." *Psychological Reports. 23.* 423-429.

Table 12.1

Means of Projected Social Distances for Each Item (in mm)
Language of instructions and gender of subjects

#	ITEMS	Hindi (Women)	Hindi (Men)	English (Women)	English (Men)
1	Hi Calm f	15.84	19.50	12.24	15.54
2	Hi Calm m	15.88	16.76	22.54	22.84
3	Lo Calm f	24.36	21.26	17.40	33.26
4	Lo Calm m	23.16	22.56	28.14	12.00
5	Hi Emotion f	43.00	54.46	59.08	48.58
6	Hi Emotion m	44.16	61.20	75.40	39.08
7	Lo Emotion f	38.08	44.24	61.20	58.50
8	Lo Emotion m	38.40	48.28	58.36	51.12

Notes: Hi= High Status, Lo= Low Status; m= Male, f= Female

119

APPENDIX:

EIGHT PROJECTED SOCIAL DISTANCE ITEMS OF PRESENT REPORT

The sticker below represents:

Experimental items numbers 1 and 2:   a female/male *superior* who *remains calm* when other people lose control of their emotions.

Experimental items numbers 3 and 4:   a female/male *aide* (assistant) who *remains calm* when other people lose control of their emotions.

Experimental items numbers 5 and 6:   a female/male *superior* who *loses control of her/ his emotions* when other people remain calm.

Experimental items numbers 7 and 8:   a female/male *aide* (assistant) who *loses control of her/his emotions* when other people remain calm.

13

Effects of Length of Stay in the United States on How the Chinese Fulfilled their Filial Obligations

Lucy C. Yu and Shu-Chen Wu

INTRODUCTION

A number of studies have documented the interaction between aged parents and their adult children. Coult and Hebenstein (1962) studied the extended kinship in Urban Society; McKinley (1966) found that ties with close relatives are maintained through visits, favors, and letters; Adams (1968) found that the greater the distance of residence between the generations, the fewer the number of contacts whether it is through visits, mail, or phone, Hill, Moss, and Wirths (1953) found that the Kinship system is the focal point of visiting and members of the kinship network are most often turned to with problems or emergencies. Shanas (1979) reported that older people are most likely to turn to family for help in times of need. Hill, Foot, Aldous, Carlson, and McDonald (1970) found that certain patterns of giving and receiving in extended kinship networks caused strain between the generations; and Staples (1980), in reviewing a decade of family literature, found very little on Asian-American families. However, Weeks and Cuellar (1981) reported that immigrants are more likely than native-born older people to turn to family members for help. The Chinese have a long tradition of honoring and supporting their aged parents (Su, 1922; Dawson, 1941; Koehn, 1944; Lang, 1946; Chen, 1947; Levy, 1949; Hsaio, 1956). Filial responsibility is considered "The virtue of all virtues and the soul of Chinese culture" (Sih, 1961). Although more recent studies of Chinese Americans have suggested that a number of Chinese and Chinese Americans in the United States are still meeting their filial responsibilities (Hsu, 1971; Wu, 1974; Yu, 1983; Yu and Wu, 1985), these responsibilities have created conflicts between generations because of different expectations of the elderly who lived most of their lives in China and the children who lived most of their adult lives in the United States (Yu and Harburg, 1980).

In view of these findings, it seems appropriate to investigate how this traditional Chinese value is affected by the length of stay in the United States among Chinese Americans.

Two basic issues in meeting one's filial responsibility in traditional Chinese society are providing financial support to and providing shelter for (or sharing housing with) one's parents and parents-in-law. This paper examines how the length of residence in the United States affects the discomfort level of this ethnic group in meeting aged parents' and parents-in-law's needs. We hypothesize that the longer the Chinese stay in the United States, the lower the distress respondents feel in meeting their aged relatives' financial needs.

METHOD

Sample

The 1970 census indicated that over 900 persons of Chinese descent resided in a midwestern University town. Combining the city directory with the University Staff Directory and the student Directory, we found 1,005 people with Chinese surnames. We then cross-referenced these directories and compiled a list of 872 unduplicated names with verifiable addresses. A self-administered, bilingual questionnaire was mailed to this sample. Five hundred and ten respondents (59 percent) returned the questionnaire. The final sample consisted of 510 respondents, 277 males and 233 females. The sample was relatively young; the age of respondents ranged from 18 to 90 years: 25 percent were under 25 years, 5 percent were 56 years or older, and 70 percent were between 26 and 55 years of age. However, some respondents were not married and some did not have living parents or parents-in law; 281 addressed their parents' financial needs, 208 addressed their parents-in-law's financial needs; 283 addressed their parents' housing needs, and 159 addressed their parents-in-law's housing needs. We classified the respondents according to their length of stay in the United States of America and divided them into four groups: the Newcomers (those who have lived here from 1-5 years); the New-Old Residents (those who have lived here from 6-15 years); the Old-Old Residents (those who have lived here 16 years or longer); and the American-Born Chinese. Twenty-seven percent (N = 136) of the respondents were Newcomers whose average stay in the United States of America was 2.5 years; 26 percent (N = 132) were New-Old Residents whose average stay in the USA was ten years; 23 percent (N = 117) were Old-Old Residents whose average stay in this country was 26 years; and 25 percent (N = 125) were American-Born Chinese who have lived in this country all their lives.

Procedure

The relevant data were organized in three groups. The first group was comprised of respondents' demographic data such as gender, age, marital status, and length of stay in the United States. The second group included a set of variables that indicated whether the respondents gave financial support to their parents or parents-in-law and whether they lived with these aged relatives. Finally, the third group consisted of variables that measured discomfort levels in meeting the parents' and parents-in-law's financial and housing needs. These two indices were constructed to measure the discomfort of providing financial support and housing for aged parents and parents-in-law.

Discomfort level was the dependent variable and the length of stay in the United States was the independent variable. Factor analysis was used to aid index construction. Analysis of variance was computed to examine if the number of years in this country decreased respondents' discomfort levels in fulfilling their filial responsibilities to the aged. The *t*-test was computed to test if there were sex differences.

Measuring Distress

Hill, et al. (1970) found that providing help to relatives caused strain. Two studies have shown that although the Chinese Americans believe in taking care of their aged parents, the actual act of providing care or not providing care created stress and strain among family members and between generations (Wu, 1974; Yu and Harburg, 1980). Based on these findings we made the following assumption about family intervention:

1. If the respondents did not discuss their filial obligation with their spouse, parents, parents-in-law, and adult siblings, there would be distress.
2. If the respondents, the spouses, the aged relatives and the adult siblings did not agree on how the filial obligation should be met (who should give, how much, and whose parents should live with them), there would be distress.
3. If the respondents, the spouses, the aged relatives, and the adult siblings were not satisfied with the situation, there would be distress.

Then we put three components, lack of discussion, disagreement, and dissatisfaction, together and measured the frequency and the intensity of these three components in relation to filial obligation and called the scale "Distress Index." We included the adult siblings because providing financial support and housing for the aged usually involves more than one adult child. Two distress indices were constructed: one to measure distress as a consequence of providing financial support and the second one to measure distress as a consequence of shared living quarters with parents-in-laws.

In constructing the indices, all variables were scored in the same direction; the maximum value of each variable indicated a high level of distress. Items with different ranges were recorded to equalize their code values. Each item within a single index contributed equally to the total score. The Distress Index for financial support has a three-point scale and was constructed with the mean score of ten items that indicated support; the Distress-Housing Index was constructed with the mean score of nine items that indicated that respondent's parents lived with them. These indices are available upon request. Each question had three possible responses: respondents with a score of 1 were considered to have low distress and respondents with a score of 3 were considered to have high distress. Cronbach's alpha and factor analysis were used to aid the development of these indices. Cronbach's alpha for Distress-Financial Support Index and Distress-Housing Index was .66 and .68. Principal component factor analysis with varimax rotation yielded two factors, satisfaction and communication for the Distress-Financial Index. Table 13.1 shows that these two factors accounted for 67 percent of the variance. Similarly, Distress-Housing Index also showed these two factors.

Questions for parents-in-law were the same as those for parents. In cases where there were missing data or nonapplicable items, the respondents were not included in the analysis (see Table 13.1).

RESULTS

We used the t-test on the entire sample to test the distress levels between males and females toward parents' and parents-in-law's needs and found no gender differences. However, looking at how long they had resided in the United States of America, we found that among the Old-Old Residents (those who had lived in the U.S. for 16 or more years), females experienced significantly higher distress levels than males in meeting housing needs of parents-in-law ($p = .03$). This means that more females than males were distressed when the husband's parents lived with them. For those who were born and grew up in the U.S., we found that more females than males were significantly distressed in meeting financial needs of parents-in-law ($p = .04$).

Furthermore, Table 13.2 shows that the length of stay did affect the distress levels regarding financial support to both parents and parents-in-law. First, looking at support for parents on the left side of the table, the Newcomers (1-5 years) experienced the highest level of distress and the Old-Old Residents (16+ years) reported the lowest distress in giving financial support to parents ($p \leq .01$). Moreover, when the four groups were compared, the Newcomers' discomfort was significantly different from the 16+ group ($p \leq .01$) and the American-Born group ($p \leq .01$); the New-Old (6-15 years) group's distress was different from the Old-Old Residents (16+ years); and there were no differences between the Old-Old Residents' distress and the American-Born group's distress.

Next, we will look at support for parents-in-law on the right side of the table. Table 13.1 also shows that the length of stay in this country significantly affected respondents' distress level regarding financial support to parents-in-law ($p \leq .01$). Again, the Newcomers reported the highest level of distress. However, with the in-laws, the U.S.-Born group reported the lowest level of distress in giving financial support.

When the four groups were compared individually for support to parents-in-law first, the Newcomers (1-5 years) did not differ significantly from the New-Old (6-15 years). However, the Newcomers differ significantly from the Old-Old residents (16 years or longer). The Newcomers also differed from the American-Born group ($p = .03$ and $p \leq .00$). Secondly, the New-Old group (6-15 years) did not differ significantly from the Old-Old residents (16 years or longer), but they did differ from the U.S.-Born group ($p \leq .00$) in their distress level when support their parents-in-law.

Table 13.3 shows that the length of stay in this country did not affect respondents' distress level significantly in regard to taking care of housing needs for both parents and parents-in-law.

DISCUSSION AND CONCLUSION

We hypothesized that respondents' length of stay in the United States decreased Chinese Americans' level of distress in meeting parents' and parents-in-law's financial and housing needs.

Our finding that the length of stay in the United States decreased the distress level of respondents regarding financial help to the aged supports our hypothesis. For both parents and parents-in-law, with the total sample in general, the longer the respondents lived in the country, the lower their distress level in regard to meeting the older generation's financial needs. This finding also supports an earlier study by Yu and Harburg (1980) that the more acculturated a person was to this culture, the more comfortable he was in meeting his filial responsibilities.

However, we did find some gender differences when we divided the group into four subgroups: we found that the US-Born females experienced higher distress levels than US-Born males in giving financial support to their parents-in-law. We know from another study that a large percentage of Chinese-American females gave money and gifts to their in-laws (Yu and Wu, 1985). The higher distress level probably was due to their lower income and their belief that they should support their in-laws (Yu, 1983); the dynamics between the daughters-in-law and parents-in-law probably also contributed to the daughters-in-law's distress.

Our second finding that the length of stay did not affect respondents' distress level in regard to parents and parents-in-law's housing needs did not support our hypothesis. Here the large proportion of relatively young contributed to this nonsignificant finding. Most of our respondents' parents and in-laws were "too young" to need help from their adult children. Many of them have never had a parent living with them in their home, although

Chinese tradition expects aged parents to live with their adult children in their child's home. Their aged relatives' geographical separation from the respondents (parents and parents-in-law were in China) was another reason given for not meeting their housing needs. In a study of Chinese-American belief and behavior toward meeting with filial responsibilities, Yu found that many Chinese Americans believed in taking care of parents' needs in the Confucian tradition. However, their behavior did not follow their belief, that is, more Chinese Americans said that they believed in giving financial support and taking care of aged parents' housing needs than they actually gave money and met the housing needs (Yu, 1983).

However, we note that among females, Old-Old residents (16 years or longer) felt significantly higher distress than males in meeting in-laws' housing needs. This was the group that was old enough to have parents who might be dependent or parents who followed the Chinese tradition and lived with their adult sons. The daughters-in-law here reported distress of having their in-laws living under the same roof, regardless of what was expected of them by tradition.

This study explored how the length of stay in the United States of America affected respondents' distress levels in meeting their aged parents' and parents-in-laws' needs. We found that the length of time that a person lived in this country had no effect on the person's distress level in regard to the housing needs of the older generation. However, the length of stay significantly affected the respondents' distress level in meeting the older generation's financial needs; we found that the longer the respondent resided in this country, the less distress he or she experienced in fulfilling their financial obligations to the aged. Our findings seem to indicate that there are some changes in how Chinese Americans are taking care of their parents. However, our findings are inconclusive for we did not have a large sample of the "old generation" to test our hypotheses. In our sample, most "aged" parents and parents-in-law were not old enough to be dependent.

REFERENCES

Adams, B. M. (1968). *Kinship in an Urban Setting.* Chicago, IL: Markham Publishing Company, 43-63, 78-83.

Chen, L. (1947). *Chinese Wisdom: Thoughts for Harmonious and Victorious Living.* Shanghai, PRC: World Book Co.

Coult, A. D., and Hebenstein, R. (1962). "The Study of Extended Kinship in Urban Society." *Sociological Quarterly, 3,* 141-145.

Dawson, M. (1941). *The Conduct of Life: The Basic Thoughts of Confucius.* New York: Garden City Publishing Company.

Hill, R., Moss, J. J., and Wirths, C.G. (1953). *Eddyville's Families.* Chapel Hill, NC: North Carolina Institute of Social Science, University of North Carolina.

Hill, R., Foot, N., Aldous, J., Carlson, R., and MacDonald, R. (1970). *Family Development in Three Generations.* Cambridge, MA: Schenkman Publishing Co., Inc., 79-80.

Hsaio, C. (1956). *Book of Filial Piety.* Kowloon, Hong Kong: Chi Shang Book Company.

Hsu, F.L.K. (1971). "Filial Piety in Japan and China." *Journal of Comparative Family Studies, 2,* 67-74.

Koehn, H. (1944). *Filial Devotion in China,* (2nd ed.) Peking, PRC: Lotus Court.

Lang, O. (1946). *Chinese Family and Society.* New Haven, CT: Yale University Press.

Levy, M. (1949). *The Family Revolution in Modern China.* Cambridge, MA: Harvard University Press.

McKinley, D. G. (1966). *Social Class and Family Life.* New York: The Free Press of Glencoe, 116.

Shanas, E. (1979). "The family as a Social Support System in Old Age." *The Gerontologist. 19.* 169-174.

Sih, P.K.T. (1961). *The Hsaio Ching.* New York: St. John's University Press.

Sonquist, J. A., and Dunkleberry, W. C. (1977). *Survey and Opinion Research.* Englewood Cliffs, NJ: Prentice Hall.

Staples, R. (1980). "Racial and Cultural Variation among American Families: A Decennial Review of the Literature of Minority Families." *Journal of Marriage and the Family. 42.* 887-903.

Su, S. (1982). "The Chinese Family System." Thesis, Columbia University, New York.

Weeks, J. R., and Cuellar, J. B. (1981). "The Role of Family Members in the Helping Networks of Older People." *The Gerontologist. 21.* 388-394.

Wu, F.Y.T. (1974). "Mandarin-Speaking Aged Chinese in Los Angeles Area: Need and Services." Thesis, The University of Southern California, Los Angeles.

Wu, P. (1946). "Kinship and Law in Feudal China." Thesis, Harvard University, Cambridge, MA.

Yang, C. (1954). *The Chinese Family in the Communist Revolution.* Cambridge, MA: MIT Press.

Yu, L. C. (1983). "Patterns of Filial Belief and Behavior within the Contemporary Chinese-American Family." *International Journal of Sociology of the Family, 13,* 17-36.

Yu, L. C., and Harburg, E. (1980). "Acculturation and Stress among Chinese Americans in a University Town." *International Journal of Group Tensions, 10,* 99-119.

Yu, L. C., and Wu, S. C. (1985). "Unemployment and Family Dynamics in Meeting the Needs of the Chinese Elderly in the United States." *The Gerontologist, 25,* 472-476.

Table 13.1
Factor Analysis of Family Interaction
in Giving Financial Support to Parents[a]

Variables	Factor 1 Loading (satisfaction)	Factor 2 Loading (communication)
Difficulty in giving	0.77	-0.00
Discussed with parents	0.36	0.69
Discussed with spouse	0.06	0.78
Discussed with your sibs	0.22	0.83
Parents' feelings	0.71	0.47
Your feeling	0.81	0.25
Spouse's feeling	0.77	0.31

Final communality estimates: Total - 4.68

Two factors explain 67 percent of common variance $\frac{(4.68}{7} = .6679)$

[a]Principal Component Varimax Rotation

Table 13.2
Analysis of Variance of Years in the U.S.
and Distress in Giving Financial Support

Overall Comparison
Parents (N=281)[a] $p \leq .01$

Overall Comparison
Parents-in-Law (N=208)[a] $p \leq .00$

Years in U.S.	N	Mean	Years in U.S.	N	Mean
1 - 5	69	1.50	1 - 5	49	1.60
6 - 15	79	1.43	6 - 15	75	1.54
16+	78	1.32	16+	62	1.44
U.S. born	55	1.35	U.S. born	22	1.26

Pairwise Comparison
Parents

Pairwise Comparison
Parents-in-Law

Years in U.S.	Sig.	Years in U.S.	Sig.
1 - 5		1 - 5	
6 - 15	.18	6 - 15	.41
16+	.00	16+	.04
U.S. born	.01	U.S. born	.00
6 - 15		6 - 15	
16+	.04	16+	.14
U.S. born	.20	U.S. born	.00
16+		16+	
U.S. born	.57	U.S. born	.07

[a]The total sample is 510; however, only 164 males and 147 females are married.

Table 13.3
Analysis of Variance of Years in the U.S.
and Distress in Sharing Living Quarters

Overall Comparison
Parents (N=283)[a] p $\leq$.13

Overall Comparison
Parents-in-Law (N=139)[a] p $\leq$.17

Years in U.S.	N	Mean	Years in U.S.	N	Mean
1 - 5	74	1.47	1 - 5	28	1.62
6 - 15	87	1.41	6 - 15	52	1.53
16+	74	1.34	16+	45	1.42
U.S. born	48	1.35	U.S. born	14	1.33

Pairwise Comparison
Parents

Pairwise Comparison
Parents-in-law

Years in U.S.	Sig.	Years in U.S.	Sig.
1 - 5		1 - 5	
6 - 15	.27	6 - 15	.42
16+	.03	16+	.08
U.S. born	.07	U.S. born	.05
6 - 15		6 - 15	
16+	.27	16+	.26
U.S. born	.37	U.S. born	.15
16+		16+	
U.S. born	.93	U.S. born	.50

[a]The total sample is 510; however, only 164 males and 147 females are married.

14

Mother-in-Law, Son, and Daughter-in-Law: A Developmental Analysis of the Relationships in the Hindu Social Context

Usha Kumar

It is not only in the folk stories and the media messages that the theme of the cruel and powerful mother-in-law, the weak and ambivalent son, and the hapless self-suffering, victimized daughter-in-law recurs. There appears to be enough documented evidence (Verghese, 1980) that these three actors, given certain conditions, enact very similar roles in live family drama as well. In addition to posing some complex social problems, especially when these interactions get exaggerated, this triad presents a curious picture of life experiences that tie them inextricably to a predetermined script of interactions.

Radcliffe-Brown (1950) noted that across cultures, the relationship of both men and women with mothers-in-law is the principal point of tension in the situation created by marriage. In American, British, and other Western societies, surveys consistently have indicated mothers-in-law to be the most disliked of all relatives. These observations could well apply to the Indian Hindu family with two major differences. In Hindu families, the "in-law problem" is with the son's wife and not with the daughter's husband. The second major difference is that one does not joke about it -- it is a dead serious business. (Mother-in-law jokes are scarce; the author has yet to hear one.) There is a saying that even if the mother-in-law or the daughter-in-law were made of 24 carat gold, they would still manage to find flaws in each other. Thus, in the "common person's" perceptions, the problem is formulated at two levels: (a) in the inherent roles and positions of the triad in the family network; (b) in the individual actor's inability to do anything about it. Besides this popular construction of the relational strains, the present analysis of these triadic dynamics here is based on three perspectives with varying degree of emphasis on each. The three perspectives mentioned below, also vary in degree of the internality-externality dimension. Without raising the controversy of the primacy of the inner versus outer world, the position subscribed to is one of congruence between the two. The task demands of the social world usually are in phase with the readiness of the inner world, or vice versa. The demands of both worlds dovetail to provide a curious adaptation of the individuals to approximate the relational network patterns expected of them in their setting.

Insofar as this chapter focuses on the developmental aspects of the triadic relationship, the more external perspectives are selected for their relevance only to the extent that they influence, support, or add to our understanding of the life experiences of the three major actors, namely, the mother-in-law, the son, and the daughter-in-law. The three perspectives are:

1. Cultural perspective;
2. Structural perspective -- triadic network;
3. Developmental perspective.

CULTURAL PERSPECTIVE

Social Context

In a mythologically instructed community, there is a corpus of images and models that provide a pattern to which the individual may aspire or a range of metaphoric identities (Bruner, 1959). In this section, an attempt will be made to provide a broad overview of ideal images held up as models to men and women as they strive to achieve their individual identities.

Hindu cosmology is feminine to an extent rarely found in other major civilizations. The feminine is the first energizing principle *(Shakti)*. It provides a conception of the world in which women are benevolent, fertile, and bestowers, as well as powerful, dangerously aggressive, and destroyers. Traditionally, this power and danger have been checked through religious laws that placed women under the control of men. The benevolent goddesses of the Hindu pantheon are precisely those who transferred control of their sexuality to their husbands. If the female controls her own sexuality, she is potentially destructive (Wadley, 1977).

The ideal of womanhood is projected in the figure of Sita, the heroine goddess of India's ancient epic, the *Ramayana*. She represents purity, gentleness, and a singular faithfulness to her husband that cannot be disturbed by his rejection, slights, or thoughtlessness. On the other hand, Ram, who epitomizes all the virtues of a hero, is also mistrustful, jealous, and very conforming to the wishes of his parents and social opinion. Thus, to be a good wife, is, by definition, to be a good woman. "By serving their husbands only can they win heaven," says the scripture.

Formidable consensus on the ideal of womanhood -- in spite of many changes in individual circumstances in the course of modernization, urbanization, and education, governs the inner imagery of individual men and women, as well as the social relations between them (Kumar, 1978).

Joint Family System

Kinship systems, role relationships, and family patterns emerge over a period of time to support and transmit certain cultural values. One key agency that trains and provides the arena for such cultural conditioning is the joint family system. Even though the traditional structures of this system are no longer as stable as they used to be, the emotional bonds and the interests of the family, which sustained joint families under the same roof, continue to be strong despite the emergence of nuclear families. For instance, the interests of the joint family demand a realignment of roles and relationships especially those initiated by marriage. The roles of the husband and wife are expected to be relegated to relative inconsequence and utter inconspicuousness. Any sign of developing tenderness within the couple are actively discouraged by the elder members of the family by either belittling or forbidding open expression of these feelings. Every effort is made to hinder the development of intimacy within the couple that might exclude other members of the family, especially the parents (Kakar, 1978).

Furthermore, there is the expectation that the daughter-in-law should sever her emotional bonds with her own family of birth to establish her loyalty with the family of her husband. This asymmetry in kinship affiliation may be overtly encouraged by the daughter's parents themselves, but emotionally they do not relinquish their concern. The in-laws, on the other hand, consider her a stranger (she is called parjai, which means "born outside the family") with the status of being a daughter-in-law and not a son's wife.

Intrusion of a stranger into a group of kin is a disturbance and a point of tension, especially for the husband's mother, who is the person most closely connected with him before his marriage. The tensions are further heightened if the daughter-in-law is a potential successor, as is the case in the patrilocal societies (Sweetser, 1963).

The Dowry System

Even though legislation exists against givers and takers in marriage, the practice is so universal that it is not possible to implement the law. There is no evidence that dowry was introduced as a voluntary gift, or a symbol of affection for a daughter. It was introduced as a nazrana. an offering, a unilateral transfer of resources by the bride's family in recognition of the other's generosity for inviting a permanent economic liability to their home. The implicit assumption is that women are economically less productive than men and are a drain on the family. Dowry is a compensatory payment to the family that agrees to harbor her. And precisely for this reason, dowry is a recurring phenomenon that lasts a lifetime (Singh, 1981).

The major tenor of complaint and tension against the daughter-in-law and her parents is that the son has not been amply compensated in the arrangement, and he could have done better by contracting another arrangement. Since this is such a persistent refrain on the part of most mothers-in-law, in all likelihood it is indicative of the unrealistic evaluation of the son's worth in the "marriage market," or the mother's unrelieved sense of deficits in herself.

It may be pertinent at this juncture to take note of the dilemmas or the content of the relational strains that repeatedly occur among the three.

The *mother-in-law* experiences relational strain due to the following perceptions of the daughter-in-law:

1. The daughter-in-law's looks and appearance;
2. Her immaturity, laziness, and inadequate training in home-management tasks;
3. Her poor upbringing in her family;
4. Her emotional investment and open expression of it towards the son-husband;
5. Continuance of emotional bonds with her family of birth, leading to fear of a gradual change in the son's loyalty to his own family;
6. Anxiety that the son may succumb to the sexual passion of his wife and may become partial in his judgments.

The *son* experiences relational strains due to the following perceptions:

1. The wife's strategy of sexual enticement may weaken him as a man and further bind him to her;
2. Guilt at having betrayed his mother by his emotional attachment to his wife;
3. Demands of the two women to act as an arbitrator in their disagreements. He perceives this as an unmanageable demand best handled through avoidance;
4. Emotional demands of the women by their very construction appear mutually exclusive;
5. Playing the indifferent husband-son.

The *daughter-in-law* feels relational strains due to the following perceptions:

1. That she is treated as a menial rather than as a member of the family with no consideration for her physical or emotional well-being;
2. That the mother-in-law circumscribes her movements, choice of friends, and contacts with family;
3. In particular, negative affect gets expressed toward her family of birth;
4. The mother-in-law's criticism, disparagement, humiliation, and rejection of her would be tolerable, if the husband gave her some protection. His noninterference is, at best, perceived as indifference and, at worst, a flaw in his masculinity;
5. Being treated as a sexual object by the husband and generally depersonalized by other members of the family;

6. Being under constant pressure to assess the moods of others in order to shape her actions. She finds herself in a double bind because of the contradictory messages transmitted to her.

It is not difficult to envisage the relational strains arising out of these perceptions. However valid these perceptions may appear from the perspective of each individual, it is the mismatched expectations of the triad that predisposes them to the relational strains. Unless merging with others is balanced by identity-establishing experiences (Askham, 1976), what follows is a false sense of stability in relationships. Stability under such conditions is the status quo obtained through interlocking conflicts, which reduce the individual's degree of freedom to find new options in interactions with others.

Structural Perspective -- Triadic Network

One way of understanding the nature of relationships in a family is to conceptually decompose the family network into a series of triads (Fischer, 1983). The most difficult triad in women's family relationships is that of the mother-in-law, son, and daughter-in-law, with the son being the significant kin who is central to the orienting and reorienting of the relationship between the other two. The mother-in-law and daughter-in-law are essentially strangers, whose relationship derives from the fact that they both have close relationships with the son-husband.

Focusing only on the essential nature of the triad without the particular actors, it presents itself as the smallest social system comprising three members in a persistent situation (Caplow, 1968). The most significant property of the triad is its tendency to divide into a coalition of two members against the third. This division leads to the formation of two *partners* and one *opponent*. Even though the rules of coalition formation are not simple, it is expected that coalition will give some advantage to the two who pair against the third.

In the present setting, the coalition of the mother with her son against the daughter-in-law is a conservative and nonutilitarian coalition. It is conservative because each member is independently more powerful than the third member, namely, the daughter-in-law-wife, and for all practical purposes does not need to form a coalition against her. It is a nonutilitarian coalition because it is based on the mutual attraction of the two partners and unrelated to the other member's control of resources. Another anomaly in this mother-son coalition is that it crosses both gender and generational barriers, factors that are ordinarily generators of potential tension in and contribute to the instability of the coalition partnership. Besides affirming allegiance to each other, the two members are ostensibly confirming the status quo in power differentials of members.

Violating some generally accepted principles of coalition formation, the rationale for this particular partnership is possibly determined by other compelling factors. Hsu's (1966) typology of kinship identified four major axes in family relationships in the world. He observed father-son, brother-brother, husband-wife, and mother-son axes in characterizing relationships in families. The Hindus, he stated, were typical representatives of the mother-son axis, in sharp contrast to families in other parts of the Orient, where the father-son axis was more prevalent. It is needless to underscore the fact that this axis is the classical oedipal situation where the libidinal element forms the basis of the tie and also turns out to be the strongest of the four ties mentioned by Hsu. "The oedipus concept is a reminder that deep-rooted unconscious libidinal motives play a large part in the selection of coalition partners and warns us against the attempt to explain family coalitions exclusively in terms of relative power" (Caplow, 1968, p. 84).

The basic assumption of the triad theory is that the relationship between any pair of actors can be best understood by examining their conjoint relationship with a significant third party. In the relationship between affinal relatives, the connecting spouse is likely to be the significant third party. Thus, we may understand the relationship between a daughter-in-law and a mother-in-law by examining the relationship of each to the man between them.

Developmental Perspective

Distinction between male and female is the basic organizing principle in every human culture. The Indian mother's nonconscious ideology (Bem and Bem, 1970) and gender schema (Bem, 1981) automatically incline her to render preferential treatment to her son when compared with the daughter. Discrimination is a built-in feature in an Indian woman's mothering.

With these general observations, the remaining section of this chapter will highlight those details of caretaking that seem important for later interactions between the son, daughter, their spouses, mother, and mother-in-law.

Mothering a Male

The birth of a male child is a deliverance for the mother in the Hindu family. For a young wife, her son, in quite a literal sense, is her social redeemer. He redeems her from insecurity about her status in the family, doubt about her femininity, and shame of infertility. She is a true wife who has born a son. It also marks the beginning of the psychological process that establishes her acceptance in the in-law's family. Upon this child she lavishes a devotion of an intensity proportionate to his importance for her emotional ease and social security.

The Indian male infant's experience of the mother is a heady one (Kakar, 1978). The mother is intensely, exclusively, and intimately attached to her son. Physical closeness extends beyond the years of infancy as manifested in rather late weaning, circumscribed locomotion for safety, and sleeping with the mother. Activities such as bathing, dressing, and eating are indulgently performed by the mother, even when the child is old enough to manage these. The mother's touch and stimulation, whether or not ministrations are deliberately seductive or overtly sexual, nonetheless infuse the mother's caretaking with an intensity that the male child's still weak and unstructured ego cannot cope with. In addition to the sensual contact, constant alertness to the child's needs before these are expressed gives rise to feelings of omnipotence in the child -- a process that is exacerbated further by his diffused sense of self-boundaries.

Mothering a female

Mothering a daughter is a distinctly different experience for a woman than mothering a son. Accolades received for the birth of a son turn to responsibility or blame for the birth of a daughter. In most families, the birth of a daughter is received with subdued feelings. It is worse for the female infant if she is the second daughter in a family of no sons. It is indeed meaningful that the incidence of postpartum depression is higher after the birth of a female than after a male infant's birth.

The femaleness of the infant possibly reactivates a sense of inferiority in the mother and memories of a history of discriminations at the hand of both adult males and females, but males particularly. She is reminded of being unnoticed by the emotionally distant father who preferred her human services but was unwilling to relate to her person. She is unable to forget the superior status accorded to her brothers who never even noticed the differential treatment accorded to her. Her lack of emotional fulfillment from the husband and his lack of independence in standing up to his mother affects her mothering and the kind of image she presents of herself to the growing female child.

There is no doubt concern for the young daughter as the mother anticipates the difficulties she is likely to encounter. There are tender moments, but these precede moments of anxiety aroused in the mother regarding her own past and frequently are followed by actions that may be considered a retaliative demonstration of aggression. Neglect, restraint deprivation, and suppression toward the female child may get displayed in different situations. For instance, the mother lets the female infant cry longer before attending to her. She may not give as nutritive foods to the female child as she gives the male. She can delay obtaining medical attention to a physical illness until the time that the malady reaches a critical stage. The daughter's interests and self-expression may be curbed lest she become more independent than is desired of her. In this context, it is not surprising to find statistical evidence that infant female mortality is higher than that of males (Kumar, 1978).

Because of the like-sex bond of the mother-daughter relationship, one would expect a greater susceptibility in the mother to consider her daughter an extension of herself. It is conjectured that in the Hindu family it is not so. The daughter's partial rejection by the mother releases the infant child from the kind of reengulfment or fusion experienced by the male infant. Her separation facilitating individuation is accelerated, and she is allowed to develop an autonomous self earlier than a son does.

From early infancy, the preparation of the female child is for marriage and motherhood. The girl grows up with the idea that she has to align herself to another family. However, strong anchors exist in the knowledge that parents know what is good for her. This is not to suggest that the girl escapes unscathed. What is damaging to the girl's sense of identity and her self-esteem is the mother-in-law's victimization of the mother and the mother's submission to it. This does not merely humiliate the mother, but also mutilates the daughter who watches her mother for clues as to what it means to be a woman. It is here that the vicious circle begins. The mother, a victim, fills her daughter with either rage or resignation; neither condition is much of a launching pad for an easy self-acceptance of femininity (Kumar, 1979).

In a dominant patriarchal culture through unconscious necessity, it is the *mater* who is of primary symbolic significance, or as Jungians would put it, the mother is the primary constituent of a man's anima. The reason for the intertwining of anima images and feminine psychology is that very early in childhood, girls learn to perceive accurately and to conform to the patriarchal images of femininity entertained by the men around them in the household. The tragic confusion for any group labeled inferior is that it absorbs a large part of untruth created by the superior group. The internalization of the dominant belief is more likely to occur if there are no other alternative concepts at hand (Miller, 1976).

Living the projections of the male anima, the girl is systematically trained in household arts and social skills. Having suffered rejection and depreciation earlier, the learning of skills is restorative for self-image and her self-esteem. She is inclined to develop a strong sense of industry.

Unravelling the Relationship Knot

One can evaluate the interaction of each member of the triad against a set of optimal and desirable interactions and accordingly analyze the genesis of deviations from their developmental histories. However, the case of mother-in-law, son, and the daughter-in-law requires a specific scrutiny of the optimal and desirable interactions for their particular application in this situation.

Even in the best of circumstances, intimacy between spouses brings unresolved conflicts and personal inadequacies to the fore, so much so that it has been recognized as the major crisis of young adulthood (Erikson, 1950). The mother-in-law, a generation removed from the son and the daughter-in-law, is naturally faced with different dilemmas in her developmental tasks. After nearly two decades of subservience, dependency, and caring for others, almost for the first time in her life she seeks self-expression, assertion, and command over what is literally her home territory. Thus, the difference in ages, sex, and developmental dilemmas of each individual add further complexity to the diagnosis of the contributing factors.

The question that arises from those observations is: when does the engagement of differences stimulate development and enhancement of the parties to the engagement, and when does it have a negative effect? Generally, relationships that stimulate development imply separateness. Separateness is achieved through clear delineation of self-boundaries and through a sense of firm identity. All three characters lack this firm sense of inner anchors: the females because of their sustained self-image of inferiority and repressed individual expression in favor of fitting the social mould of conformity, and the male with his diffused boundaries and narcissistic orientation. In the interaction, the male is looking for a safe merger with the other without commitment. Intimacy for the young couple is hardly for mutuality but for finding a confirmation of their idiosyncratic preoccupations. A recreation of the mother image through projections on the wife stifles the relationship. The young wife is not ready to take the projections of the mother image of the husband on herself. She fights hard to get away from it. Her need is to get evidence of her physical attractiveness, her lovableness, and her acceptability -- confirmations of which are hard for her to obtain from the husband.

All three individuals, conditioned by their early psychosocial history, find themselves limited in traits such as insight, empathy, and accurate perception of the other, which are all factors facilitating close relationships (Waring, McElrath, Lefcoe, and Weisz, 1981). For example, the more experienced member of the triad, the mother-in-law, displays no empathy for the younger woman or sees no likeness of her daughter in the daughter-in-law. Possibly being a victim to sustained and unwarranted aggression lowers sensitivity and empathy for others. This, of course, speaks to the power of unconscious projections in relationships. It also spells for the power of the outer roles that shape the person's denying the truth or existence of the inner person (Wickes, 1927). The mother-in-law, who took refuge in roles and social prescriptions in her youth, now finds herself encrusted in the outer shell of roles and out of touch with her inner world of feelings. Both women have built up "too good a person" image and now pay a price for their overconformity and need for social approval, which led to the neglect of those elements that were true representations of self.

An aggressive destructive impulse toward the male child is one distinct probability of female reaction, especially in a society that blatantly derogates and discriminates against women. Yet surprisingly, this dimension toward the male child is weak. The anger suppressed earlier is focused on the daughter-in-law, who jeopardizes the mother's position. This focused anger and hostility is possibly reciprocated in full measure by the ego-alien anger of the daughter-in-law against her mother. And the vicious cycle starts. The mother-in-law's open aggression is met with covert hostility and negativism by the daughter-in-law, who shies away from open verbal confrontation by keeping up the facade of subservience and respect.

The daughter-in-law's reactions are determined by yet another factor. Her anger at her mother's discrimination is incorporated in her overall self-image as a split-self and ego-alien part of her identity. Preliminary interview responses indicated that the personal constructs used for the mother are the bipolar opposites of those used for the mothers-in-law. The mother is idealized as benign, the mother-in-law as a malefic figure. Both are exaggerated and unrealistic images. The mother-in-law now becomes the living Rorschach to receive the hostile projections of the daughter-in-law. The appropriateness in the choice of the object fits the stereotypes of the mother-in-law. It is suggested that even if the daughter-in-law did not have a mother-in-law, she would create one in the family of the husband to give vent to her anger. However, the mother-in-law turns out to be a strong adversary with her own confused sense of boundaries between assertion and aggression.

Since the norms of the relationship give a superior role to the mother-in-law in the relational network, the balance of power is temporarily in her favor. However, unsupported by her husband and uncertain about her son's continued loyalty, she is apprehensive of her decline in status. On the other hand, the daughter-in-law, in her willingness to be a sexual object for the husband, hopes to win him over some day. Intimacy starts to develop with the birth of the child whose care becomes the central issue in her relationship with the husband. If she gives birth to a son, she anticipates a winning coalition with the infant against her mother-in-law.

The husband, caught between the two women and unsure of his own capabilities handling them, feels relieved when one of them physically leaves the field. Or if that does not happen, he can emotionally leave the field. It is not an easy arrangement because of his overwhelming need to be served by females and his dependence on relationships. His ambivalence makes him change his stance, to the chagrin of both females. Though the existence of the ideal mother image is only in his fantasy, his attachment to the mother in the home brooks little interference.

In the end, what is very apparent in this analysis is the fact that similar patterns in child rearing appear again and again in response to certain needs generated in the mother and the mothered. The psychic structures become as irreversible as the biological ones. Furthermore, the deeply ingrained inequality of the sexes proves disadvantageous to both in forming healthy relationships in adult life. Unlabeling the female sex as inferior may minimize the heterosexual asymmetries by encouraging fathers to take a primary role in the nurturance of infants. The infant's sense of self is frail. The foundation of all self-esteem is grounded in the first closeness with the caretaker. The curiously close dovetailing of the social reality with the inner world only underscores the fact that intervention for change has to keep pace with both fronts, the inner as well as the outer, to be enduring in its effectiveness.

SUMMARY

Briefly, this paper analyzed the triadic relationships of the mother-in-law, son, and daughter-in-law to suggest some contributing factors in their relational strains. The analysis focused on the relevant aspects of three perspectives: the cultural, the structural, and the developmental. The models held up to males and females revealed powerful women who subjugated themselves to males. The triadic nature of the relationship predisposed the two members to form a partnership against the third. The developmental features of mothering males and females differentiated subsequent differences in their self-images and identities. Prolonged infancy, unresolved oedipal conflicts, diffuse sense of self, and weak ego strength in the male; and rejection, inferiority, and role learning in the female were considered basic to the interactional difficulties in intimacy. The distant father figure and heterosexual asymmetries provided a further relational knot in this triad. The support of the social customs and joint family orientation toward people tended to make psychic structures irreversible in their effect on the three members of the group.

REFERENCES

Askham, J. (1976). "Identity and Stability within the Marriage Relationships." *Journal of Marriage and Family,* 535-547.

Bem, S. L. (1981). "Gender Schema Theory -- A Cognitive Account of Sex-Typing." *Psychological Review, 88,* 354-364.

Bem, S. L., and Bem, D. J. (1970). "Case Study of a Nonconscious Ideology: Training the Woman to Know her Place." In *Social Foundations of Beliefs and Attitudes,* edited by D. J. Bem. Belmont, CA: Brooks/Cole, 89-99.

Bruner, J. S. (1959). "Myths and Identities." *Daedalus.*

Caplow, T. (1968). *Two against One: Coalitions in Triads.* Englewood Cliffs, NJ: Prentice-Hall, Inc.

Fischer, L. R. (1983). "Mothers and Mothers-in-Law." *Journal of Marriage and Family,* 187-192.

Erikson, E. H. (1950). *Childhood and Society.* New York: W. W. Norton.

Hsu, F.L.Y. (1966). "Kinship and Ways of Life: An Exploration." *Psychological Anthropology.* Homewood, IL: R. D. Irwin, 149-158.

Kakar, S. (1978). *The Inner World.* Delhi, India: Oxford University Press.

Kumar, U. (1978). "The Functional and the Dysfunctional Role of Interpersonal Communication Patterns in the Hindu Joint Family in India." *International Journal of Group Tensions, 8,* 120-129.

Kumar, U. (1979). "Indian Woman's Quest for Identity." *International Journal of Group Tensions, 9,* 149-168.

Miller, J. B. (1976). *Toward a New Psychology of Women.* New York: Penguin Books.

Radcliffe-Brown, A. R. (1950). *African Systems of Kinship and Marriage.* London, England: Oxford University Press.

Singh, N. (1981). "Dowry Deaths." *Indian Express,* October 31.

Sweetser, D. A. (1963). "Asymmetry in Intergenerational Family Relationships." *Social Forces, 4,* 346-352.

Verghese, J. (1980). *Her Gold and her Body.* Ghaziabad, India: Vikas Publishing Press.

Wadley, S. (1977). "Women in Hindu Tradition." *Signs, 3,* 113-125.

Waring, E., McElrath, D., Lefcoe, D., and Weisz, G. (1981). "Dimensions of Intimacy in Marriage." *Psychiatry, 44,* 169-175.

Wickes, H. (1927). *The Inner World of Childhood.* New York: Appleton-Century-Crofts.

15

From the Psychoanalysis of a Greco-American Man: Death of the Father

C. Edward Robins

My father's death -- that is to say, the most important event, the most poignant loss, of a man's life. Having discovered that this was so, I felt unable to obliterate the traces of the experience (Sigmund Freud, 1908/1953). *(The Interpretation of Dreams.)*

Freud wrote those words in 1908, four years after he suffered his only psychotic-like experience, which occurred when he was on vacation in Athens in 1904. He does not tell us about that experience until 1936, three years before his own death. He tells that, at the very moment he was enjoying the sublime historical significance of the Acropolis and its surroundings, he was overwhelmed by a powerful "splitting" (*Spaltung*) of his consciousness: he wasn't sure of his position in reality any more. He later traced a chain of associations back to the image of his then-failing father, who, without even a high school education, could never understand what the Acropolis meant. Somehow, he had betrayed his father (Freud, 1964).

ANAMNESIS

The following is the story of another man -- from a very different culture -- who likewise cannot "obliterate the traces" of the experience of his father's death. Let us call him "S." He is a 47-year-old man who came to me three years ago for analysis, referred by his firm's personnel department. He is a tall, attractive man with thinning black and silver hair combed back. He dresses very casually, often with black pants and/or black shirt. In the first consultation, he immediately stated the reason he had come: "I want you to help me break up with my girlfriend and go back home to my wife and children." He then went on to tell me that he has been separated from his wife and three children for the last five years, and that he sees them only about every other weekend. For the past two years, he has been getting up in the middle of the night feeling "nervous and paranoid," having had terrible nightmares about his children being consumed by tragedies. S. then went on to describe his father as "a stifler of women," and added "I may be repeating his lifestyle."

Subsequent sessions revealed the following history. He was born of Greek immigrant parents. His father was the only survivor of many siblings. During our first interview, he responded to my query about the deaths of the siblings: "Oh, they just died. I guess there was a lot of child mortality in those days." It is only recently that he has revealed that they were slaughtered in the so-called "Disaster of Asia Minor" in the early 1920s, an event that is considered to be decisive in the formation of contemporary Greek cultural identity. This debacle, in which nearly two million died, is referred to in contemporary Greek discourse as "The Humiliation of Asia Minor." It figures into contemporary Greek identity much as the Holocaust does for contemporary Jewish identity, according to Drs. Steve Demakopoulos and Spyros Orfanos (personal communications, February and March, 1987).

According to S., his father "went AWOL" and came to New York; then, after making some money, he returned to Greece with a dowry to arrange the marriage with S.'s mother. When she protested to her father (who had been a celebrated guerrilla fighter against the Turks) that she did not know this young man nor did she want to go to America with him, "her father slapped her and that was that." The couple settled in a Greek ghetto in New York City, known as the site of violent street crimes (it bordered on "Hell's Kitchen"). Once, while walking with his father, S. remembers the stabbed hulk of a thief being thrown through a street-level window just in front of them; the man's blood, S. recalls, went "running like urine down the gutter." When he registered his horror to his father, his father jeered, "Don't be afraid, be a man!"

S. is the third of three children. Yet when he reported their age differences, he said that K., the oldest brother, is two years older than he, and that N., his sister, is two years younger than he. At the beginning of his treatment, S. recalled his childhood and the many beatings at the hands of his father and mother. One experience he vividly remembers and often speaks about was his father hitting the three children with a shoe for "sex play underneath the covers;" their mother had caught them at it during the day and warned them they would get a beating when their father came home. It was especially painful to S. that his mother was "standing by, ready to hand my father another shoe when one had flown out of his hand during the beating."

S. was called "Nick" in school, an Americanized version of many Greek names, which he adopted until young adulthood. In school he felt alone, left out, and miserably stupid. Since he did not understand English until the third grade or so, he felt especially isolated. In third grade he contracted ringworm, which necessitated his staying out of school for six months. Upon returning to school, his shaved and "pitted" scalp (because of electrolytic treatments his father insisted would "make your hair grow back more thickly") made him feel "humiliated."

S. remembers his father and mother fighting violently in front of the children, and that he played the role of "mother's protector" against the physical abuse of his father. He was continually afraid they would get a divorce.

At the age of 12, "everything changed." (Three years before, S.'s father had tried to break up a fight between a couple in their building because the man was physically beating the woman; the couple turned on him and tried to throw him out the window, banging S.'s father's head on the window sill.) Now S.'s father dies of a brain tumor. S. brought in photos to show me that, since that time, he has "always been depressed." (The photos did show a slumping lifeless boy.) It is immediately following his father's death that the calamities quickly mount. S. is himself hospitalized for an appendectomy; the family apartment is broken into several times, once by the building's superintendent, who "left a trail of coat hangers down the back staircase to his apartment." Another time, the back door was forced open, the apartment was ransacked, and an ominous machete ("the Jim Bowie kind") was left on a table: "They could have cut us up with it." Shortly after, S. found the new superintendent (the former one ran off after the burglary) murdered in a hallway.

It was also right after his father's death that S.'s terrifying nightmares began. During that time, S. remembers: "a smothering feeling....Mom grouped us kids together and said: 'He has left you *orphans*!...We've gotta be one person now, and stick together in everything.' She laid out the law, the Greek tradition.... I remember her declaring: 'I want to make up our own laws, now that Papa's dead.' But I opposed her because I didn't want to be called a Mama's boy.... I don't know who the fuck I am." Mother went to work and the children all helped out to run the home. On Saturdays the children were expected to go with their black-clad mother to their father's grave in the cemetery. "We never had Christmas for three years; that's the Greek tradition," he sadly said. (Note that S.'s statement that he didn't know who he was immediately follows his recollection that his mother tried to abrogate "the father's law" (*nomos* in Greek). This may be a telling sequence, since according to Lacan (1977), the true subject is founded on the father's law, the "symbolic function" that ruptures the incestuous imaginary bond between the mother and child.

S.'s two siblings left for jobs in another part of the country while they were in their late teens. S. was left with mother at home; "it's the Greek way that the youngest stays with mother." Later, when S. attended a college in New York, he found his first girlfriend, a non-Greek girl. His mother refused to accept his new relationship. It was during this time that S. sought out his first analyst; he also was encouraged by his older brother who had already been in treatment in California for several years, and who kept urging S. to start analysis "because our parents have so fucked us up."

At the age of 26 years, S. met and married a Greek girl (whose first name is the same as his mother's), even though he strongly objected to her undue attachment to her own mother. "I felt invisible around her; her mother always came first." Within one year they moved to the suburbs, and he stopped his analysis. Even though he and his wife had a stormy relationship, they had three children: two boys and then a girl, spaced roughly three years apart. S. continually felt "invisible" at home with his wife, which led to fights and mutual resentment. He began having affairs after their first child was born (whom he named "C." after his father). Their three children have played reminiscent roles in the war between father and mother. The familiar script goes like this: he angrily declares that he is leaving, and the children plead "Dad, don't go!" Their pleading is a poignant moment for him, and he repeats the scene time and again. He says "it's just like the Greek ghetto, the three of us seeing our father for the last time."

S. insisted that he and his wife begin marriage counseling during the fifth year of their marriage. His wife soon considered it futile, so S. stayed and continued in individual psychotherapy for three years. At the end of that time, he left the family and took up residence in a large city, a two-hour distance from the family home. It was at the end of his first session with me that he said: "Whenever I try to break off with my girlfriend, I get nauseous and remember my father's death."

THE NAMES

During the first session, S. proudly told me that his given name means "the resurrection of Christ." Literally, the name means "standing up again," or "making the dead to stand up again." He reported that he had used his Americanized nickname ("Nick") since he was a child, but reassumed his real name (that is, "the resurrection of Christ") *after* the death of his father; yet, it is only as an adult that he has fully asserted it. His name further implies "setting up or erection of a building; an erection."

What may be most revealing is that his name is spelled in an idiosyncratic way that indicates "having been driven from one's home, homeless; without a hearth." This usage of "homeless" is found in the *Iliad* (9:63). Nestor is deploring Achilles' insatiable revenge: "a clanless lawless *hearthless* man is he that loveth dread strife among his own folk." See also Cicero's imitation of this line and his conclusion that "such a man I would exclude from membership in the human race, banish beyond the confines of human nature" (Philippics 13:1). Dr. Demakopoulos (personal communication, February, 1987) says that this meaning of his name ("homeless") "could only be used viciously." (It may be that the lurking presence of a "bag man" in his dreams signals his homeless destiny. Homeless may also be related to *Heimlos* or *Unheimlich* in German, the latter being Freud's word to describe what we translate as "uncanny, weird." Lacan (1983) has made much of this concept.)

At the American school he was called Nick, a name he has always felt uncomfortable with. It calls up images of "poor little Nicky" for him, a "wimpish kid," and indicates more "a mechanic" than a professional. At home, his father called him "Microvio," which literally means "microbe," or more exactly, "vermin." This nickname is unusual; Drs. Demakopoulos and Orfanos (personal communication, February, 1987) had never heard of it being used for a child. Further, the combination of "micro" plus "bios" into "microvio" signifies a small life, but also, and the way any native speaker would understand it: a *short* life, that is, the opposite of longevity.

According to S., the name of his father is uncertain, for after the slaughter of the family, his father, "the sole survivor, probably took a passport from one of his dead older brothers and came to America. We never knew his real name or age. He never told *anyone*. My mother didn't even know. He was afraid he'd be sent back. He might not have been 65 when he died, but 47." (Of course, S. is 47 years old.) Finally, his father was popularly known -- and nicknamed -- for his large collection of stylish hats.

"Orfanos" (orphans) was the word mother used to name the three children after their father's death; it signals the most sorrowful state imaginable, a state of undeserved and intolerable abandonment. This usage attests to the importance of the father in Greek culture, since the term orphans would not be so readily applied if "only" the mother had died.

Note in Figure 15.1 that the paternal grandfather's name is not remembered; yet the paternal grandmother's name resurfaces in S.'s sister, which is proper Greek custom (that the father name the first daughter after his own mother). What is more problematic is shown in the next row down, with S.'s father "C." This father has totally suppressed his real name and now does not name his first son after his own father, which is strict Greek custom, but gives him the name K. Thus, C., this father-without-a-name, cannot pass on his own father's name, and thus takes an undefined and illegitimate position, rather like a fugitive ghost.

On the maternal side, note that the grandfather's name is the same as S.'s. This revelation of the grandfather's name came only recently in S.'s treatment; before, the grandfather was always referred to by his "generic" name, "Papou." This was the vicious fighter against the Turks about whom the following story was at the heart of the family lore: his mission was to retrieve the Greek women from their Turkish captors: if they refused to return to the Greeks, he would torture them ("cut off their nipples and make necklaces out of them") and then kill them. Note also that S's wife's name is the same as his mother's, which serves to reactivate his previous experience with his own mother.

Regarding S.'s position in the family tree, he stands directly under his maternal grandfather, because they share the same name. Moreover, he seems -- at least on an unconscious level -- to have identified with his grandfather. Take, for example, S.'s first sexual experience. At age 11 he was playing alone in a cardboard-box fort he had made; he suddenly had the clear image of biting an attractive girl's nipple, and at that instant experienced his first orgasm. Orgasmic fantasy since then continues to picture the woman as "being hurt" in some way. It may be that, in his early experience, the violence of the Greek ghetto replays the Disaster of Asia Minor and the sadistic glory of grandfather. S.'s near-sadistic fighting with his wife can also be seen as a continuance of the same warfare. Certainly, his dreams are filled with wars, battles, armies fighting, and being defeated. A further, linguistic connection between S., his grandfather, and violence is in his story of being beaten for sex play. His father hit them with a shoe and his mother was "standing by, ready to hand my father another shoe when one had flown out of his hand during the beating." The common word for shoe is *papoupsi*, which homonymically identifies the name of his grandfather, Papou. Thus, in this affect-laden memory, "shoe" (= papousi = Papou) is associated with violence and torture. Grandfather S. is somehow present in the hand of S.'s father as a "stifler" of the sexual, and held tight in the hand of his mother, eager to pass him on to her offspring.

S. had confused the birth order of his own siblings during the first session, making himself the second, and not the youngest child. Note that his confused sequence is the actual birth order of his own children (boy-boy-girl). He is consciously identified with his second son, D., "because D. is the same age I was when my father died, twelve." S. is thus reliving his own childhood experience in the present experience of his children.

THE REPETITION COMPULSION

In his present reality, during the years 1980 to 1986, S. has been recreating the drama of a past reality that he is not able to cope with, that is, the trauma of the death of his father. For at least six years, the following compulsive behavior persisted: S. would return home after about a two-week absence, and soon would get into a fight with his wife. He would proclaim his final departure, and the children would weep and implore him to stay, crying "Dad, don't go!" He would give them "last hugs" and take "last looks," prolonging the moment, and then finally leave. Sometimes he would not go far; always he would return to hugs of reunion and sobs of relief. Then he would leave for another two weeks or so. Throughout this experience, he focused especially on the plight of the children, left without a father, "orphaned" into the world of violence, the world of the Greek ghetto. We can understand his repetition as a reliving now what occurred at another time, in another place (Freud's *andere Lokalität*), that is, as a reexperiencing of the death of his father in its affective dimension, but now with S.'s imposing his own resolution to the trauma: the resurrection of the father in himself (and in his name, which he asserted after his father's death). The father is really alive and has come back. S. also derives a cathartic joy from this imaginary world because he identifies with the position of his second son (who is the same age as S. at the time of the father's death).

During the first year of his treatment, S. spoke very much about his acting out of this compulsive drama at home; in the past year, he has not mentioned its reoccurrence. Yet it is with his girlfriend and, as we will see, within his treatment, that S. continues to recreate his trauma: he is constantly threatening to leave and then comes back.

EXCERPTS FROM THE TREATMENT

The following are chronological excerpts from the treatment. S.'s words are placed in quotation marks and the author's are in brackets.

S. plays a tape of his previous night's dream: "I'm on the phone with my brother....He said 'Papa died just now.' I had a strange reaction within me of fear and someone breaking into the house....I just had a sense of it...horrible....How could he have died if he was just over visiting me? I was afraid somebody'd break into the house....I feel tired, like I've gone backwards. [Somebody's dead.] "Yes. If he did die, somebody broke into our apartment. Three to four weeks after. And my appendectomy. We were ripped off, I got sick, and went to the hospital in the ambulance." [You went to the hospital too.] "Do you think I'm imitating my father? In that too?" [Maybe you are.]

At the beginning of treatment, S. told me the date of his father's death. Each year he does not allude to it directly, but before or after that day he has invariably brought in dreams in which he -- S. -- is "shot in the stomach," "left for dead," etc.

"My son D. is my age when my father died, twelve. His father's still alive -- and it feels great! I get paranoid when the father's not with the son. This is what I want: *the father will be with the child!* (Pause) Hmmm, I'm just getting a fantasy right now. I was seeing my oldest son, then saw my girlfriend and wanted to end this thing with her; then I saw myself as being single, like in "Man with One Red Shoe," seducing a beautiful girl in my apartment. Being with more women. It feels nice for the ego." [If the father is with the son, then the son can seduce beautiful women.] Note that the relationship between shoe, papoupsi, and Papou reappears again. S. had told me that before killing the women traitors, his grandfather and the other fighters would have most surely raped them.)

"I had a dream about the three-cornered hat and the fantasies. There was a kid about my son D.'s age, twelve, who looked like Oliver Twist, who was supposed to visit his father in a field in Central Park. I'm not sure I'm with him or I'm him. A soldier with a three-cornered hat on a white horse, with gray hair like George Washington, teases and beats him up emotionally by saying: 'You're late! You can't go see your father! Your meeting with your father is cancelled. Your father won't be able to see you because you're late.' There was another soldier more sympathetic to the kid. He knows the first soldier is trying to break the kid's heart. The kid turns to me with tears in his eyes and says *'I'm going to miss him again!'* and begins to sob. I realize the second soldier sympathizes with the kid and me, and he comes over and says 'It's not true. You can always see your father. You do have time to see your father.'"

S. associated to the dream by first seeing in it his relationship with his own son, that his son would have a broken heart if he couldn't see his father again. Then he said that he himself was the boy who always gets a broken heart because he can't see his father. I pointed out that he wore a cowboy hat to the session, to which he responded that he wants *me* to say it's not too late, but if I won't, then *he*'ll have to be the "hopeful soldier." During the following sessions, he returned to the scene of his father's death and funeral. He described in plaintive detail the old widows wailing to his mother "He left you with three orphans!" and then his looking from his dead father in the casket to his bereft mother, and then his "grabbing onto her" and breaking down in agony. He cried openly when he said "I can't let go of anything....It's the *not seeing him again* that I can't take....My brother and sister hated him. He was a bastard for them....But did I...do I...love him?" As S. unlocks his painful memories, a more positive view of his father begins to emerge -- one evidently all S.'s own, since it is not shared by his brother and sister. Also, note the dilemma of S., personified by the two soldiers. The first, George Washington -- "father of his country" -- says it is already too late: "you can't see your father." The second, hopeful soldier assures S. that "you can always see your father, you do have time to see your father." The first is the harsh reality-principled father, the bearer of the law of death who announces to the son that it is already too late: "You've lost. Death is closed to the living. You can never see your father again." The second soldier "sympathizes with the kid" and posits an imaginary resolution to the law of death: "It is never too late." At this point in the treatment, S. was perceiving me as the first harsh soldier; and if he is to accept the reality of his father's death, he will have to be "beaten up emotionally."

At the beginning of the session, he said, "Maybe analysis won't work for me." [Maybe it won't.] The next session he went back to my saying maybe his analysis won't work. He was angry and said, "Now I have to work, like for the love of my parents, like I did as a child. Like having to prove at work how good I am. It's the father! So, when you say 'you've got to work,' it's the same. I have to work!...But I don't want to be responsible! (Pause) I don't know how my wife and girlfriend put up with me."

S. went on to say: "My oldest son C. had a dream that I died. Then he got *up in* the middle of the night and had to force himself to accept that he'd never see me again." Isn't it curious how the same trauma recurs in the dream of his son? The father is dead and he will never see him again. Evidently, S.'s son is wrestling with the same demon as his father: death is final, there is no reprieve, and, of course, that fathers and sons kill each other, at least in dreams and fantasies. In this regard, "C" here stands for the name of the father. S.'s early dreams are filled with images of killing boys the ages of his own sons. Does a mythic awareness of fathers and sons killing each other -- from Tantalus and Pelops down through the revenge of the house of Atreus -- penetrate all cultures, and dwell in all fathers' and sons' fantasies and dreams?

S. had been tape-recording sessions for the past several months and now commented: "The tape recorder isn't working. That means I'll have to do it on my own. The tape is my Pop. I'd be a threat to him if I can do it on my own. Then I'd show him that I don't need him if I do it myself, and then he'd be gone....If I'm really myself, then Pop'll die and leave me. That's why I can't feel myself and be me. So I give myself up more because I can't stand being abandoned. I'm afraid to speak...even though I want to hit that woman (in group)!" [That you can't stand letting your father die?] He then told me that his older brother was in town, and that during their conversation of the previous night, his brother was so furious when talking about their inadequate parents that S. thought: "the veins in his neck'll pop!" [Pop?] "Aw, you and your word games....I guess I haven't told you yet that I had a stress test for my heart last week because I've been worrying that I might drop dead like my father." S.'s identification with his father is now much more conscious. He feels that if he is really himself, that is, unique, different from his father, then his father will die. So S. shoulders a burden of pathological identification with his father to "keep him alive." Searles (1965) and others have elaborated on this "compassionate sacrifice" of the child to save the parent by identifying with the parent's pathology, especially to keep the parent alive.

S. has brought in the tape of the conversation he had last night with his 12-year-old son, D. In the tape, the son tells how frightened he was listening to his father and mother fighting, and in a choked voice says "I thought you were leaving." S. then told me that his "session with his son" gave him the feeling that "the father is with the son." He said, "I'm being the father I didn't have, the understanding father who won't treat his son the way he was treated...." [Your son felt like you were leaving.] "Yes. He gets frightened. I get frightened that I'll lose him....C., my oldest son, gets independent and takes off; I get angry when he leaves, as though he doesn't love me." [C.'s leaving too.] "But I'm always leaving -- leaving the analysis too!" He had been saying that analysis wasn't working for some months already, and was threatening to leave.

"I need to show that I exist!" he stated at the beginning of the session. Then he pointed to his yellow and white notes, saying, "400 to 500 pages.... Maybe I should write a novel." [How would you cast me in the novel?] "The strong silent guy, the Gregory Peck role, very quiet, says very little, but people listen." [Peck?] "In contrast, I'd make myself (he laughs) a chicken running around with its head cut off!" [Without a Peck-er?] "You're stronger than I am....Gregory Peck evokes really powerful images, he's got his shit together...Have you seen "The Big Country," a Western?...He doesn't have to prove himself to anyone. I suddenly feel very excited right now! I've always wanted to be like that. Like Gregory Peck." [But you make me Gregory Peck.] "I'm angry with you too! You don't say enough! But I'm still glad I don't have my brother's doctor; good old Ed makes me do all the work! It does work better if I'm my own father...But speaking of peckers, my girlfriend had a dream last night about John Wayne with no pants, no underwear, and a huge schwanz -- that's what she calls it." Can S. be himself? And not be just a son waiting for the father's permission to be sexual, to be strong? In the next session, S. revealed that he "forgot" and left his diary for his wife to see and that divorce proceedings are now under way. He said "I guess I wanted the honest truth."

S. wonders, "Do I have a sense of myself beyond the two women? No, I'm stifled alone....My book doesn't get me through any more. I can't find the answer in there. I can't find...myself in there. Nor here in the analysis. I'm too stupid....And you're not doing enough for me."

S. expresses how angry he is at me for not being more like "the good father who puts me on track. Time is the only thing changing things for me in here; I'm not doing anything myself....Right now I feel like I'm alone in here....I burnt incense over the weekend. It's for the dead." [Time won't cure your heart, the analysis won't change you.] "Yeah. But I still want *you* to put me on track....I still wake up at 2 A.M. That's when my father died. But the babysitter had tried to convince me that it wasn't true, told me to go back to sleep. I prayed to God that it wasn't true. Then about 4 A.M the apartment filled with whining neighbors; then I knew it was true."

CONCLUSION

Psychoanalysis, in my view, does not really resolve conflicts, nor "change" anyone; at best, it can free a paralyzed subject of its bonds, but it is still up to that subject to struggle and create itself. It strikes me that S. is beginning to see his own causation of his predicament and has taken some steps to clear it up, especially his policy of honesty with his wife, girlfriend, and children. He reported feeling "invisible" at the beginning of treatment (was that his identification with his ghost-like father?); more recently, especially in his work, he feels more visible, but it is at the cost of a great deal of pain, especially of "staying with my own feelings." His improvement is most striking in group therapy: at the beginning he was quite hostile toward and afraid of women, and now he is more open and friendly with them.

S. is looking for himself, but where does he really come from? His identification with his father? For me, it is decisive that S. is beginning to realize that his father is not able to be resurrected, that death is closed. For it is only by facing this loss at the heart of his existence that S. becomes capable of *speaking* from his true maimed reality. Authentic desire becomes possible only now, born out of his basic lack; so, too, responsible decisions are possible, since once his life is limited to the possible, he can make his life a project for which he is accountable. In this light, his conscious and unconscious identifications with father and grandfather have been repressing his own identity as a subject.

A final, countertransferential occurrence that has figured into my understanding of this case was a dream I had just after S. told me the name of his grandfather this past summer. I dreamt that I looked into a mirror and saw an olive-skinned woman with long "baubly earrings." I took the earrings off and felt relieved that my ears were not pierced. But then I looked at my feminine, pointed chin and wondered: can I change this structure? The dream indicated two things for me. First, my position in the treatment as a "mirror" for S., akin to the mother's function in the mirror phase for Lacan (1977), and my consequent discomfort at being in that position. Second, the dream contained the words "baubly earrings." I looked up the strange word "baubly" in the dictionary; and then remembered that S. had been telling me about his grandfather "making necklaces out of the nipples," which immediately connected with my image of the long, threaded earrings. Then, Dr. Richard Boothby (personal communication, April 25, 1987) pointed out that "baubly" sounds like "Papou" (grandfather). Add to this the fact that S. often pronounces the word for grandfather so it sounds like "Babou" (which means "father"). The letters p and b can sound almost identical, and their confluence suggested to me the confluence of the Papou-Babou identifications. Thus, I felt the point of my dream was this: If I am a somewhat faithful mirror of S., then if *S.* removes *his* earrings of sadistic torture and glory -- if he "takes off" his identification with his grandfather's and father's sadism -- will he then be a woman? S. has recently affirmed that, indeed, this is a major dilemma for him.

Most recently, S. has decided to leave analysis and seek treatment with someone else ("who will tell me what to do"). I pointed out to him that this is the month and week of his father's death, during which he will be dealing with our separation. He did not want to face the fact that he would "never see" me again, and gave me quite a tender hug good-bye. At this writing, I am not sure whether he will return or not. If he does not return, it may actually mean that he is facing and integrating the traumatic loss of someone close to him -- his father and me.

In this paper I have attempted to show the importance of names and cultural identity in determining the identifications (and destiny) of this Greco-American man, and his struggle to free himself of those identifications and become his own subject. I have considered only the impact of his own name and his father's death, and the repetition compulsion it has spawned; important issues in the "maternal field," especially the position of the woman, are not discussed.

REFERENCES

Freud, S.(1953). "Preface to the Second Edition." *The Standard Edition, Vol. 4.* Interpretation of Dreams. London: Hogarth Press. (Originally published in 1908.)

Freud, S. (1964). "A Disturbance of Memory on the Acropolis." *The Standard Edition, Vol. 22.* London: Hogarth Press. (Originally published in 1936.)

Lacan, J. (1977). *Ecrits: A Selection.* Translated by A. Sheridan. New York: W. W. Norton.

Lacan, J. (1983). "La Psicoanalisi al Rovescio (V), Seminario del 21 Gennaio 1970," In *Il Piccolo Hans: Rivista di Analisi Materialistica,* Translated by P. Mieli. *37,* 37-57. Bari, Italy: Edizioni Dedalo.

Searles, H. (1965). *Collected Papers on Schizophrenia.* New York: International Universities Press.

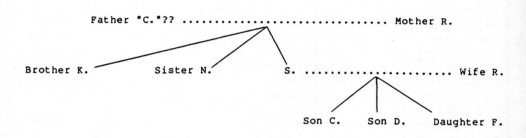

Figure 15.1. Map of Names

Grandfather ... Grandmother   Grandfather ... Grandmother

    E.??   N.   S.   ??

         Father "C."?? .... Mother R.

Brother K.   Sister N.   S. .... Wife R.

                               Son C.   Son D.   Daughter F.

16

Stages and Ages in Adult Development: A Commentary and Research Note

John D. Hogan and Gary G. F. Yorke

Adult development is a relatively new area of study for psychology. Compared with other segments of the life span, there has been little research done on this period until recently. Developmental psychologists are realizing what lay people have long known: the course of adulthood does not flow in one smooth continuous line. As Shakespeare put it, "one man in his time plays many parts, his acts being seven ages." Each of us has our own personal markers, some shared and some unique, which signify changes and transitions in adulthood: graduation, marriage, first job, a major reconciliation, and so on.

From the beginning, developmental psychologists have tended to minimize the importance of these transition markers and have viewed the period as fixed and static. The belief has been commonly held that personality is set by early adulthood and that change during adulthood is rare or impossible (Schaie and Geiwitz, 1982). The role of developmental psychology was to describe the formation of adult personality; personality psychology studied only the vicissitudes of adulthood (Basseches, 1984).

In those infrequent instances when adulthood was studied, the main source of interest has been the older adult. Of the seven reviews appearing in the *Annual Review of Psychology* from 1951 to 1980 on adult development and aging, the most commonly cited journal by far was the *Journal of Gerontology* (Birren, Cunningham and Yamamoto, 1983). It is a fact that the developmental period which is the longest, the period of greatest accomplishment and leadership, the period when people marry and raise families, is the period which is the least researched and the least understood.

There have been a handful of researchers who have made significant contributions to adult development over the years, some in the early part of the century. A few, working in the 1950s, published work that is still considered to be of pivotal importance. These researchers, however, were not in the mainstream of developmental research. By the 1960s, interest in adult development began to grow rapidly (Lerner, 1986). Theorists came to realize what is now generally acknowledged: not only is there life after adolescence, there is also the possibility for growth and change, that is, the potential for true development. With that understanding, the whole of developmental psychology began to shift to that of a life-span approach.

It might be argued that the area is so new, it is plagued by its own methodological problems (Gutmann, 1977). In fact, psychologists are becoming increasingly aware of the need to integrate cross-cultural data into their theories of development. As Robert LeVine has said of his work in Africa: "It is a long way from the life course in one African society to a general conception of human adulthood ... but ... even a single instance of cultural variation can indicate how well our homegrown ideas travel ..." (1980, p. 77).

Developmental psychologists have not been particularly adept at weeding out their ethnocentric biases. Despite voluminous literature on the most studied of all human subjects, the child, there seems to be only a dim understanding that the child is to a significant degree a cultural invention (Kessen, 1979) -- that we do not know the child in an absolute sense apart from the culture in which that child resides. If this is true for the much-studied child, how bleak our understanding must be of the understudied adult.

Despite its short history, the psychology of adult development is being dominated by assumptions that some would advertise as fact. Two of these assumptions, that development proceeds in stages and that development is very closely age-linked, have found a number of powerful adherents. Perhaps both are true, but it would be useful to examine other cultures before we posit universals. To be fair, there is no one acceptable model for describing adult development. None of the researchers has completely ignored cross-cultural questions, although for the most part they have had no discernible impact. It is a question of watching the speed with which some of the new assumptions are being taken as fact and the manner in which they are being interpreted. Stage theory is perhaps the most obvious example.

In the beginning, the stage theory approach seemed to be simply a carry-over from child psychology, a debt owed to Rousseau, and a style that found favor in the works of Freud, Piaget, Kohlberg, and even Montessori. Few would argue that stage descriptions have had a great deal of success in describing the child and adolescent. Whether they are equally useful in describing the adult is, however, still a matter of debate. Yet, everywhere there are labels suggestive of the age-stage approach, labels such as era, phases, passages, seasons, transitions, and transformations. Gail Sheehy's *Passages* (1976), a popular account of some theories of adult development, is the most visible example of this trend. Whatever the label, the basic idea remains the same: there is a progressive unfolding of behaviors leading to something new. For some, the age at which the behavior occurs does not matter all that much; the sequence is the thing. Nonetheless, for many, age is still a matter of considerable importance.

Even as the assumptions of the stage approach dominate thinking about adulthood, a change is being seen in the flexibility given to the stages. One has only to compare the ideas of the two earliest theorists, Carl Jung and Erik Erikson, to those of more contemporary theorists.

Jung proposed a system that could be interpreted as a stage theory, although a very simple one. It contained only two units or periods: before the midlife and after the midlife. The theory was quite flexible. It allowed for different styles of development in the first half of life, which could be addressed and, perhaps corrected, in the second half. In his theory, as adults strive for "wholeness" and "centeredness" and "meaning," each will achieve different levels of success, none fully realizing established goals, and all responding in ways reflective of the culture in which they live. Clearly, the man and his theory meant to include cultural variation as an important part of the theory (Crain, 1985).

In a similar fashion, Erikson introduced his now-familiar ego stages of young adulthood, adulthood, and old age. He was the first to make it clear there are genuine adjustment problems at each stage of adulthood, not just residuals from childhood. As the individual works through the stages of intimacy versus isolation, generativity versus stagnation, and ego-integrity versus despair, there is nothing rigid about the system. Erikson is clearly aware of the vast differences among cultures, and in fact, one of his stated goals is to show how different cultures handle the stages differently (Crain, 1985). What Erikson *does* claim is that all cultures address themselves to the same issues. For instance, every culture must address itself to the issue of generativity. If not, there is no care for the next generation and the culture will die. The manner in which the issue is addressed, however, is subject to vast variation, and that variation becomes a study in itself.

Most contemporary theories do not espouse the same "open-ended" approach. This is best illustrated by the work of Daniel Levinson, who wrote one of the most detailed accounts of adult development. Levinson's work first came to public attention as the basis for *Passages* by Gail Sheehy in 1976, the book that spearheaded popular interest in the study of adulthood. Levinson and his associates published their own book two years later (Levinson, Darrow, Klein, Levinson, and McKee, 1978).

In their original work, the Levinson group studied 40 men, ten men from each of four occupational groupings. Though similar in age, the subjects were educationally diverse. Based on a series of intensive interviews with them and their families over the course of several years, Levinson proposed the notion of a life structure, a master plan by which life unfolds. Since the completion of that first study, he has continued to investigate the life structure in other groups. For example, in a companion piece to the first book, he has studied the lives of 45 women for his forthcoming book, *The Seasons of a Woman's Life*. He has studied the lives of more than 100 men and women of different countries and historical periods who have been depicted in plays, novels, biographies, and autobiographies. For another book in preparation, he has investigated the lives of another group of men and women in middle adulthood (Levinson, 1986).

From all of these findings, he has reached a number of conclusions that he admits have been hard for many social scientists to accept. As before, he provides a road map to the underlying order that he finds in the unfolding of a human life. What he now emphasizes with greater clarity, and what he states as the most controversial of his findings, is the discovery of age-linked periods in adult development. These are described as nine standard series or periods, each beginning at a well-defined point, with a range of only two or three years on each side. The first is "early adult transition, from age 17 to 22" and last is "the late adult transition, age 60 to 65." He emphatically states that this is a finding, not a hypothesis (Levinson, 1986).

This is all rather startling and exciting. It is also somewhat problematic. Gone is the flexibility of Jung and Erikson. In their place is a grand plan of adult life that is proposed to hold for all cultures and people and, in fact, Is very closely linked to age. For the theorist or researcher in search of a well-rounded theory that would include cross-cultural and cross-ethnic data, these ideas present a great challenge.

In fairness to Levinson, he welcomes input from other cultures. There is one immediate problem with this. He believes the only acceptable way the theory can be tested is through intensive studies of life structures over a span of years. This may prove a formidable obstacle for many researchers. One study that did attempt to use Levinson's methods found that Indian adult males engage in certain developmental tasks, such as leaving home, at a much later age than American adult males (Mines, 1981). This would seem to suggest that Levinson's stages may not be as fixed as he has stated.

THE STUDY

Even within our own Western culture, different ethnic groups may have different expectations regarding age-linked behaviors. We proposed to look at what kinds of differences might be found across several ethnic groups. The impetus for the design was provided by a simple, straightforward, and classic paper by Neugarten, Moore, and Lowe (1965) on age norms and adult socialization.

In that paper, the authors argued that expectations about age-appropriate behavior and the behaviors themselves were closely related and, further, there was general agreement in American society when various events should occur. To illustrate their point, the authors present data gathered from a 19-item questionnaire. Each item asks the respondent to state a specific age fulfilling the requirements of the item stem, for example, the best age for a man to marry. In their original sample of about 100 subjects, characterized as middle-class and middle-aged, the responses show a great deal of agreement. Unfortunately, the statistics used were only descriptive statistics. Nonetheless, the authors concluded that despite differences in value patterns, life styles, and reference groups, there was a high degree of consensus in the responses. Other samples, which were diverse in age, race, and geographic location, were also alluded to although no data were offered for these groups.

The authors simply conclude that each additional set of data yielded essentially the same pattern.

We questioned the findings at the same time that we agreed with them. Certainly there is a great deal of consensus, but the data are arranged to highlight that point. For each statement, an age range is given and the percent agreement of the sample to that age range is reported. Presumably the range was picked based on the results; it was not stated a priori. For Instance, to the item "What is the best age for a woman to marry?," the range given is 19-24 years. In their sample, 85 percent of the women and 90 percent of the men gave responses within that range. Other items generate less agreement. For the item "When do most men hold their top jobs?," 71 percent of the males gave a value within the 45-50-year range but only 58 percent of the females did so. There may be significant agreement here but there is also a good deal of variability.

We proposed to look at these same items using different groups and a different type of analysis. It seemed to us more likely that clear differences would be found among groups -- that essentially the same pattern would *not* emerge for each of the groups tested.

The sample consisted of undergraduate students enrolled in psychology courses at the same university. In addition to responding to the items, the students were asked to state the group with which they most identified. For this analysis, three groups were found large enough for analysis: a Hispanic group with 35 subjects, a Black group with 18 subjects, and a Caucasian group with 40 subjects. There were no significant differences in their mean ages, which overall were approximately 20 years. Although the sample included almost twice as many females as males, there were no significant differences in their representation within groups. It is worth noting that the sample is very homogeneous on many counts: all were college students, in the same age range, at the same university, from the same geographic area, and so on. This is, of course, a way of controlling a number of variables that could misrepresent the results. At the same time, such a selection is likely to obscure differences that exist in the real world. For example, the fact that the subjects are all college students must result in some intellectual and socioeconomic similarities that would not be the case in a non-college sample.

The first inspection of the data revealed that, for all the items, there was only one that was significantly different between the sexes. This was **Item #3**, the age when most people should become grandparents. Males had a mean of 54.6 years, and females a mean of 51.9 years, a difference significant beyond the .05 level. The difference may not be entirely unexpected. **Item #3** is one of the few items that does not ask the respondent to differentiate between the sexes. Perhaps subjects are simply responding to the reality of the situation: men marry later than women and, in fact, do become grandparents at a later age. What was the most striking about this particular analysis was, that of all the items, only one demonstrated a significant sex difference.

In the comparisons that were the main focus of the study, one-way ANOVAs revealed four statistically significant items. These comparisons, with probability levels, means, and differences can be found in Table 16.1. In order of item number, the differences were these:

Item #3: The age when most people should become grandparents. The Black and Hispanic subjects both place that age at about 51 years and do not differ from one another. Caucasians generate a value closer to 55 years and differ from the other groups beyond the .01 level. It could be argued that these figures reflect the circumstances of the families from which these groups come, that is, the earlier age of marriage and hence of grandparenting among Blacks and Hispanics. However, these differences are not reflected elsewhere. All three groups agree on **Item #1**, the best age for a man to marry, and on **Item #2**, the best age for a woman to marry. Parenthetically, the figures that they give for both items tend to be high, 27 years and 25 years, respectively.

Item #6: The age most men hold their top jobs. Blacks gave the lowest value at 34.1 years, and were not significantly lower than Hispanics, who gave a value of 35.7 years. Both were significantly different from the Caucasian group, who gave the age as 38.8 years. All of the groups gave a relatively young age. The thirties are usually seen as a time of job building and consolidation, not a time when one is expected to reach the top of their chosen profession.

Item #14: The age when a man has the most responsibilities. For this item the Hispanic group gave the lowest value at 32.6 years, but were not significantly different from the Black students at 33.7 years. Both were significantly different from the Caucasian group at 37 years.

Finally, **Item #19:** The age of a good-looking woman. This time it was the Caucasian group who gave the lowest age at 25.7 years, not significantly different from the Hispanic group at 26.9 years. The Black students gave a value of 32.6 years, clearly higher and significantly different from each of the other groups.

What does all this mean? The data are tentative at best, and perhaps clearer judgments should be left until larger samples are evaluated. However, two things are suggested. One is that there *is* a great deal of agreement regarding expectations of age-linked behaviors, although it is not nearly so certain that these expectations translate directly into behavior. In fact, based for norms available on adult development, it is quite clear that they do not. Second, if these data are to be seen as accurate, they suggest that in spite of the agreement, there are a number of pockets of diversity, and rather provocative ones at that.

Why is it that the Black sample sees the age of a good-looking woman to be almost seven years later than that of the Caucasian sample? Remember the Black sample is no different in age from the other groups. Surely there are implications of that judgment felt in early and middle adulthood, for both Black males and females. Why does the Hispanic group see a man with the most responsibilities at age 32 or 33 years while the Caucasian subjects put the time at 37 years? Are the responsibilities of adulthood seen differently? Is one group responding more to the requirements of parenting and the other to occupation? The answer is not in the data but any attempt to describe adulthood must take those differences into account. A span of four or five years is a very important one in some theories.

Similar statements could be made for the other items, and remember only 19 items were sampled. There was no attempt to cover the population of potential items about adulthood. However, the point should be clear. Even in a relatively homogeneous sample such as the one described here, differences can be identified that may have considerable impact on the course of adult development. Uniform theories of adulthood, at least to the extent that they are closely age-linked, seem premature.

George Vaillant, who authored the book *Adaptation to Life.* which was based on the Grant study sample, a follow-up of students selected while in college, put it this way:

> Patently, the Grant study is not cross-cultural. Over and over again, my credibility is undermined by the fact that the sample includes no women -- and only college graduates; no Blacks -- and only Americans; no one born after 1924 -- and only men born after World War I began.
>
> Readers must decide for themselves when the Grant study men reflect human beings and human wound healing, and when they merely reflect the arcane folkways of a small, perhaps unfamiliar tribe (Vaillant, 1977, p. 365).

It needs only to be added that until the data are in, the same can be said for all our modern theories of adult development.

REFERENCES

Basseches, M. (1984). *Dialectical Thinking and Adult Development.* Norwood, NJ: Ablex Publishing Company.

Birren, J. E., Cunningham, W. R., and Yamamoto, K. (1983). "Psychology of Adult Development and Aging." *Annual Review of Psychology. 34.* 543-575.

Crain, W. C. (1985). *Theories of Development: Concepts and Applications.* 2nd ed. Englewood Cliffs, NJ: Prentice-Hall.

Gutmann, D. (1977). "The Cross-Cultural Perspective: Notes toward a Comparative Psychology of Aging." In *Handbook of the Psychology of Aging.* edited by J. E. Birren and K. W. Schaie. New York: Van Nostrand Reinhold.

Kessen, W. (1979). "The American Child and other Cultural Inventions." *American Psychologist, 34.* 815-820.

Lerner, R. M. (1986). *Concepts and Theories of Human Development*, 2nd ed. New York: Random House.

LeVine, R. A. (1980). "Adulthood among the Gusii of Kenya." In *Themes of Work and Love in Adulthood*, edited by N. J. Smelser and E. H. Erikson. Cambridge, MA: Harvard University Press.

Levinson, D. J. (1986). "A Conception of Adult Development." *American Psychologist, 41*, 3-13.

Levinson, D. J., Darrow, C. N., Klein, E. B., Levinson, N. H., and McKee, B. (1978). *The Seasons of a Man's Life*. New York: Ballantine Books.

Mines, M. (1981). "Indian Transitions: A Comparative Analysis of Adult Stages of Development." *Ethos, 9*, 95-121.

Neugarten, B. L., Moore, J. W., and Lowe, J. C. (1965). "Age Norms, Age Constraints and Adult Socialization." *American Journal of Sociology, 70*, 710-717.

Schaie, K. W., and Geiwitz, J. (1982). *Adult Development and Aging*. Boston, MA: Little, Brown and Company.

Sheehy, G. (1976). *Passages: Predictable Crises of Adult Life*. New York: Dutton.

Vaillant, G. E. (1977). *Adaptation to Life*. Boston, MA: Little, Brown and Company.

Table 16.1

Mean Scores for Items Differentiating Ethnic Groups1

Item #3.   The age when most people should become grandparents

p = .029	Hisp.	51.5	cauc/hisp	.01
	Blacks	50.8	cauc/blac	.01
	Cauc.	54.5	hisp/blac	NS

Item #6.   The age most men hold their top jobs.

p = .025	Hisp.	35.7	cauc/hisp	.01
	Black	34.1	cauc/blac	.01
	Cauc	38.8	hisp/blac	NS

Item #14.   The age when a man has the most responsibilities.

p = .022	Hisp.	32.6	cauc/hisp	.01
	Black	33.7	cauc/blac	.05
	Cauc.	37.0	hisp/blac	NS

Item #19.   The age of a good-looking woman.

p = .021	Hisp.	26.9	cauc/hisp	NS
	Black	32.6	cauc/blac	.05
	Cauc.	25.7	hisp/blac	.05

17

Perceptions of Middle Age and Old Age

Leonore Loeb Adler, Nihar Ranjan Mrinal, Helmut E. Adler, William M. Davis, Joan Goldberg, and S. Patricia Walsh

Recently Neugarten and Neugarten (1986) stated that: "In all societies lifetime is divided into socially relevant units, and biological time is translated into societal time....Societies from the simplest to the most complex define various periods of life." (p. 32). Several years earlier Neugarten, Moore, and Lowe (1965) reported on the age-norm timetable, which society uses to identify the expected age for major events to occur. Based on their findings, they concluded that these age norms were used to determine the "best time" for many critical social behaviors. However, Kimmel (1980) concluded that many people established their own personal age norms by using society's "best age" determination as guidelines. Therefore society was, in fact, defining appropriate actions for people at different ages. It turned out that conforming to these social clock norms led to favorable results; violations, on the other hand, did not. These social norms identified the standards shared and conformed to by the members of different cultural, social, or ethnic groups. Another approach was explored by Hogan and Yorke (1986), who wanted to see whether there were developmental stages during adulthood. Earlier D. J. Levinson (1986) had raised the following question: "Are there age-linked developmental periods in adulthood?" To this Question he responded with: "The discovery of age-linked periods in the adult development of the life structure is one of the most controversial findings of my research....I do propose, however, that there is an *underlying* order in the human life course, an order shaped by the eras and by the periods in life structure development" (1986, p. 11).

Neugarten, Moore, and Lowe (1965) also had clearly identified a problem associated with the overuse of age-linked normative patterns. They pointed out that behaviors which were forced into so-called "normal" patterns were actually being constrained. An expected age for specific behaviors raised the possibility, that if the behavior occurred at other times, it might have been perceived as deviant, or at least "odd" by the individual, the society, the ethnic group, or by all of these. Furthermore, issues of social pressure from significant others to conform, as well as the level of anxiety generated by nonconformists, became important topics. Since the general trend in Western culture was youth-oriented, the thought of getting older may have been anxiety-arousing and tension-producing in middle-aged and older-aged persons.

It might be correct, as Levinson (1986) proposed, that there was "an underlying order in the human life course," which could be interpreted as age-linked or age-related periods in adulthood. However, the next question would necessarily lead to the query: *Does the actual (chronological) age at which the "life-events" or age-related periods in adulthood take place correspond with the perceived age of their occurrences?*

Some years ago, Leonore Loeb Adler (unpublished research) conducted informal studies to investigate the perception of age for two age-linked periods in adult life. The results gathered in this way showed that 20- to 30-year-old college women perceived "middle age" as ranging from around 40 to 45 years, while 35- to 45-year-old college women perceived "middle age" as occurring around 50 years. When the younger group was asked about "old age," they perceived it either as after 65 or as 70 years (probably because of the social security laws and the retirement age). The older age group responded to the same question with ages ranging from 75 to 80 years. In other words: *the perception of age varied depending on the age of the perceiver.*

During the past few years Adler, Davis, Ray, Deitch, and Hill (1986) and Adler, Davis, and Adler (1987) conducted research with large triethnic populations in New York City's colleges. The results of these studies revealed that with increasing age of the perceivers, the perceptions of age-related stages, or life-events, increased as well. In addition, the data showed that the females' ages were perceived as younger than those of their male counterparts.

Based on these findings, a pilot study was started (Davis, Mrinal, and Adler, 1987) with an Indian (Asian) population and then expanded in the current investigation. The underlying thought of the present research was as follows:

1. To see whether there were similar perceptions of age-related periods during the life-span, with a population, that was geographically far removed from the U.S. sample and that was culturally and ethnically different.
2. Would females' age-related stages be perceived as younger than those of males?

To find the answers to these questions, the present study compared the responses of an Indian (Asian) population with those of a population from the United States of America.

METHODS

Subjects

One hundred fifty-one subjects from Nagpur, India, participated in the present study. These Asian subjects were compared with the U.S. sample of 180 participants from the greater New York area. These populations included 77 Indian men and 74 Indian women, and 54 U.S. men and 126 U.S. women. All were grouped by the following age-categories: the "young" groups included students from 16 to 34 years of age; the "middle" groups included subjects who were between 35 to 54 years of age; and the "old" groups included participants who were 55 to 80 years old. See Table 17.1 for distribution of the 331 subjects who participated in this cross-cultural research. Almost all U.S. subjects -- except for a few U.S. men in the "middle" group, who were faculty members or college administrators were college and continuing education students. The Indian sample was made up of college students in the "young" groups, and of mostly professionals and faculty members in the "middle" groups; no demographic information about the "old" groups is available at this time. The majority of the Indian subjects were Hindi, though a few were Muslims or followed other religious teachings; the U.S. population, however, was a mix or the major religions found in Western societies, with the majority belonging to the Catholic denomination. All participants were tested in their native vernacular.

Procedure

Each participant received one questionnaire. The U.S. subjects received the original English version. For the Indian population, the instructions and questions were translated into Hindi and then back-translated into English for additional confidence in the accuracy of the translation. There were 25 questions that represented age-related events and "milestones" during the life-span. Each question was responded to with regard to males and females, totaling 50 items. Two questions, that is, four items, were analyzed and are reported here. These were: (1) "The age of a middle-aged (male, and female)"; and (2) "The age of an old (male, and female)". Some demographic information was collected for each subject. The questionnaires were handed out either individually or to entire classes (groups). It took approximately ten minutes to fill out the questionnaires.

RESULTS AND DISCUSSION

Two age-related stages, or age-linked periods, in adulthood were analyzed for the present study. These life-events were "middle age" and "old age," which were perceived for both males and females. The results confirmed the first inquiry, which was undertaken to see whether there were similar perceptions of age-related periods during the life-span with a population, that was geographically far removed from the U.S. sample and that was culturally and ethnically different. Inspection of Table 17.1 revealed that the schemata in both populations followed similar trends. The means of the two age-linked stages (middle age and old age) were categorized by countries (USA and India), by gender of subjects (men and women), by age groups (young, middle, and old), and by sex of items (male and female). (See Table 17.1.) The statistical analyses consisted of analyses of variance and Newman-Keuls tests for critical differences. Comparisons of means for age perceptions by U.S. and Indian subjects for both the age-related stages during adulthood, for males and females, followed the same trends and schemata in both populations, though they lived in different cultures and countries. However, the Indian sample perceived both age-linked periods as being earlier than their U.S. counterparts did. (See Figures 17.2 and 17.2.)

The second query inquired whether the females' age-related stages would be perceived as younger than those of males. Only a partially positive answer was possible. Both men and women from India in all three age groups perceived the ages of males to be approximately three to four years older than those of females, in both age-related stages. These results were not found in the U.S. responses, where perceived age differences between males and females were mostly negligible, at least for these two stage categories in adulthood. (See Figures 17.1 and 17.2, and Table 17.1.)

Compared with U.S. men, U.S. women's responses showed an increase in the perceptions of age from two to five years in both adult stages. For example, in the "middle age" category, U.S. women of the middle group responded to the female's age with a mean of 49.33 years, while U.S. men's answers resulted in a mean of 45.92 years. The same U.S. women's group responded to the "old-age" category for a female with a mean of 76.95 years, while the U.S. men's perceptions for a female resulted in a mean of 71.67 years. (See Table 17.1.) There were no such distinct differences in the perceptions of Indian men and women. To illustrate this, here is a comparative sample: the middle groups rated "middle age" for females with a mean of 40.35 years by women compared with a mean of 39.68 years by men. With the "old-age" category for females, the same Indian women's middle group responded with a mean of 58.08 years, whereas the equivalent middle group of men responded with a mean age of 57.96 years. (See Table 17.1.) No explanation can be offered at this time for these variations between the two populations.

All U.S. age groups perceived an age difference of approximately 20 to 25 years to exist between "middle age" and "old age." However, the Indian population saw "middle age" as about five to nine years younger than the U.S. women did, and about 11 to 18 years younger than their perceptions of "old age." In all comparisons between the means of the U.S. and Indian subjects' perceptions of age, a significant difference existed ($p < .01$) for both genders. (See Figures 17.1 and 17.2.)

Based on these results, the following question arose: Why are both age-related stages perceived to be so much younger by Indian subjects than by

U.S. subjects? Could the answer lie with the life-expectancy of the country of origin? That possibility might be plausible. Another question also needs to be answered: How is the "old" person perceived by the respondents? Neugarten and Neugarten (1986) advanced two classifications of "young-old" and "old-old." The two authors explained that these terms had become part of everyday parlance and were based originally on health and social characteristics, rather than on chronological age. A young-old person could be 58 or 85 years old. Neugarten and Neugarten (1986) explained that the term represented the social reality in which the line between "middle age" and "old age" was no longer clear. Most often the "old-old" persons were particularly vulnerable and were in need of special care. However, in the present study there was never any overlap of the two age-linked stages of adulthood. In other words, the present results showed two distinct stages of age-related periods in the different cultural groups of the two countries. In addition, the same results revealed a pervasive trend that, with the increased ages of the perceivers, the perceptions of age increased in both countries. Such findings, of course, corroborated the results of previous studies by Adler, et al. (1986, 1987). In summary, it can be stated that: (1) the perceptions of age-related stages in adult life may vary depending on the age of the perceiver; and (2) the responses by subjects from different countries revealed that, though the actual age norms may vary due to ethnic or cultural differences, the schemata remained the same cross-ethnically and cross-culturally.

REFERENCES

Adler, L. L., Davis, W. M., and Adler, H. E. (1987). "The Perception of Life-Events with Regard to Age: A Cross-Ethnic Comparison." Paper read at the Annual Meeting of the Society for Cross-Cultural Research at Miami, FL, February 14.

Adler, L. L., Davis, W. M., Ray, J. W., Deitch, I., and Hill, O. O. (1986). "The Perception of Age: A Cross-Ethnic Comparison." Paper read at the Conference on Research in Cross-Cultural Perspective, cosponsored by the Department of Psychology, St. Francis College, and the Institute for Cross-Cultural and Cross-Ethnic Studies, Molloy College, at Brooklyn, NY, October 25.

Davis, W. M., Mrinal, N. R., and Adler, L. L. (1987). "'Milestones' Events Perceived by an Indian Sample: Age and Gender Group Comparisons." Paper read at the Colloquium on Cross-Cultural and Cross-Ethnic Research, cosponsored by the division of Social Psychology of the New York State Psychological Association and the Institute for Cross-Cultural and Cross-Ethnic Studies, Molloy College, at the City University of New York, New York, NY, March 20.

Hogan, J. D., and Yorke, G.G.F. (1986). "Stages and Ages in Adult Development: A Commentary and Research Note." Paper read at the Conference on Cross-Cultural Research in Human Development: Focus on Theoretical Aspects. Institute for Cross-Cultural and Cross-Ethnic Studies, at Molloy College, Rockville Centre, NY, March 15.

Kimmel, D. C. (1980). *Adulthood and Aging: An Interdisciplinary Developmental View,* 2nd ed. New York, NY: John Wiley and Sons.

Levinson, D. J. (1986). "A Conception of Adult Development." *American Psychologist, 41*(1), 3-13.

Neugarten, B. L., Moore, J. W., and Lowe, J. C. (1965). "Age Norms, Age Constrains and Adult Socialization." *American Journal of Sociology, 70,* 710-717.

Neugarten, B. L., and Neugarten, D. A. (1986). "Age in the Aging Society." *Daedalus, Journal of the American Academy of Arts and Sciences, 115*(1), 31-49.

Figure 17.1

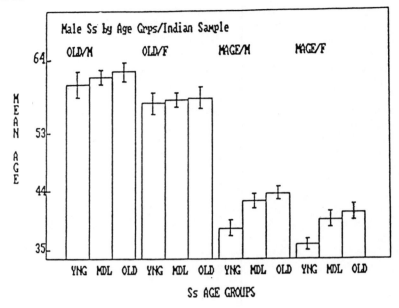

Male Ss by Age Grps/Indian Sample

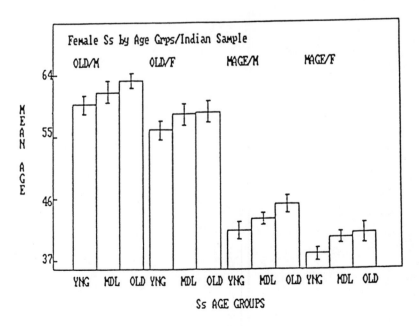

Female Ss by Age Grps/Indian Sample

YNG=16-34
MDL=35-54
OLD=55-80

Figure 17.2

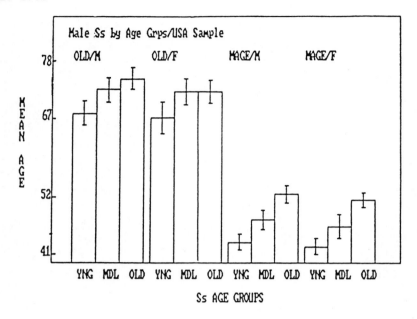

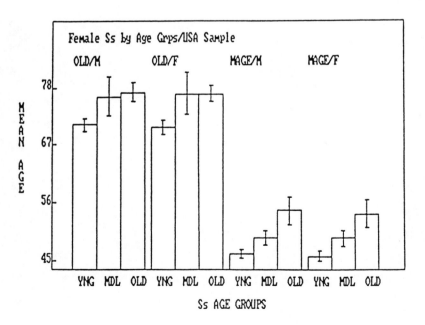

YNG—16-34
MDL—35-54
OLD—55-80

Table 17.1

Perceptions of Age for "Middle Age" and "Old Age"

by populations of different age groups from India and U.S.A.

(Means for each age level.)

(Groups of Ss: Young = 16-34 years; Middle = 35-54 years; Old = 55-80 years)

Age Groups	n	Middle Age "male"	"female"	Old Age "male"	"female"
US Men (N = 54)					
Young	28	42.89	42.07	67.64	66.64
Middle	12	47.25	45.92	72.08	71.67
Old	14	52.14	51.14	74.23	71.62
US Women (N = 126)					
Young	87	46.35	45.97	70.88	70.49
Middle	23	49.48	49.33	76.37	76.95
Old	16	54.60	53.93	77.15	76.92
Indian Men (N = 77)					
Young	23	38.30	35.87	60.35	57.48
Middle	25	42.56	39.68	61.48	57.96
Old	29	43.66	40.72	62.28	58.28
Indian Women (N = 74)					
Young	26	41.40	38.00	59.81	56.00
Middle	26	43.12	40.35	61.35	58.08
Old	22	45.18	41.00	63.14	58.91

Cross-Cultural and Interdisciplinary Perspectives in the Research on Human Religiosity

Halina Grzymala-Moszczynska

As a psychologist working at the Institute for the Science of Religions, I face questions in everyday life and everyday cooperation, along with my colleagues who represent other branches of an interdisciplinary field of science, concerning goals of two partners, that is, psychology and the science of religion.

The literature concerning this problem brings very different and often confusing ideas about possibilities or very often the lack of possibilities, of such day-to-day cooperation. A great deal of this confusion depends upon the fact that very often the psychology of religion, as a part of the science of religion, is a subject of interest for psychological dilettantes, people who have never completed a rigorous psychological education but have tried to practice the psychology of religion as a "born philosopher" or comparative historian of religion. Also, in the educational process of psychologists and scientists of religion, there is rarely a chance to get acquainted with the possibilities of fruitful cooperation between both disciplines.

A psychological look at religion might be described from one of four standpoints delineated by Professor James Dittes from Yale University:

1. *Instancing*. In events regarded by participants as religious, the same variables and relationships are found as in other events. For example, the same effects of the salience of group membership are found when the group is the Catholic Church as when it is the student body of a particular college. This position might be called the most reductionistic or parsimonious, depending on the values being emphasized.

2. *Uniquely prominent relationships*. Certain relationships among certain variables, which may exist outside religion, are particularly discernible within religious events. For example, the evocation of affiliative behavior by ambiguous or stress situations may be especially prominent in religious phenomena. The relationships discerned in religion may hold

true in other situations, though in an attenuated or masked or (otherwise less observable) fashion, so that their study in religion may help to illuminate other behavior. This is analogous to the study of abnormal psychology, in which particular relationships, such as defensive reactions to anxiety, may be discernible and their study may illuminate normal behavior as well.

3. *Unique relationships.* The basic variables in religious behavior are essentially those found in any behavior, but they interact with some variables within religion (e.g., absolute sanctions, or freedom ensuing from absolute acceptance) to provide relationships unlike those found elsewhere.

4. *Basically unique variables.* The basic variables operating within religion (e.g., a "religious" sentiment) are different and separate from those discerned outside religion (Dittes, 1969, p. 604).

·Psychological research reports concerning religiosity appear most often from the second and third standpoints. The second standpoint, namely, "uniquely prominent relationships," used to be present in the research on the influence of attitudes toward religion on reasoning and remembering certain kinds of information. Attitudes toward religion are treated as rather constant and central. So, research results illustrate a relationship between attitudes and cognitive processes of human beings. The standpoint seems to be the proper one in research on the internal structure of religiosity and its correlates (i.e., dimensions of personality and biographical variables). The danger connected with this standpoint seems to be twofold: (1) searching for identity in the processes that are similar only superficially; and (2) easily made attributions of the conclusion from the analysis of one of the processes to another (e.g., searching for similarities between brainwashing and proselytizing action of new religious movements).

Another danger connected with acceptance of this standpoint might be an unjustified limitation of research conclusions in order to adapt them also to nonreligious subject matter. Because of the aforementioned limitations, a most secure and fruitful theoretical basis for psychological research on religiosity seems to be created by acceptance of the statement that variables analyzed in research on religiosity are common also for other fields of human activity yet in the research on religiosity, they appear not only exclusively clear but also in a quite unique relationship, which is the standpoint belonging both to Dittes' points two and three.

The next point of our analysis concentrates on gains derived by the science of religion from psychological studies. Major gains depend upon psychological terminology and psychological theories. Psychological language seems to be far more precise and suits a description of individual or group religiosity much better than the terminology existing within the history of religion or philosophy of religion. Unfortunately, the meaning of some notions within psychology and other branches of the science of religion differ, so a special caution in using psychological terms is needed. For example, a description of a certain person as very submissive means for the psychologist somebody who has not reached full emotional autonomy, or somebody searching for support from surrounding persons; the same expression for a representative of the science of religion sounds very neutral or even in the theological tradition quite positive (e.g., a person submissive to God). Therefore, we have to employ very precise notions for particular terms; otherwise we will not avoid misunderstandings (Scobie, 1975).

As a good example of the usefulness of psychological terminology to the psychology of religion, religious experience could be analyzed in terms of disturbances of cognitive processes, that is, under- or oversensory stimulation (van der Lans, 1977). The same very fruitful result was achieved by the Swedish psychologist Ernst Arbman, who has employed clinical psychological terminology in analyzing religious experience and related psychopathological states (Arbman, 1963).

Psychological theories could also inspire new directions in the analysis of empirical data gathered in field studies. Among the most inspiring theories are those of cognitive dissonance by Leon Festinger, locus of control by Julian Rotter, and of authoritarian personality by Theodor W. Adorno.

Unfortunately, the aforementioned possibilities of utilizing psychological theories for enriching and enhancing the analysis of processes of structuring human religiosity are used very seldomly. They are usually restricted to the problems of religious motivation (i.e., motivation of being a religious person as well as motivation of irreligiosity), (Beit-Hallahmi, 1980).

Several authors try to adapt general developmental theories to explain the development of human religiosity. They mostly base their theories (not always explicitly) on Piaget's theory, and they restrict themselves to the age limits of adulthood. A very interesting attempt to cross age boundaries was made by Michael Riccards (1978) in his scheme of development of religious susceptibility.

In spite of all the attempts mentioned, those theories and theoretical schemes lack a sociodynamic background. They characterize the average process of development, but rarely specify typical features of religious development in a certain historical period. At this very moment, religious developments in Polish religiosity could serve as a very good example of the relationship between man's sociopolitical situation in certain historical periods and changes in religiosity. Regarding the most characteristic feature of these changes, I want to point out the consequential and ritualistic dimensions of religiosity. Religiosity among youths became much more active, in the sense of practices and in the sense of attachment to the Church. A traditional period of religious crisis also does not appear. In addition, the traditional decline of religiosity among the age groups from 30 to 50 years has been replaced by real interest and engagement in religious life.

It would be very interesting to compare, in cross-cultural studies, to what extent all these changes are conditioned by the current political situation in Poland or how far they are illustrative of cultural changes in developmental trends of contemporary religiosity in general.

REFERENCES

Arbman, E. (1963). *Ecstasy or Religious Trance*. Uppsala, Sweden: Svenska Bokförlaget/Norstedt.

Beit-Hallahmi, B. (1980). "Psychology of Religion - What Do We Know." *Archiv für Religionspsychologie, 14*, 228-236.

Dittes, J. (1969). Psychology of Religion." In *The Handbook of Social Psychology,* edited by G. Lindzey and L. Aronson, Reading, MA: Addison-Wesley, *5*, 603-618.

Riccards, M. P. (1978). "The Structure of Religious Development." *Lumen Vitae, 1*, 97-123.

Scobie, G. (1975). *Psychology of Religion*. London, GB: B. T. Batsford, Ltd.

PART FOUR: FOCUS ON OLD AGE

Photo credit: Maric Productions

19

Real-Ideal Residence Environment: Perceptions of Older Women Religious

S. Patricia Clark

Institutionalization of "retirement" is new to the American scene and relatively new to communal living groups. The growth of institutional retirement environments has increased the need for accurate descriptions of these settings.

A review of the literature with regard to the institutionalization of retirement living by religious communities reveals numerous anecdotal or observational reports, but little evidence of systematic study of either the "objective" environment or the perceived environment of the aged members themselves.

This research is an attempt to characterize the diversity found in three environmental settings of women religious, aged 65 years and over, who are members of one lifelong communal group with foundations in Rockland County, New York, since 1886. Since the present aged members have initiated the process of institutionalizing retirement, this study begins at this source to tap their perceptions of their actual and preferred environments through use of Moos' Sheltered Care Environment Scale. We seek the answers to these questions of interest to practitioners in the field of aging: What are the dimensions underlying Moos' Sheltered Care Environment Scale? How do the dimensions underlying perceptions of the Real environment differ from those underlying the Ideal environment? How do three environmental settings for retired women religious relate to each of these dimensions?

The relationship between environment and aging was first addressed by the gerontologist Robert Kleemeier (1959). He recognized the possibilities for both theory development and application in addressing the person/environment transactional system. He encouraged knowledge development in the "sensory-perceptual mediation of person-environment transactions, the definitions of milieu in social terms, the self as it interacts with different environmental contexts, and more specific social and physical aspects of housing and institution" (Lawton, 1980a).

In the past decades, some theoretical models have been proposed as ways to approach the study of how environment affects the behavior of old people. Campbell's (1981) general model proposes linking the physical design to important outcome variables for older people such as high/low morale and physical health/illness. He suggests studying people whose sense of cognitive control may be more influenced by the difference between what they have and what they desire. This theory is useful both in the recognition of negotiability and of discrepancy between the real and the preferred, but operationalizing these concepts is "in process."

Lawton and Nahemow's much-revised theoretical statement, the Adaptation Model, recognizes the broad range of individual resource differences and both the positive and negative influences of the environment. Here again this theory poses many operational problems.

Meanwhile, other researchers were motivated differently from the theorists. Physical environment and aging became a popular study in the 1960s when architects asked behavioral scientists for design guidelines. Surveys of design research on the microenvironments of the elderly may be found in Campbell (1981), Lawton (1980a, 1977), and Carp (1976). Design research using environmental manipulation has proved difficult to conduct. However, the "natural environments" of newly created facilities for the elderly accounts for many of the thematic studies concerning planned housing and institutions. These correlational studies have indicated needs for security, territory, safety, and social outlets. The results of these research studies have been translated for use into the recently evolved consumer-based technology for environmental design.

Meanwhile researchers were looking to operationalize the psychosocial milieu of the institutionalized older adult. Kleemeier (1959) suggested studying such dimensions as the segregate, the congregate quality, and the organization. Factor analyzing the Home for the Aged Descriptive Questionnaire (HDQ), Pincus (1968) suggested further studies on four environmental dimensions: Public/private; structured/unstructured; resource-sparse/-resource-rich, and isolated/integrated.

Moos and associates in the Social Ecology Lab at Stanford have developed various social climate scales to measure the environmental press of family settings, groups, work settings, schools, and treatment settings. To date, Moos has developed the most sophisticated measurement system for reflecting both the "objective" environment and the experienced environment of older adults in his Multiphasic Environmental Assessment Procedure (MEAP). Moos selectively measures the "objective" environmental resources in physical, organizational, human aggregate, and behavioral setting terms. The experienced environmental resources are measured in social-climate terms by using the consensual judgments of staff members and/or residents to assess the typical behavior in one's environment for the selective dimensions of Relationship, Personal Growth, and System Maintenance and System Change. These dimensions bear many similarities to other investigators' works in the field of aging studies.

Using Moos and Lemke's (1979) experiential instrument, the Sheltered Care Environment Scale (SCES), this initial study will characterize three retirement settings of a subgroup of lifelong communal-living aged women religious.

STUDY DESIGN

Today's interest in consumer perception stirred the overall research approach. The nonexperimental design is both descriptive and exploratory. It is descriptive since the objective is to convey and assess selected demographic and perceptual characteristics of a specific group on a given subject. The study has an exploratory feature as well. It statistically examines a rationally developed instrument, the SCES, toward detecting new patternings of variables, which may lead to the discovery of new concepts. The SCES has not been previously subjected to such statistical analysis.

Subjects

The total population (N = 175) of women religious, aged 65 years and over, who were members of the religious Congregation of Our Lady of the Rosary, at Sparkill, New York, was chosen to be the study population.

Initially, a letter requesting a meeting to explain the study was sent to the Executive Board of the Congregation. This meeting resulted in permission to conduct the research study.

Two letters were drafted and sent out a week apart to each congregation member, 65 years and older, requesting her participation in the study. Fourteen sisters were not able to complete the study because of health reasons, twelve sisters refused, and four sisters could not be reached. Cognitive and demographic data were collected on 145 persons who willingly completed both forms of the measurement instrument.

Respondents range from the ages of 65 to 94 years. The mean age is 72.95 years. The educational level of the respondents show that six have doctoral degrees, 52 master's degrees, and 66 others have completed their undergraduate collegiate work. One hundred thirty sisters were born in the United States of America, and 15 were born in Ireland. The mean years of professed service for this group is 49.46 years. There are 72 members living in Sparkill (16 in the Infirmary and 56 in the Motherhouse), and there are 73 members living in various local convents.

Settings

Three global settings are chosen by the members as residences. The Motherhouse is a 30-acre complex located in Sparkill, Rockland County, New York, just behind the Palisades. The main residence building is comprised of two units: an Infirmary and a Residence Hall. The two-floor Infirmary has individual rooms, nurses' stations, medical rooms, large sitting rooms, and a chapel. Meals are brought on trays to most of the Infirmary residents.

The four-floor Residence Hall for Sisters of all ages, called the Motherhouse in this study, is comprised of individual rooms, solariums, very large communal rooms, a congregate dining hall, chapel, and offices for congregational administrators. An active Resident Council is in operation here.

Not only are the two units separated physically, but they also denote different psychological identifications. In the Infirmary, a sense of being a "patient" is fostered. On the other hand, the Motherhouse encourages a strong identity with its long-standing tradition of congregational customs and rituals.

The third global setting, called Local Convents, is represented in 31 locations with each residence averaging seven occupants of all ages. Each house has its own council and is responsible for its own governance.

Measures Used

Two forms, Real (actual) and Ideal (preferred), of the Sheltered Care Environment Scale (SCES) were administered to measure the consumers' perceptions of the social climate. Both forms are identically worded except for the verbal; for example, Real item number one reads "Do residents get a lot of attention?" while Ideal item one reads "Would residents get a lot of attention?" The SCES contains 70 dichotomous items, with the last seven items serving as fillers.

The SCES purports to measure three global dimensions and seven subscales. The Relationship Dimension contains subscales named Cohesion and Conflict. The Personal Growth Dimension contains subscales named Independence and Self-Exploration. Subscales named Organization, Resident Influence and Physical Comfort are included in the global System Maintenance and System Change Dimension. Each subscale contains nine items.

Reference data on the Real form has been established in a range of 93 sheltered care facilities in California as follows: 590 residents and staff in 40 skilled nursing facilities (SNFs); from 950 residents and 239 staff in 27 residential care facilities (RCs); and from 1,524 residents and 112 staff in 23 apartment facilities (APTs). Results show considerable variability in the social environments both among and within the three types of sheltered care facilities.

Real-SCES subscale internal consistencies and intercorrelations were calculated for a sample of 374 residents and 655 staff members from a representative group of facilities. Results indicate adequate to high internal consistencies on the seven subscales at this time. Normative data for the Ideal SCES were not available at the time of this study.

Data Collection

Group sessions were scheduled in the Motherhouse setting at Sparkill, New York, and in various local convents both in New York and Missouri. A one-to-one approach was used in the Infirmary setting located in Sparkill, New York.

To replicate Moos' findings as closely as possible, the wording was not altered in the SCES forms. However, a suggestion was made to all respondents to read the word "staff" as "other Sisters," for more relevancy. The original YES-NO response set was also held fast.

Approximately one week elapsed between the administering of each of the two forms of the SCES to the subjects. The ordering of the completion of the Real and Ideal forms was randomly assigned. Subjects were asked to identify their completed forms. Administration time on each rating occasion was approximately 25 minutes.

The circled responses on the questionnaire were transferred to answer sheets.

Data Analysis

The Real and Ideal responses were factor analyzed separately. Factors scores using Ideal form responses and Real form factors were correlated. All correlations were done using Pearson's r. Simple Analyses of Variance were carried out separately for each of the three Real factors and for each of the three Ideal factors.

RESULTS

Factor Analysis: Dimensions Underlying SCES

The responses to both forms of the SCES (Real and Ideal) were factor analyzed using the PA2 factor program of the 1975 SPSS. The number of iterations was fixed at one in order to use the squared multiple correlations as communality estimates to replace the I's in the diagonal of the correlation matrix. Varimax rotations were obtained for 3-, 4-, 5-, 6-, and 7-factor solutions. The 3-factor solutions were retained for both the Real and the Ideal forms because they satisfied the arbitrary criterion that a factor be extracted only if the eigenvalue exceeded 3.0 (approximately 5 percent of the total variance), as well as the criterion that the factor structure be psychologically meaningful. The criterion used to define each factor was that the loading for a variable must have an absolute value greater than .40.

REAL FORM

This three factors solution accounted for 27.3 percent of the total factor variance. Items that constitute the three "Real" factors have been named "Comfort Negotiability," "Resident Influence," and "Activity Level." It is evident that Moos' seven subscales in the SCES have clearly taken on new structuring.

Real Factor I

Sixteen items clustered in this "Comfort Negotiability" factor, accounting for 52.2 percent of the variance in this 3-factor solution. This array reflects items in Moos' subscales as follows: Conflict 6, Comfort 4, Organization 3, Self-Exploration 2, and Cohesion 1.

Semantically, this factor reveals the presence of negotiable P-E interactions on the interpersonal, personal comfort, and organizational levels. Specific negotiable interpersonal behaviors among residents themselves include: voicing criticisms and complaints, talking about money problems and about fears, starting arguments openly, and getting impatient with each other. Between staff (other Sisters) and residents, a negotiable behavior is seen as upmanship on the part of the staff.

Negotiable personal comfort behaviors concern temperature, noise, and odor control, and also includes personal appearance.

Negotiable organizational behaviors perceived in the environment include remarking about confusing situations.

Real Factor II

Ten items clustered in the "Resident Influence" factor, representing 27.1 percent of the total variance in this 3-factor solution. This array reflects items from Moos' subscales as follows: Resident Influence 4, Independence 3, Physical Comfort 2, and Cohesion 1.

Semantically, the residents perceive the presence of resident influence in the following behaviors: having privacy whenever wanted; having a say in making the rules; setting up and taking charge of activities; being able to change things if they try; being strongly encouraged to make their own decisions; seeing their suggestions acted upon; not being asked to leave when one breaks a rule; not merely passing time here; and not experiencing a crowded milieu.

Real Factor III

Nine items clustered in this "Activity Level" factor, representing 20.7 percent of the total variance in this 3-factor solution. The items found in this array reflected in Moos' subscales as follows: Cohesion 3, Independence 2, Resident Influence 2, Self-Exploration 1, Organization 1.

Semantically, the residents perceive the staff's (other Sisters') behaviors as including: teaching of new skills; teaching of "how to" deal with practical problems; planning residents' activities carefully; having socials; sharing a great deal of individual attention; listening to residents' past dreams and ambitions; trying out new and different ideas; and spending a great deal of time with the residents.

IDEAL FORM

The 3-factor solution accounted for 26.5 percent of the total variance, with the three factors accounting for 51.9 percent, 27.8 percent and 20.4 percent of this variance, respectively. Items that constitute the three "Ideal" factors have been named "Comfort Negotiability," "Enabling," and "Open Communication." Note that Ideal Factor I is labeled the same as Real Factor I. However, the similarities in both perceived environments are not pronounced in Factors II and III.

Ideal Factor I

Nineteen items clustered in this ideal "Comfort Negotiability" factor representing 51.9 percent of the total variance in this 3-factor solution. These items break down to Moos' subscales as follows: Conflict 7, Organization 5, Cohesion 4, and Physical Comfort 3.

Semantically, the residents prefer such negotiable interactions among themselves as: complaining; criticizing others and the setting; becoming impatient; and, starting open arguments. Preferred negotiations with staff (other Sisters) would be involved in the cases of upmanship, or criticism over minor things.

Residents prefer personal comfort behaviors to remain negotiable such as temperature and noise control, privacy, activities, discussions, and personal appearance.

Residents prefer organizational behaviors to remain negotiable, in situations of marked confusion, with people changing their minds, unclear matters, or situational changes.

Ideal Factor II

Thirteen items clustered in this factor labeled "Enabling" representing 27.8 percent of the total variance in this 3-factor solution. These 13 items break down to Moos' subscales as follows: Cohesion 4, Resident Influence 3, Independence 2, Organization 2, and Physical Comfort 2.

Semantically, residents prefer aesthetic use of colors and decoration to create warm, cheerful effects, as well as the inclusion of comfortable and homey furnishings.

Preferred enabling behaviors would include the teaching of how to deal with practical problems; healthier residents helping the less healthy ones; residents getting a great deal of individual attention; the presence of challenging activities for the residents; and staff (other Sisters) spending a great deal of time with residents.

Preferred governance is: Residents having a knowledge of sanctions; residents' suggestions and requests being acted upon; residents being able to change things if they try; and the provision of a well-organized setting with the residents having a say in making the rules.

Ideal Factor III

Nine items clustered in this "Open Communication" factor, accounting for 20.4 percent of the variance in this 3-factor solution. These nine items break down to Moos' subscales as follows: Self-Exploration 4, Resident Influence 3, Physical Comfort 1, Conflict 1.

Semantically, residents prefer that staff (other Sisters) allow minor infractions of the rule; residents prefer not having to keep neither personal problems nor disagreements to themselves; being able to talk openly about their fears and their personal problems; and keeping the noise regulated.

Correlations of Real and Ideal Environments

The qualitative differences among the "Real and the Ideal" factors have already been detailed. However, it is also of interest how the factors underlying the Real form of the SCES differ from the factors underlying the Ideal form. Unit-weighted factor scores were computed and standardized to yield a mean of 50 and a standard deviation of 10. Three additional factor scores were computed, using Ideal Form responses and the Real Form factors in order to gauge the relation between how the subjects perceive their actual environment, and how they might want their actual environment to change. Pearson product-moment correlation coefficients were computed.

The correlations among the Real factors (using Real Form responses) and the Ideal factors range from -.14 to .37, and indicate that the way the Real environment is perceived differs from the way that the Ideal environment is perceived. The correlations among the Real factors using Real Form responses and the Real factors using Ideal Form responses range from -.08 to .42, and show that there is an implicit desire to change the real environment.

Since these last correlations are not close to 1.0, it is an indication that what is desired in the Ideal environment is different from that which is perceived in the Real environment. The correlation of .40 between Comfort Negotiability based on the Real form and Comfort Negotiability based on the

Ideal form of the SCES indicates that considerably more Comfort Negotiability is desired in the Ideal environment than exists in the Real environment. Likewise, the correlation of .42 between Resident Influence based on the Real Form and Resident Influence based on the Ideal Form of the SCES indicates that considerably more Resident Influence is desired in the Ideal environment than exists in the Real environment. Again, the correlations of .29 between Activity Level based on the Real Form and Activity Level based on the Ideal form of the SCES indicates more Activity Level is desired in the Ideal environment than exists in the Real environment.

Analysis of Variance for Three Settings

To determine the ability of the instruments to discriminate among three distinct environments (Infirmary, Motherhouse, and Local Convents), statistical tests of significance (3 x 1 simple ANOVAs) were carried out separately for each of the three Real factors and for each of the three Ideal factors.

The Analysis of Variance of Real Factor 2 (Resident Influence) shows a significant effect due to residence. Scheffe contrasts of the means show that residents in Local Convents have a significantly higher score on Resident Influence than either Motherhouse or Infirmary residents. Moreover, residents of the Motherhouse show a significantly higher score in this factor than the residents of the Infirmary. Inferentially, a hierarchial order of dependency increases and involvement decreases from Local Convent to Motherhouse to Infirmary, which agrees with this finding.

However, the analysis of variance of Real Factor 3 (Activity Level) shows a significant effect due to residence. Scheffe contrasts of the means show that residents in the Motherhouse have a significantly higher score on Activity Level than Local Convents' residents. Inferentially, a semantic item-analysis reveals that programmed packages are included in this array. The Motherhouse is the central site for educational activities for the Community. Also, the Motherhouse residents are more of a captive audience due to transportation problems than residents of the Local Convents would be.

The Analysis of Variance of Ideal Factor 3 (Open Communication) shows a significant effect due to residence. However, Scheffe contrasts of the means shows no single pairwise difference.

This study has presented data on environmental perceptions of aged women religious for the purpose of studying the underlying dimensions of the SCES, for studying the differences in Real and Ideal perceptions and for detecting whether three levels of specialized Sheltered Care results in cognitive variations.

DISCUSSION

The factor analysis of two separate forms of the Sheltered Care Environment Scale supports the original conception of social climate scales as including three global domains: Personal Growth, Relationship, and System Maintenance and System Change. By inference, in the Real-SCES components analysis, the Personal Growth domain is represented by the first factor labeled "Comfort-Negotiability." This grouping can be viewed as an array of personal identification statements showing assertiveness, involvement with reality, and a responsiveness to sensory comfort, interpersonal interactions, and systems negotiability.

By inference, the System Maintenance and System Change domain is represented by Real Factor 2, Resident Influence. This array of items may be viewed as a press towards the residents accepting responsibility for formulating policies and running the residency.

By inference, the Relationship domain is represented by Real Factor 3, Activity Level. This clustering of items may be viewed as the degree of socialization encouraged by programmed activities and formal structures.

By inference, in the Ideal-SCES components analysis, Personal Growth is again represented by the first factor labeled "Comfort-Negotiability." This cluster can be seen as personal identification statements showing assertiveness, reality, and a concern with privacy and changing situations.

By inference, the System Maintenance and System Change domain is represented by the Ideal Factor 2, "Enabling." This array can be seen as containing statements promoting enablement through such environmental contingencies as a stable organization, a supportive network, and aesthetic furnishings.

By inference, the Relationship domain is represented by the Ideal Factor 3, "Open Communication." This grouping can be seen as preferential statements for open and honest communication and for flexible structures for rule enforcement.

The results of the two separate components analysis do not support Moos' rational groupings of the SCES into the seven dimensions, which he labels Cohesion, Conflict, Independence, Self-Exploration, Organization, Resident Influence, and Physical Comfort. Despite the fact that Moos defends his subgroupings as conceptually distinct, though moderately highly correlated, these areas were collapsed in both the Real and the Ideal factor analysis. The combining of original dimensions reflects the high intercorrelations among items on different original dimensions, and hence this study focuses only on the newly structured factors.

Also, there appear to be some relatively weak items in the original scale. Nine items were not reflected in either factor solution. Twenty-eight items did not appear in the restructuring of the Real form; twenty-two items did not appear in the Ideal restructuring. The items that clustered in both factor-analytic solutions also suggested a stronger semantic style than was suggested by the original subscale clusterings.

The restructuring and relabeling of Moos' subdivisions in this factor-analytic solution suggests further study of the SCES semantics toward operationalizing the concepts of environmental "negotiability" and of "enabling" in social ecological studies.

By inference, the Real factors and the Ideal factors semantically present the residents' perceptions of an evolving environment. The Real factors reflect the "consciousness awareness" process that women religious have experienced in the past two decades in personal growth (Comfort Negotiability), governance (Resident Influence), and interpersonal relationships (Activity Levels). The Ideal factors reflect the preferred directional trend in the global domains of personal growth (Comfort Negotiability), governance (Enabling), and interpersonal relationship (Open Communication).

Having direct responsibility for the functional milieu and having a lifelong investment in the Congregational environs, the aged women religious are likely to have more realistic expectations of both themselves and their environs as they are committed to evolving a more humane environment.

An alternative explanation may be that aged women religious are likely to view the environmental interface from a transcendent perspective and hence the Ideal preferences may be beyond human experience.

The very low to low correlations between the Real and the Ideal Scale Scores reflect different response patterns between existing environmental perceptions and preferred environmental perceptions. Even though some of the cross-measures were significant, there simply is not much match between the way the real environment is perceived and the way the ideal environment is perceived. Clearly, no halo effect was revealed.

The low moderate correlations using the Real Form responses and the Real factors using Ideal Form responses fall short of the perfect match, thereby reflecting an implicit desire to change the real environment.

These quantitative differences suggest further study to this consumer group in reworking concepts and themes toward future programming.

One explanation for this wide gap between the Real and Ideal perceptions may be related simply to the effects of women religious in transition. The current renewal process of women religious involves a reconceptualization of religious life and a new historical way of expressing what it means to be a woman religious. The low correlations between the perceived Real and the Ideal environments could reflect the current tensions present in all sorts of concrete expressions in this transitional period.

The Analysis of Variance revealed some significant effects due to residence. By inference, the three environments represent three hierarchial levels of care for the elderly. In an ascending order of respondents' assumed dependency, the Infirmary parallels a skilled nursing home; the Motherhouse parallels a residential care community; and the Local Convents parallel planned apartment living.

Statistically, Real Factor 2, Resident Influence, shows a significant effect due to residence. Residents of the Local Convents perceive a significantly higher involvement in governance than the Motherhouse residents or Infirmary residents, respectively. Inferentially, one might expect a greater involvement level in Local Convents because of the increased hierarchial order of dependency assumed present in the three types of settings.

Statistically, Real Factor 3, Activity Level, shows a significant effect due to residence. The Motherhouse residents perceive more programmed packages in their environment than the residents of the Local Convents. Inferentially, this is true when one considers that the Motherhouse is the center of most of the Community's "programmed packages." The semantics of this factor give no hint of either organizational or individual spontaneity present. With this semantic information, the statistical finding sounds true.

Ideal Factor 3, Open Communication, shows a significant effect due to residence, but no significant pairwise difference. Inferentially, this may reflect a preference for a strong supportive network on all levels.

Consistent with the theoretical perspective of social ecology, this study illustrates the importance of characterizing environments in actual practice. The results show the SCES, even though in its embryonic stage, to be a potentially functional assessment catalyst toward creating a more humane environment.

Limitations

The present study was only an initial step toward developing a stronger knowledge base for the Sheltered Care Environment Scale. This study has important limitations:

1. The unique study population was a highly educated aged group who presently is deeply involved in many environmental restructurings within their holistic life space.
2. The SCES is designed for newly come-together residential lay groups and not for lifelong committed religious groups.
3. The original YES-NO response choice might have been converted to a four-point format to effect more variability.

Implications

The emergence of three meaningful basic factors provides confirmation on the basic dimensions suggested by the gerontological researchers over the last two decades: personal referents, relationship, and organization. The restructuring of Moos' subdimensions would call for further research on the semantics and the relevancy to older adults of these subdimensions. Also, further studies are needed to explore the concepts of "negotiability" and "enabling."

The quantitative differences between the Real and the Ideal solutions suggest to the respondent group that they might pursue a variety of strategies to validate the gap and determine their predictive usefulness.

The results of the Analysis of Variance performed with these data show some sensitivity to the presence of residence differences. These agree with inferences about the hierarchical order of dependency in the later years.

At this time, it is most appropriate to call for more statistical studies of the rationally-developed Sheltered Care Environment Scale in order to explore its predictive usefulness.

REFERENCES

Campbell, D. E. (1981). "Microenvironments of the Elderly." In *The Dynamics of Aging*, edited by F. J. Berghorn. Boulder, CO: Westview Press, Inc.

Carp, F. M. (1976). "Housing and Living Environments of Older People." In *Handbook of Aging and the Social Sciences*, edited by R. H. Binstock and E. Shanas. New York: Van Nostrand Reinhold Co.

Kleemeier, R. W. (1959). "Behavior and the Organization of the Bodily and the External Environment." In *Handbook of Aging and the Individual*, edited by J. E. Birren. Chicago, IL: University of Chicago Press.

Lawton, M. P. (1977). "The Impact of the Environment on Aging and Behavior." In *Handbook of the Psychology of Aging*, edited by J. E. Birren and K. W. Schaie. New York: Van Nostrand Reinhold Company.

Lawton, M. P. (1980). *Environment and Aging*. Belmont, CA: Wadsworth, Inc.

Lawton, M. P. (1980a). In Introduction, *Environmental Context of Aging: Life Styles, Environmental Quality, and Living Arrangements*, edited by T. O. Byerts, S. C. Howell, and L. A. Pastalan. New York: Garland STPM Press.

Moos, R. M., (Ed.). (1976). *Human Adaptation: Coping with Life Crises*. Lexington, MA: D. C. Heath and Company.

Moos, R. H. (1976). *The Human Context: Environmental Determinants of Behavior*. New York: Wiley-Interscience.

Moos, R. H. (1980). "Specialized Living Environments for Older People: A Conceptual Framework for Evaluation." *Journal of Social Issues, 36*, 75-94.

Moos, R. H., and Insel, P. M., (Eds.) (1974). *Issues in Social Ecology: Human Milieus*. Palo Alto, CA: National Press Books.

Moos, R. H., and Lemke, S. (1979). *Multiphasic Environmental Assessment Procedure: Preliminary Manual, Social Ecology Laboratory*. Palo Alto, CA: Stanford University, School of Medicine.

Pincus, A. (1968). "The Definition and Measurement of the Institutionalized Environment in Homes for the Aged. *The Gerontologist, 8,* 207-210.

20

Friends of Older Black and White Women

Hedva Lewittes and B. Runi Mukherji

Friendship is critical both to the mental and physical health of older women (Eisenberg, 1979; Hess, 1979; Lowenthal and Haven, 1968). Social participation is frequently related to measures of life satisfaction and happiness, and in one study of widows, contact with friends contributed more to high morale than did visits from children (Arling, 1976). Throughout adulthood, friendship serves important functions in women's lives. It has been suggested that friendships have therapeutic value, provide a broader social network for women isolated in the home, and may complement marriages in which husbands are unable to fulfill their wives' needs for emotional intimacy, (Hess, 1979). Within friendships women are continuously socialized into the qualities of nurturance and sensitivity. Throughout the life cycle, women's friendships are characterized by emotional expressiveness and self-disclosure and concerned with reciprocity, intimacy and assistance (Bell, 1981; Booth, 1972; Candy, Troll, and Levy, 1981; Hacker, 1981). As people get older, friendships often become increasingly important because retirement and loss of family members can disrupt social integration and lead to isolation. Studies suggest that women are more likely than men to maintain old friends and make new friends. Indeed, women's relational abilities appear to contribute to their greater flexibility and adaptability in old age (Lewittes, 1982).

While importance of friendship for older women is fairly well documented, few studies examine the content and meaning of older women's friendships. To begin with, research on older people tends to focus on number of interactions and size of networks and these measures provide insufficient information (Cohen and Rajkowski, 1982). Especially for older people who are limited by lack of money and mobility, frequency of contact may not indicate the perceived quality of a relationship and does not adequately delineate the particular nature of friendships that may have lasted for decades or even a lifetime. Much of the research that delves into the content of friendship is based on younger, college-educated populations.

These studies define friendship as a relationship that is voluntary and chosen. Yet for many older people, certain relatives are considered to be friends. In addition, measurement scales developed on younger subjects focus on intellectual stimulation, common work interests, and shared activities (Safilios-Rothschild, 1981; Wright, 1974) and did not include items that reflect the specific nature of intimacy and kinds of help and shared activities relevant to the life circumstances of older people. Further, most studies of older people fail to look at ethnic differences in friendship.

In particular, there is insufficient research on the friendships of older Black women, and the majority of the studies that have been done have methodological and conceptual shortcomings that limit their validity. As a result, it is unclear whether the previous discussion of friendship applies to Black women. Several studies suggest that older Blacks' friendships are less intimate than those of older Whites and that the Black elderly have a loose definition of who is a friend (Sterne, Phillips, and Rabushka, 1974). However, to begin with, these studies investigate only the urban poor, many of whom have been uprooted. Secondly, the data on friendship are often not reported separately for Black women. The results for Black women are either combined with the data for Black men (Sterne, Phillips, and Rabushka, 1974) or with the results for White women (Arling, 1976). Further, these studies do not distinguish between close friends and casual acquaintances and do not examine the patterns and characteristics of the close friendships.

In order to obtain a valid picture of Black women's friendships, it is important to define and measure friendship in a way that reflects their economic circumstances, family patterns, and cultural history. Quite possibly, Black women have different but equally meaningful needs and values in regard to their friends than do White women. A study of widows suggests that Black women are more likely to have been independent from their spouses, and thus loneliness is less of a problem for them than for White widows. However, money is more of a problem (Lopata, 1973). Thus, concrete assistance may be more important in Black women's relationships than in White women's. While practical aid is often considered to be the responsibility of family members rather than friends, for Black women there may be more overlap between the functions of friends and family. For example, a study of an urban Black poor community suggests that friends who exchange services and fulfill obligations that contribute to mutual survival, come to be considered as kin. In addition, a recent study of the church friends of elderly Blacks characterized these relationships as "pseudo-extended families," which may fill the void in helping networks left by children and siblings, who have moved. These church friends had an impact on the subject's psychological well being while nonchurch friends did not.

In sum, the objective of this study was to examine the meaning and content of both Black and White older women's relationships with their closest friends. The subjects in this study were asked to respond to a series of questions about their best friends (who could be relatives, if the respondent chose to name a relative as a best friend). The questions were constructed to reflect the life circumstances of the elderly women, both Black and White, and were directed at the nature of intimacy, helping behaviors, and activities shared by them and their friends. The respondents included Black and White single women from a variety of socioeconomic backgrounds.

METHOD

Subjects

The subjects were recruited through senior citizens centers and clubs, women's groups, church groups, or were obtained via community networks. Groups were contacted in both urban and suburban locations, and every effort was made to get both Black and White samples that represented a range of socioeconomic backgrounds. In the final sample for this study, there were 97 White respondents and 83 Black. The mean age of the sample was 71 years old, with the range being from 59 years to 91 years old.

Materials

The data for this study were collected by means of a questionnaire called the Older People's Friendship Schedule (OPFS), which consisted of 71 items and was subdivided into two major parts:

1. The first 14 items requested demographic information from the respondents, such as, age, marital status, ethnicity, income, etc.
2. The second part consisted of two sets of 30 items, where the respondent was asked to select two of their best friends and answer questions pertaining to the specific content of their friendship. For each friend selected, the respondent was asked for the following types of information:
    a. Descriptive characteristics of friend, such as whether the friend was a relative or not, how long the friend had been known, and frequency of interaction. Example:
        22. How long have you known this friend?
        ____ less than 1 year   ____ 1 to 5 years
        ____ 5 to 20 years   ____ 20 to 40 years
        ____ more than 40 years
    b. Content of friendship with respect to categories of:
        (i)   helping
        (ii) intimacy
        (iii) shared activities

Example (intimacy):

34. I tell this person things I do not tell anyone else.
___ very often   ___ a fair amount
___ not very often   ___ never

Construction of Questionnaire and Procedure

The OPFS was constructed and pilot tested by the authors in consultation with professionals who worked with the elderly. The questionnaire was administered by a research team that included Black and White members who aided the subjects if they had difficulty reading the questionnaire.

RESULTS

Demographics of Sample

An examination of the demographic data reveals clear differences between Black and White subjects. Black women had significantly lower incomes, $t(165) = -2.86$, $p < .005$; less education, $t(177) = -2.83$, $p < .0052$; and their spouses' occupations were of lower status, $t(126) = 3.9$, $p < .001$. Black women were most likely to have been domestics, and Whites, housewives. However, despite these significant differences in the means of the two samples, an examination of the actual frequency distributions for these two samples show overall similarities (see Tables 20.1, and 20.2).

The majority of both Blacks and Whites were in the three lowest educational and occupational categories. The significant mean differences occur because on each variable, there is a large group of Blacks clustered in the lowest category and a large group of Whites in the next higher categories. It's not that the Whites were rich and the Blacks were poor. Rather the Whites had low incomes and the Blacks had lower. The Black sample is significantly younger than the White, $t(175) = -2.49$, $p < .05$, with the average age of the Black women being 69.6 years, and the White, 72.5 years.

Regarding residential and family patterns, both Blacks and Whites are most likely to live in a private house, and both groups have lived in their current location for an average of 17 years. While both Black and White women are most likely to live alone, significantly more Blacks live with family members, $t(177) = 3.29$, $p < .005$. Black women have been without a spouse for an average of 18 years, which is significantly longer than Whites, who have been separated for an average of 12.75 years.

Descriptive Characteristics of Friends

There is a great similarity in the general characteristics of Black and White women's friendships. There was no difference between the two groups as to the number of friends who were relatives. Overall, about 68 percent of the friends named were *not* relatives. For both Blacks and Whites, the majority of all friendships named were long term, with 60 percent being over 20 years' duration; the modal response to this question was 20 to 40 years. However, there was a significant difference between the length of the first and second friendship described. While over half the second friendships were still 20 years or longer, that is, the second friendships were also long term, many more of the first friendships were over 40 years. Most of the friends lived within 50 miles, and there were no differences between Blacks and Whites in the frequency of interaction or phoning their friend. On the average, both Blacks and Whites see or call their friends either daily or a few times a week. Very few subjects name male friends or name friends met at work.

Comparisons of Blacks' and Whites' Ratings for Content of Friendship

Since there was a significant difference between Black and White subjects on a socioeconomic status; it could be argued that any Black/White differences in the content of friendship were due to economic rather than cultural/ethnic differences. In order to test for this possibility, we performed two-way, ethnicity by income, ANOVAs on all the questions concerning helping, intimacy, and shared activity. For these analyses, the ratings for the first and second friends were combined. These analyses revealed no main effect for income and no significant interaction between income and ethnicity on any of the items.

Intimacy appears to be important in the best friendships of both Black and White women. For example, there were no group differences in response to the following items: "I share my thoughts and feelings," "My friend listens without judging," and "My friend makes me feel better when I am upset." The modal rating for both groups on these three questions was "very likely." However, for Black women, in addition to intimacy, concrete help is also important in friendships. There was a significant difference between Black and White subjects on the following items: "My friend visits me when I am sick" and "I borrow change and household items from this friend." A breakdown of the responses to these questions by income category reveals that Blacks of every income level are more likely to rate these kinds of help as important. However, the largest Black/White discrepancies occur in the middle-income categories, and the lowest-income Blacks are least likely to report that they receive this kind of help. Overall, both Black and White women rated shared activities as less important than intimacy or helping.

Comparisons of ratings of the first and second friends (Friend 1 and 2)

The striking Black/White differences emerge in the ratings of the first and second named friends. Blacks make a distinction between the content of the two friendships, while Whites do not. For Blacks, Friend 1 is seen as more intimate than Friend 2, while concrete help is rated similarly in both. Whites do not differentiate between friends as sharply. Intimacy is central to both first and second friendships of Whites, and help less important in both, than it is to Blacks (see Table 20.3).

An example of the distinction that Blacks and Whites make between Friend 1 and Friend 2 can be seen in the analysis for the item, "I tell my friends things I do not tell anyone else." A two-way (Ethnicity x Friend) ANOVA on the responses to this question reveals no main effect of ethnicity, a main effect of Friend, $F(1,116) = 7.07$; $p < .01$, and a significant interaction, $F(1,116) = 7.92$, $p < 006$. Similarly, two-way (Ethnicity x Friend) ANOVAs on the responses to "I share my thoughts, feelings, and experiences with my friend," show no main effects of Ethnicity or Friend, but do show a significant interaction, $F(1,116) = 3.70$, $p < .056$.

DISCUSSION

This study reveals both significant similarities and differences in the friendships of Black and White women. Contrary to previous studies that characterize older Black people's friendships as less intimate and less clearly defined than Whites, the picture of older Black women's friendships that emerges is of relationships that serve somewhat different functions than those of Whites, but are meaningful and vital.

There are several features of this study that distinguish it from previous research and may account for its findings. In this study, subjects were asked to describe their best friends, not all friends or friends in general, and further they were allowed to name relatives as friends if they wished. Secondly, intimacy was defined on the schedule as a series of concrete items on which subjects could indicate levels of importance for each particular type of intimacy. In addition, the types of items regarding help and activities were designed to reflect the particular circumstances of older women. Given that women make and maintain more intimate friendships than men, it was critical that the data were compiled and analyzed for Black women separately from Black men, as well as White women.

Some of the demographic characteristics of the sample in this study also differentiate it from previous research on the friendships of the Black elderly (Sterne, Phillips, and Rabushka, 1974). There is a socioeconomic diversity in our Black sample. A sizeable number of Blacks are not at the lowest income level, have finished high school, are suburban, and have not recently been uprooted. A majority of our Black sample lives in private homes. These demographic characteristics are intentional. Our research team sought out groups serving the Black elderly in which members were not all destitute. We did so because we wanted a sample of Blacks that were not representative of only poor Blacks, so that we could make valid comparisons between the Black and White samples. Nonetheless, the Blacks in our sample are poorer and have less education than the Whites. These differences in education, income, and occupation are perhaps not surprising, but they do raise the question as to whether Black/White differences in friendship patterns are a result of the socioeconomic factors. However, the pattern of Black/White differences that emerges in these data is difficult to account for, purely by socioeconomic variables. Two-way (Ethnicity x Income) ANOVAs were performed on the questions concerning the content of friendship and did not show any main or interaction effects for income. These findings suggest that Black/White differences in the study reflect ethnic/cultural factors. Methodologically, Black/White differences in socioeconomic status in the society as a whole create a difficult dilemma for cross-ethnic research. On the one hand, a study in which Blacks and Whites are matched for socioeconomic variables would enable cleaner statistical comparisons to be made and would resolve more conclusively the issue of whether differences between the two groups were primarily cultural. However, since in the population as a whole, a larger percentage of Black single women (compared with White single women) are poor, such matched samples would not be representative of the general population distribution.

To turn now to a discussion of the data, one of the most striking results in this study is that so many women, both Black and White, described relationships of long duration. Other research has also confirmed the preponderance of long-term friendships among the elderly. Psychological theory stresses the importance of a sense of continuity for mental health in later life (Butler, 1982). This finding suggests that friends as well as family may be an important source of connection with the past. The data indicate that, although the friendships had been formed many years ago, they were still active. Sixty-seven percent of the women reported seeing their friends a few times a month, and most friends lived within 50 miles. Telephone contacts were frequent. The finding of stable, meaningful relationships in this study is probably related to the fact that the subjects had lived in their current residences for an average of 17 years. In addition, the fact that many of the subjects were obtained through centers and groups suggests they are a fairly active and well-functioning group. Nonetheless, distance and transportation were seen as obstacles to maintaining ties. Seventy-eight of the subjects said they had friends whom they would not see as much as they liked because they no longer lived close by.

The most important finding gleaned from a comparison of Black and White women's responses is that the friendships of the Black women *do not* appear to lack intimacy, as was found in previous research. On the contrary, there are no Black/White differences in the mean ratings on any of the items that describe intimacy in friendship. Since intimacy is highly valued in popular modern psychology, the assertion that Blacks are less intimate could easily be interpreted as a negative judgment, although this is never explicitly stated in the previous research. Thus, the finding of this study that elderly

Black women are aware of and put high value on intimacy in their relationships will hopefully dispel the notion that Blacks are less emotionally deep or complex.

Additionally, previous studies also hypothesized that Blacks have a loose definition of friendship that includes almost anyone. This hypothesis is also not supported in our data. Sixty-eight percent of both groups named friends who were not relatives. Furthermore, Blacks -- far from having a vague notion of friendship -- made clearer distinctions between their two friends than did Whites. It is important to note that the questionnaire used in this study did not suggest to subjects that the first friend they named was a better or best friend as compared with the second. Nor did the questionnaire indicate that subjects ought to differentiate between their two friends. Nonetheless, the subjects themselves made some distinction. For both Blacks and Whites, there is a significant difference between the length of friendship 1 and 2, and Blacks described different functions and meanings as well.

The distinctions that Black subjects make between their two friends do suggest that the relative value of intimacy for them is somewhat different than for White women. White women describe intimacy as the most important aspects of their two friendships. For Black women, intimacy is rated high in the first friendship but not in the second. Helping is more important for Blacks even in describing the first friendship, and the second friendship is described primarily as a helping relationship.

Given that Black women report that they get more practical assistance from their friends, one might expect that they help each other more because they are poorer. The fact that this is not upheld by our statistical analysis does not convince us that these cultural differences are not at least partly due to economic factors. Other research suggests that Blacks develop strategies of mutual aid as an adaptation to adverse economic circumstances (Stack, 1974). Indeed, such helping networks have been utilized by many poor and immigrant groups. In these data, however, there is no linear relationship between helping friendships and income. This occurs because among Blacks, the poorest groups are least likely to rate help as part of their friendships. It seems quite possible that the poorest subjects are less able to see and phone their friends, and less likely to participate in activities that would enrich their helping networks. Further investigation is needed to clarify this issue.

The finding that concrete help, particularly assistance such as visiting when sick, is important in the friendships of Black women suggests that there is more overlap in the functions of friend and family for Black women. In addition, the fact that this study found that Black women are more likely to attend church with their friends than Whites, confirms previous research on the importance of church friends to the psychological well-being of older Blacks (Ortega, Crutchfield, and Rushing, 1983). Further, studies of older people in Black and White families find that, particularly, Black women give and receive more functional aid than their White counterparts (Mindel, 1986). Thus friendship patterns seem to reflect broader cultural values and an understanding of the meaning and content of friendship provides a fuller picture of the roles of older Black women.

REFERENCES

Arling, G. (1976). "The Elderly Widow and her Family, Neighbors and Friends." *Journal of Marriage and the Family, 38,* 757-768.

Bell, R. (1981). "Friendships of Women and of Men." *Psychology of Women Quarterly, 5*(3), 402-417.

Booth, A. (1972). "Sex and Social Participation." *American Sociological Review, 37,* 183-192.

Butler, R. N. (1982). "Toward a Psychiatry of the Life Cycle." In *Readings in Aging and Death.* edited by S. Zarith. New York: Harper and Row.

Candy, S. G., Troll, L., and Levy, S. G. (1981). "A Developmental Exploration of Friendship Functions in Women." *Psychology of Women Quarterly, 5*(3), 456-472.

Cohen, C. I., and Rajkowski, H. (1982). "What's in a Friend. Substantive and Theoretical Issues." *The Gerontologist, 22,* 261-266.

Creecy, R. (1977). "Close Friendship: A Correlate of Morale among Low-Income Black Aged?" *Gerontologist, 17*(5), 50.

Eisenberg, L. A. (1979). "A Friend, Not an Apple a Day Will Keep the Doctor Away." *The American Journal of Medicine, 66,* 551-553.

Hacker, H. M. (1981). "Blabbermouths and Clams: Sex Differences in Self-Disclosure." *Psychology of Women Quarterly,* (Spring) *5*(3), 385-402.

Hess, B. (1979). "Sex Roles, Friendship, and the Life Course." *Research on Aging, 1,* 494-515.

Lewittes, H. (1982). "Women's Development in Adulthood and Old Age: A Review and Critique." *International Journal of Mental Health: Women and Mental Illness.* (Spring/Summer), *11*(1,2), 115-134.

Lopata, H. Z. (1973). "Social Relations of Black and White Widowed Women in a Northern Metropolis." *American Journal of Sociology.* (January), *78*(4), 1003-1010.

Lowenthal, M. F., Thurnher, M., and Chiriboga, D. (1977). *Four Stages of Life.* San Francisco, CA: Jossey-Bass.

Meyerhoff, B. (1978). *Number Our Days,* New York: Simon and Schuster.

Mindel, C. H. (1986). "The Elderly in Minority Families." In *Growing Old in America*. 3rd ed., edited by B. B. Hess and E. W. Markson. New Brunswick: Transaction Books.

Ortega, S. T., Crutchfield, R. D., and Rushing, W. A. (1983). "Race Differences in Elderly Personal Well-Being." *Research on Aging, 5,* 101-118.

Safilios-Rothschild, C. (1981). "Toward a Social Psychology of Relationships." *Psychology of Women Quarterly, 5*(3), 377-384.

Stack, C.B. (1974). *All Our Kin*. New York: Harper and Row.

Sterne, R., Phillips, J. E., and Rabushka, A. (1974). *The Urban Elderly Poor*. Lexington, MA: D. C. Heath and Co.

Wright, P. H. (1974). "The Delineation and Measurement of Some Key Variables in the Study of Friendship." *Representative Research in Social Psychology, 5,* 93-96.

AUTHOR NOTES

This research was funded by the State University of New York University Awards Program grant (Summer, 1983) to the first author. The authors wish to thank Doretha Custis, who was a research assistant on the study. Her extensive experience in working with the elderly and her contacts in the Black community were invaluable. We also wish to thank Michael Palij for the many hours of expert assistance he provided on the data analysis. Finally, we wish to thank Lynn Iredell, Zelda Meyers, and Teresa Morrissey, who were also research assistants and whose energy and commitment greatly contributed to the project.

Reprints of the chapter and copies of the questionnaire can be obtained from Dr. Hedva Lewittes, Department of Psychology, SUNY, College at Old Westbury, Old Westbury, NY 11568.

Table 20.1

Percentage Distribution Across Income Categories for Black and White Women

	Income Category				
Ethnicity	0-$300	$351-800	$801-1500	$1501-2500	Above $2500
Black	25.00	41.67	16.67	8.33	8.33
White	14.29	42.86	21.43	14.29	7.14

Table 20.2

Percentage Distribution Across Education Categories for Black and White Women

	Education						
Ethnicity	0-8 years	some high school	finished h.s.	vocational training	some college	college grad	post grad
Black	30.00	20.00	25.00	5.00	10.00	5.00	5.00
White	18.18	18.18	22.73	13.64	13.64	4.54	9.09

Table 20.3

Group Means for Content of Friendship for Blacks and Whites

for Friends #1 and #2

		Content of Friendship		
Ethnicity		Psychological Intimacy	Concrete Help	Shared Activities
Black	Friend #1	1.6	1.68	2.40
	Friend #2	1.85	1.59	2.45
White	Friend #1	1.59	1.85	2.67
	Friend #2	1.62	1.97	2.66

21

Cross-Cultural Perspective of the Changing Role of the Care Provider for the Aged in a Chinese Context

Lucy C. Yu

Women in the middle generation have been known as the "kin keeper," or care provider for the aged, and serve as the link between the grandparent and the grandchildren generations in the United States of America, (Hill, Foot, Aldons, Carlson, and MacDonald, 1970; Shanas, 1979; Civcivelli, 1980; Brody, 1981; Weeks and Cuellar, 1981). Studies about Chinese Americans in this country found that Chinese-American women in the middle generation are taking care of their own aged parents, as well as their parents in-law (Wu, 1974; Yu and Harburg, 1980, 1981; Yu and Wu, 1985). However, in the Chinese tradition, it is a woman's duty to take care of not her own but her husband's parents (Lang, 1946).

After the establishment of the People's Republic of China in 1949, everyone is required to work, and women no longer have to justify their working outside the home in order to save face for themselves or their husbands More important, women theoretically should be financially independent. This independence gives them the right to take care of their own parents instead of their husband's parents.

The purpose of this study is twofold: (1) to examine whether or not Chinese men and women are still adhering to the Chinese tradition by taking care of the husband's parents; and (2) to examine whether or not Chinese women are taking care of their own parents and/or taking care of their husband's parents.

METHOD

Sample

The data were collected at one of the most prestigious technical Universities in China. The university has reestablished ties with several major academic institutions in the United States, and exchanges between its faculty and students and those at American universities are taking place. Most of the respondents were physicists or engineers. Their monthly salaries were between 100 and 200 yuans in 1979, which is equivalent to 50-100 U.S. dollars. Most of the scientists were assigned their university job because of their technical training. Their wives were usually college graduates. Both spouses worked.

The respondents ranged in age from 20 to 75 years. Over half were 36 years or older. Eighty percent were married, 11 percent single, and 6 percent widowed. Fifty-six percent were males and 40 percent females. All of the males and 86 percent of the females were employed. Eighty percent of the males and 48 percent of the females had finished college.

Procedure

This investigator visited a university in the People's Republic of China during various stays in China on three separate trips. She carried 50 copies of a bilingual questionnaire with her during her visit and, while there, after much negotiation with the University officials, was given permission to administer a questionnaire regarding the support of aged parents to a group of university staff and their families. This paper reports the findings from that study.

In 1979, people were emerging from the shock of the Cultural Revolution. Because life had been extremely difficult during the Cultural Revolution, the respondents' answers to the questionnaire may be guarded. The questionnaire was distributed by a professor from the host university to the university staff and their families. The investigator did not meet any of the respondents. She explained to the professor that the contents of the questionnaire were nonpolitical, that the questionnaire posed no potential threat to the psychological health of the subjects, that participation was voluntary, and that anonymity of respondents and confidentiality of their answers would be guaranteed. How much that guarantee meant to the Chinese, and whether or not they believed the guarantee, is unknown. The completed questionnaires were collected by a professor one day before this investigator left China. Forty-eight respondents returned the questionnaires.

It is hoped that this pilot study will be viewed as one of the many attempts and quantitative data collection in the People's Republic of China after 30 years of isolation.

Instrument Used

Two bilingual questionnaires, developed by this investigator and validated for a Chinese-American university population in the United States, were used for this study (Yu and Harburg, 1980). The purpose of the questionnaires was to explore both the belief and the behavior of respondents vis-à-vis giving financial support to and sharing housing with their own aged parents. Married couples were asked to answer questions about their own parents and their in-laws.

Whenever there were missing data in a particular question, those cases were excluded from analysis. Therefore, although the total sample contained 48 subjects, the number of respondents varies from table to table. A number of questions pertained to respondents' siblings; they were included because in China, the care of the aged is traditionally the responsibility of male siblings. The financial and housing questionnaires asked for respondents' beliefs concerning filial responsibility and examined their actual behavior in fulfilling their financial responsibility. The questions also explored whether or not the respondents, their parents, their spouse, and their siblings were satisfied with what was being done for the parents in terms of financial support and housing. In traditional China, parents expected to live with their sons; they were considered unfortunate if they did not have sons and had to live with their daughters. In order to test whether or not this tradition is changing, the housing questionnaire asked respondents where they thought their aged parents would like to live, and where they themselves would like to live after retirement. Cronbach's alpha for the Financial and Housing Indices were .66 and .68, respectively. Sociodemographic information was collected, and frequency distributions were computed for variables under consideration.

RESULTS

Financial Support

Respondents were asked whether adult children should help their aged parents financially. We found that 89 percent agreed that they should. Eleven percent felt that it depended on children's and parents' situation. There were no significant differences between males and females.

Table 21.1 shows that most respondents not only gave money and gifts to the aged, but they also gave on a regular basis (86 percent). Only 14 percent did not give anything to their parents; 43 percent gave monthly support to their parents; and 19 percent gave yearly. The question of financial support was not applicable to four respondents either because of the respondent's young age and that of their parents, whom they did not support, or because their parents had died. More males than females gave on a monthly basis; females tended to give more often than males on a yearly basis.

Although the Chinese in this survey reported giving financial support to their parents regularly, Table 21.2 shows that 77 percent reported that they did not find it difficult to give money, while 23 percent found it sometimes difficult and very difficult to give financial support to their parents. Eighty-three percent of the adult children who gave financial support to their parents stated that their parents were satisfied with the support they received; 63

percent were satisfied with the support they gave their parents; 62 percent said that their spouses were satisfied with how much they gave; and 52 percent felt that their siblings were satisfied with the responding sibling's contribution to their parents.

Because of page limits, we cannot provide all findings in tabular form; therefore, some of our findings will be presented in the following narratives. We also found that 79 percent of the respondents discussed financial support with their parents; 17 percent did not because their parents felt uncomfortable talking about money. Ninety-five percent of the respondents discussed with their spouses giving money to their own parents. Eight percent did not because they or their spouses did not feel comfortable discussing this topic. Fifty percent of the respondents communicated with their siblings about giving money to their parents; the other 50 percent said that either their siblings or they felt uncomfortable talking about giving money to their parents.

Living Arrangements

Traditionally, the Chinese have lived in multigenerational households. We tried to find out if the respondents still believe in multigenerational living. Two questions addressed this issue: (1) do you believe in multigenerational living; and (2) adult children should share housing with aged parents. We found that over 80 percent of both males and females believed that even though there are problems with multigeneration living, it is still a good idea. Over 84 percent of both males and females felt that the adult children should share housing with their aged parents.

Further analysis indicated that about half of the respondents never had a parent live with them in their house. Tables 21.3A and 21.3B show that 50 percent of the respondents never had their parents live with them after the adult children became independent. Forth-eight percent had their parents live with them for at least one year. Within this segment of the sample, 14 percent had their parents living with them ten or more years. Of the parents who lived with adult children for more than six years, 43 percent lived in their son's homes; 16 percent lived in their daughter's homes; and no one lived with other relatives or in nursing homes. Moreover, 52 percent of males and 32 percent of females had their parents live in their son's homes.

Since half of the respondents had their parents living with them, we asked the respondents whether or not this living arrangement was satisfactory to all concerned. We found that 76 percent of the respondents said that their parents were satisfied, and 71 percent said that they themselves were satisfied with their living arrangement. Seventy-three percent said that their siblings agreed with them on where their aged parents should live.

Communication Regarding Parents' Housing Needs

Although 76 percent of the respondents said that their parents were satisfied with the living arrangement, only 68 percent said that they had discussed the issue with their parents. Ten percent of the respondents and 22 percent of the parents reportedly felt uncomfortable discussing the housing issue. Although 73 percent said that their siblings agreed with them on living arrangements for their parents, we found that only 60 percent had discussed the issue with their brothers and sisters; 36 percent of the respondents felt uncomfortable discussing the issue with their siblings.

Spouse's Role

Since we are examining the role of the middle generation, we wanted to find out if husbands and wives are consulting each other about their parents. Sixty-five percent of our respondents said that they discussed the living arrangements with their spouses, 25 percent said that they felt uncomfortable talking about it with their spouses, and 10 percent said that their spouses felt uncomfortable talking about it. Seventy-seven percent of the respondents reported that their spouses agreed with them, and only 17 percent said that they never discussed the issue with their spouses; 6 percent said that their spouses disagreed with them about where their parents should live. Our findings indicate that husbands are consulting their wives and vice versa, whereas in the old tradition, husbands would not have to consult their wives about "his" parents.

Generation Differences

Chinese tradition strongly advocates that adult children take care of their aged parents' housing needs by bringing the aged parents into their homes, and this tradition is further reinforced by law in the People's Republic of China (*Ren Ming Daily,* 1986). We wanted to find out where the older generation would like to live; where the younger generation thinks the older generation should live; and where the younger generation would like to live after retirement.

We found some differences between generations. Table 21.4A shows that 61 percent of respondents reported that their parents prefer to live in their son's home; 26 percent of respondents reported that their parents would like to live in their daughter's home, and 14 percent of respondents reported that their parents would like to live either in their son's or daughter's home.

However, when we queried the respondents themselves "where would you like to live after retirement," they seemed to divide 48 and 42 percent, respectively, along male and female lines that they would like to live in their son's home (Table 21.4C). Thus, we found that more older people prefer to live in their son's home than daughter's home.

DISCUSSION AND CONCLUSION

Although the care of aged parents is a long-established Chinese tradition, the interaction and communication among extended family members concerning the aged are complex and sometimes stressful. In this study, we focused, superficially, on two critical issues for the elderly and their families: financial support and living arrangement.

This study indicates that there are some changes in the male and female role in support of aged parents. All of our male and 86 percent of the female respondents were employed, giving the women certain financial independence, whereas traditional Chinese women were totally dependent on their husbands. We found that both men and women still believed in supporting their parents and having their parents live with them; they backed up their belief by giving monetary support regularly to their parents and by having their parents living with them for extended periods at one time or another.

Both men and women in our atypical sample were better educated than the national norm; although we cannot conclude that all men and women are better educated in China today than before, we know that in traditional China (before 1911) women did not receive any formal education (Yao, 1983). The fact that 57 percent of the female sample received some college education is an indication that opportunity for formal education for women has increased.

Older people still tend to follow Chinese tradition and prefer to live in their son's home; more older males prefer to live in their son's home than older females. Fifty percent of men still would like to follow Chinese tradition of fulfilling male children's filial responsibility by having their parents live with them, but only 25 percent of women thought their parents should live with sons. We don't know whether or not these were daughters-in-law. These findings suggest a gender difference in both generations. We did not perform a Chi-square test because we did not have enough cases for some cells.

Several studies of Chinese Americans in this country found that overseas, Chinese still adhere to the principles of filial piety (Hsu, 1971; Wu, 1974; Yu and Harburg, 1980; Yu, 1983) and that filial responsibility did create stress among Chinese Americans (Yu and Harburg, 1981; Yu, 1983).

We also found that although most of the respondents (61 percent) reported that their parents would like to live in their son's home, among the respondents themselves, 49 percent thought they would like to live in their son's home and 42 percent thought they would like to live in their daughter's home, again indicating that a change is taking place in regard to the old tradition of depending on the son, and only the son, in old age.

Contrary to the old tradition, that care of aged parents was the responsibility of sons, daughters in our sample are sharing the responsibility of providing financial support and shelter for their own parents. We realize that respondents in their twenties and thirties may not have elderly parents, or if they do, they also may have older siblings on whom responsibility for care would fall; responses of those young people were not included in the analysis if they checked the response category "not applicable." These findings suggest that in contemporary China, women seemed to have emerged as having decision-making power in the care of the aged.

Finally, any finding from this study must be interpreted with caution. Our small sample was biased and restricted to urban intellectuals. Since there are no normative data with which to compare our study, any inference of change is speculative. This study, however, does point to the need for a larger, more systematic sociological study of present patterns of family interaction in the care of the aged.

REFERENCES

Brody, E. M. (1981). "Women in the Middle and Family Help to Older People." *The Gerontologist, 21,* 471-480.

Chen, L. (1947). *Chinese Wisdom: Thoughts for Harmonious and Victorious Living.* Shanghai, China: World Book Co.

Civcivelli, B. G. (1980). "Social Services and the Kin Network: View of the Elderly." *Journal of Home Economics, 3,* 34-37.

Hill, R., Foot, N., Aldons, J., Carlson, R., and MacDonald, R. (1970). *Family Development in Three Generations.* Cambridge, MA: Schenkman Publishing Co.

Hsu, F. (1971). "Filial Piety in Japan and China." *Journal of Comparative Family Studies, 2,* 67-74.

Lang, O. (1946). "Chinese Family and Society," New Haven, CT: Yale University Press.

Shanas, E. (1979). "The Family as a Social Support System in Old Age." *The Gerontologist, 19,* 169-174.

Weeks, J. R., and Cuellar, J. B. (1981). "The Role of Family Members in the Helping Network of Older People." *The Gerontologist, 21,* 388-394.

Wu, F.Y.T. (1974). *Mandarin-Speaking Aged Chinese in Los Angeles Area's Needs and Services.* Los Angeles, CA: University of Southern California, Unpublished Ph.D. Dissertation.

Yao, E.S.S. (1983). *Chinese Women: Past and Present.* Mesquite, TX: Ide House, Inc.

Yu, L. C. (1983). "Patterns of Filial Belief and Behavior within the Contemporary Chinese-American Family." *International Journal of Sociology of the Family, 13,* 17-36.

Yu, L. C., and Harburg, E. (1980). "Acculturation and Stress among Chinese Americans in a University Town." *International Journal of Group Tensions, 10,* 99-119.

Yu, L. C., and Harburg, E. (1981). "Filial Responsibility to Aged Parents: Stress of Chinese Americans." *International Journal of Group Tensions, 11,* 47-57.

Yu, L. C., and Wu, S. C. (1985). "Unemployment and Family Dynamics in Meeting the Needs of Chinese Elderly in the United States." *The Gerontologist, 25,* 472-476.

Table 21.1
HOW OFTEN DO YOU GIVE MONEY OR GIFTS TO YOUR PARENTS?

	Male n	Male %		Female n	Female %		Total n	Valid %	
Never	3	13		3	15.8		6	14.3	
Weekly	0	0		0	0		0	0	
Monthly	12	52.2⎤		6	31.6⎤		18	42.9⎤	
Yearly	2	9 ⎬ 87.3		6	31.6 ⎬ 84.3		8	19 ⎬ 85.7	
Other	6	26.1⎦		4	21.1⎦		10	23.8⎦	
Total	23			19			42		
Missing	2			2					

Table 21.2
SATISFACTION IN GIVING FINANCIAL SUPPORT TO PARENTS

	Frequency (N)	Percent (%)
DIFFICULT FOR RESPONDENTS TO GIVE		
Not difficult	34	77
Sometimes difficult/very difficult	10	23
TOTAL	44	100
PARENT'S FEELING ABOUT THE SUPPORT YOU GIVE THEM		
Satisfied	33	83
Somewhat satisfied	6	15
Not satisfied	1	2
TOTAL	40	100
YOUR FEELING ABOUT THE SUPPORT YOU GAVE TO YOUR PARENTS		
I am satisfied	25	63
Somewhat satisfied	13	33
Not satisfied	2	5
TOTAL	40	100
YOUR SPOUSE'S FEELING ABOUT THE SUPPORT YOU GAVE TO YOUR PARENTS		
Spouse satisfied	24	62
Somewhat satisfied	13	33
Not satisfied	2	5
TOTAL	39	100
YOUR SIBLING'S FEELING ABOUT THE SUPPORT YOU GAVE TO PARENTS		
Siblings satisfied	25	52
Somewhat satisfied	6	13
Not satisfied	17	35
TOTAL	48	100

Table 21.3

A. NUMBER OF YEARS YOUR PARENTS LIVED WITH YOU

Yrs.	Male n	%	Female n	%	Total n	Valid %
0	8	33.3	14	77.8	22	52.3
1-5	8	33.3	3	16.7	11	26.2
6-10	3	12.5	0	0	3	7.1
11-15	1	4.2	1	5.6	2	4.8
16-20	2	8.3	0	0	2	4.8
21-25	2	8.3	0	0	2	4.8
TOTAL	24		18		42	
Missing	1		3			

B. WHERE DO YOUR PARENTS LIVE NOW?

	Male n	%	Female n	%	Total n	Valid %	
son's home	13	52	6	31.6	19	43.2	⎤
daughter's home	3	12	4	21.1	7	15.9	⎥
other blood relatives' home	0	0	0	0	0	0	⎥
senior citizens' home	0	0	0	0	0	0	⎥ 63.6
son and daughter's home	2	8	0	0	2	4.5	⎦
their own home	7	28	9	47.4	16	36.4	
TOTAL	25		19		44		
Missing			2				

214

Table 21.4

A.   WHERE WOULD YOUR PARENTS LIKE TO LIVE AFTER RETIREMENT?

	Male		Female		Total	Valid
	n	%	n	%	n	%
Son's home	15	62.5	11	57.9	26	60.5
Daughter's home	5	20.8	6	31.6	11	25.6
Other blood relatives	0	0	0	0	0	0
Senior citizen's home	0	0	0	0	0	0
Son or daughter's home	4	16.7	2	10.5	6	14
TOTAL	24		19		43	
Missing	1		2			

B.   WHERE DO YOU THINK YOUR PARENTS SHOULD LIVE AFTER RETIREMENT?

	Male		Female		Total	Valid
	n	%	n	%	n	%
Son's home	13	52	5	25	18	40
Daughter's home	3	12	7	35	10	22.2
Other blood relatives	0	0	0	0	0	0
Senior citizen's home	0	0	0	0	0	0
Son or daughter's home	9	36	8	40	17	37.7
TOTAL	25		20		45	
Missing	0		1			

C.   WHERE WOULD YOU LIKE TO LIVE AFTER RETIREMENT?

	Male		Female		Total	Valid
	n	%	n	%	n	%
Son's home	11	47.8	9	50	20	48.8
Daughter's home	10	43.5	7	38.9	17	41.5
Other blood relatives	0	0	0	0	0	0
Senior citizen's home	0	0	0	0	0	0
Son or daughter's home	2	8.7	2	11.1	4	9.8
TOTAL	23		18		41	100.1
Missing	2		3			

22

Social Support in the Elderly:
A Cross-Cultural Comparison

Cynthia L. Frazier and Chavannes Douyon

During the mid-1960s, research findings appeared that explored the relationship between life stress and the onset of illness. Holmes and Rahe (1967), originators of the Social Readjustment Rating Scale, advanced the following rationale: the greater the life change or adaptive requirements involved in stressful events, the greater the vulnerability, or lowering of resistance, to disease and the greater the severity of a resulting condition. In most of this work, correlations between life stress and illness were found to be positive.

This type of research has been criticized for failing to recognize factors such as social support that might contribute to a fuller understanding of the etiology of physical and psychiatric illness. In subsequent research, social support was believed to act as a buffer against physiological and psychological consequences (Nuckolls, Cassel, and Kaplan, 1972).

Two divergent trends have evolved in the literature. While many investigators were concerned with the effects of the actual amount of social support available to the individual, others were interested in the extent to which one perceives that his/her needs for support are being fulfilled. Despite this difference in construct, both approaches obtained similar results. Social support was found to be negatively related to physical and psychological dysfunctioning (Caplan, Cobb, French, Van Harrison, and Pinneau, 1965; Miller, Ingham, and Davidson, 1976; Surtees, 1980).

A related finding is that the actual amount of social support received is not always commensurate with the perception of being supported. Gore (1978) found that subjects who had actually received considerable help from both family and friends perceived substantial support only on the part of family members.

One subgroup subjected to continuous reevaluation of social support is the geriatric population. During this phase of life, the individual undergoes physical, psychological, and social changes. Implicit in the notion of change is the experience of stress. The most common stress-related events include widowhood, retirement, physical deterioration, and threat of imminent death.

Despite the life changes concomitant with aging, many individuals appear to adapt successfully to accommodate change and seem to maintain healthfulness. It is conceivable that the stressful changes associated with aging may be mediated by supportive systems that may reduce the likelihood of illness occurring. Lowenthal and Haven (1968) found that the presence of a confidant played a mediating role between social deprivations of aging and psychological adjustment.

While social support for the aged is intuitively regarded as an important factor, its effects upon health for this group have not been sufficiently examined. The relative effects of actual and perceived social support have not been adequately compared. Therefore, the aim of the present study is to determine the type of social support that is a better predictor of psychological health in the geriatric population in two cultures: an American (New York) sample, representing an industrialized society; and a Haitian (Port-au-Prince) sample, representing a nonindustrialized society.

METHOD

Participants

New York Sample. The participants in this study were 126 community-based individuals recruited in the greater New York area. Eighty subjects were interviewed at their respective senior centers; the remaining in their respective homes. Ninety-eight percent of the sample were Caucasian; two percent were Black. Participants ranged in age from 60 to 95 years (M = 74.6, SD = 7.6). Seventy-seven females outnumbered 49 males. Forty subjects were married, compared with 86 participants who were either widowed (N = 60), single (N = 15), or separated/divorced (N = 11). The average length of education was 8.6 years. Ninety-four percent of the sample were retired (N = 119), while six percent (N=7) maintained part-time employment.

Port-au-Prince Sample. Thirty-eight subjects were interviewed in their homes and in social service agencies in the Port-au-Prince area. Participants ranged in age from 60 to 93 years (M = 69.9; SD = 8.9). Twenty-nine subjects were married, while only nine were single. Marital status (i.e., widowed, separated/divorced) was not further differentiated by the Haitian administrator. Fifteen subjects (39 percent) reported being unemployed, while nine subjects (24 percent) were retired. Thirty-seven percent of the sample were employed either on a full-time basis (N = 8) or on a part-time basis (N = 6). While income was not reported, the Haitian sample was predominately middle class. Subjects of a lower socioeconomic status could not successfully comprehend the type of questions posed and were not included in the sample.

Measures

Psychological healthfulness was measured in terms of absence of depression and presence of self-esteem. The Beck Depression Inventory (Beck, Ward, Medelson, Mock, and Erbaugh, 1961), and the Self-Esteem Scale (Rosenberg, Silber, and Tippett, 1965) were used as indexes of psychological healthfulness. Perceived social support was measured by the Perceived Social Support Inventory, using the Family-based and Friend-based scale (Procidano and Heller, 1983). Actual social support was measured by the Social Support Index (Surtees, 1980).

All measures were translated from English into French by Dr. Chavannes Douyon with the exception of the Beck Depression Inventory. A French translation was obtained directly from Dr. Beck.

Procedures

The Perceived Social Support Inventory, using the Family-based and Friend-based scales, was administered after demographic data were collected. While some of the subjects had the capability of self-administration, others with physical limitations (e.g., poor eyesight) did not. Therefore, in order to ensure that each subject received a standardized presentation, the content of each measure was read aloud. The examiner recorded each subject's responses regardless of ability.

Since depression and self-esteem have been found to be related (Beck, 1967), administration of the Beck Depression Inventory and the Self-Esteem Scale was alternated to prevent any bias that one variable might have on the other. Next, the Surtees' Social Support index was administered. This measure of support, representing the actual level of available resources, was presented last to prevent any influence on the Perceived Social Support measure. The average length of time required to administer the entire battery of questionnaires was 30 minutes.

RESULTS

New York Sample

A series of regression analyses was conducted to explicate the relationships among the demographic variables, actual social support, perceived social support, depression, and self-esteem.

Demographic Variables. The results revealed that married subjects are less depressed than subjects who are not married ($F(1,119) = 4.91$; $p < .05$; $B = -.21$). Marital status was also found to be positively related to actual social support ($F(1,121) = 39.09$; $p < .01$) which suggests that married individuals possess more actual support than unmarried individuals.

Regarding the demographic variable of sex, the only significant influence of this factor was on total perceived social support ($F(1,120) = 6.72$; $p < .05$). The positive Beta weight (.21) suggests that females perceive more social support than males. While there was no significant difference in the actual amount of support for males and females, females tended to have more actual sources of support than males ($F(1,112) = 3.02$; $p < .10$).

The demographic variable of age had no significant influence upon actual support, perceived social support, depression, nor self-esteem.

Actual Social Support. Actual social support contributed significantly to total perceived social support ($F1,120) = 27.02$; $p < .01$), with a positive Beta weight (.47) indicating that those who report high actual support likewise perceive more support. The perception of social support is thus a function of the actual resources available to the individual. Contrary to expectation, actual social support did not influence the proposed health variables of depression or self-esteem.

Perceived Social Support. Total amount of perceived social support was discovered to be significantly related to depression ($F(1,119) = 21.92$; $p < .01$). The negative Beta weight (-.44) signified less depression in those subjects who perceive more support. Closer examination revealed that both sources of perceived support, family-based and friend-based, contributed significantly to level of depression ($F(1,118) = 6.75$, $p < .05$); and $F(1,118) = 7.87$, $p < .01$, respectively).

Total amount of perceived support was also found to significantly contribute to self-esteem in subjects with a positive Beta weight (.40) denoting higher self-esteem in subjects who perceived greater support. Furthermore, family-based perceived support and friend-based perceived support both had significant effects upon self-esteem ($F(1,118) = 4.89$, $p < .05$; and $F(1,118) = 6.59$, $p < .05$, respectively).

Predictor. The relative influences of actual social support and perceived social support were examined to ascertain which was the better predictor of depression and self-esteem. Unexpectedly, actual social support had no significant influence on the dependent variables when the effects of other variables were controlled. While there was a significant and negative correlation between actual social support and depression ($r = .17$; $p < .03$), the direction of this relationship reversed (Beta = .16) and fell to a nonsignificant level ($F(1,119) = 2.44$, $p < .10$) when the variance of perceived social support was held constant in the regression equation. Overall, the perception of support was the better predictor of depression and self-esteem than actual social support.

Validation Results. To ascertain the concurrent validity of the actual social support measure, subjects' self-reports were compared with informant's ratings for a subset of the sample (N = 40). A Pearson product-moment correlation of .61 ($p < .001$) was obtained, indicating that the Surtee's Social Support Inventory is an adequate index of actual supportive resources.

Port-au-Prince Sample

Demographic Variables. The results of the multiple regression analyses revealed that marital status was significantly related to total perceived social support ($F(2,35) = 8.05$; $p < .007$) with a positive Beta weight (.39) indicating that married subjects perceived more social support than single subjects. The demographic variables of sex and age were not significantly related to actual social support, perceived social support, depression, or self-esteem.

Actual Social Support. Similar to the New York sample, actual social support was found to be significantly related to total perceived social support ($F(2,35) = 9.87$; $p < .004$). The positive Beta weight (.44) suggests that those who reported high actual support likewise perceived more social support. Furthermore, actual social support did not influence depression nor self-esteem in the Haitian sample.

Perceived Social Support. Perceived social support was found to be the only factor significantly related to depression ($F(1,36) = 15.5$; $p < .001$). The negative Beta weight (-.55) indicates that subjects who perceived more total support were less depressed. Interestingly, when perception of family-based support and perception of friend-based support were analyzed, the results showed that only the perception of support from family members was significantly related to depression ($F(1,36) = 16.47$; $p < .001$); $B = 1.56$). Unlike the American sample, the perception of support from family members appears to play a more important role in ameliorating depression than the perception of support from friends in the Haitian sample.

Similar results for self-esteem were obtained. Total perceived social support was significantly related to self-esteem ($F(1,36) = 9.57$; $p < .004$). The positive Beta weight (.46) suggests that those who perceive more social support have higher self-esteem. Upon closer scrutiny, it was discovered that only the perception of family-based support contributed significantly to self-esteem ($F(1.36) = 15.36$; $p < .001$; $B = .54$).

Predictor. The overall results of the data analysis for the Haitian sample showed that perception of social support from family members was the better predictor of depression and self-esteem than actual social support and perceived support from friends.

DISCUSSION

The aim of the current investigation was to determine the relative influences of actual and perceived social support in predicting psychological health in the geriatric population. Two cultures were selected for examination. An American sample from the greater New York area was selected to represent a predominately white, urban sample of older adults from an industrialized society. A Haitian sample from the Port-au-Prince area was selected to represent a predominately black, urban sample of older adults from a nonindustrialized society.

Based on the results of multiple regression analyses, the perception of social support appears to be the only factor that significantly predicts level of depression and self-esteem in both the New York sample and the Port-au-Prince sample. While the perception of support was derived from both family and friend resources in the American sample, Haitians tended to rely primarily upon family-based support. This result may be explained, in part, by the difference in the role of the family in each culture. Treas (1977) commented on the forces of societal change in the United States that limit the involvement of the family, who have traditionally provided support for aging parents in the form of companionship, services, advice, and financial assistance. The family network has also been divided into autonomous nuclear family units, thus excluding members of the extended family from obligation. Increased mobility has reduced the availability among family members. The changing role of women has fostered competition between the woman's traditional responsibility for the aging parent and her current commitments to her job and nuclear family. Furthermore, friendship bonds have become an important resource of support for the aged as family members are less available. In the Haitian sample, a more traditional role of the family was portrayed (e.g., the subject lived in same household with children and grandchildren). Additionally, Haitian subjects tended to report less involvement with neighbors, church members, and coworkers.

Interpretation of these results should be viewed in light of the following limitations:

1. *Possible discrepancies in translation.* Future research should consider the back-translation method for ensuring accuracy in the translation of the measures-employed.
2. *Differences in samples.* While the results of the study are similar for both samples, it is questioned whether the samples are comparable due to differences in sample size and demographics (i.e., the Haitian sample contained more subjects who were younger, married, and employed).
3. *Communication difficulties between coauthors.* The typical communication difficulties of conducting research in two countries limited the amount of collaboration and discussion necessary for comparing cultural differences.

The overall results point to the important role that perception plays in mediating between actual social support and the psychological responses of depression and self-esteem. Since actual support contributes to the perception of support in both cultures, one's awareness of support may increase as actual sources of support are augmented. However, the older Haitian would be best bolstered by increased family support, while the older American would benefit by increased support from family members as well as friends. As actual sources of support are increased, perception of support is enhanced. In this way, perception of being supported may protect against depression and elevate self-esteem in the older adult.

REFERENCES

Beck, A. (1967). *Depression: Clinical, Experimental, and Theoretical Aspects.* New York: Harper and Row.

Beck, A., Ward, C., Medelson, M., Mock J., and Erbaugh, J. (1961). "An Inventory for Measuring Depression." *Archives of General Psychiatry, 4,* 561-571.

Caplan, R., Cobb, S., French, J., Van Harrison, R., and Pinneau, S. (1965). "Job Demands and Worker Health: Main Effects and Occupational Differences." *NIOSH Research Report.*

Gore, S. (1978). "The Effects of Social Support in Moderating the Health Consequences of Unemployment." *Journal of Health and Social Behavior, 19,* 157-165.

Holmes, T., and Rahe, R. (1967). "The Social-Readjustment Scale." *Journal of Psychosomatic Research. 11,* 213-218

Lowenthal, M., and Haven, D. (1968). "Interaction and Adaptation: Intimacy as a Crucial Variable." *American Sociological Review, 33,* 20-30.

Miller, P., Ingham, J., and Davidson, S. (1976). "Life Events, Symptoms, and Social Support." *Journal of Psychosomatic Research, 20,* 515-522.

Nuckolls, C., Cassel, J., and Kaplan, B. (1972). "Psychosocial Assets, Life Crisis, and the Prognosis of Pregnancy." *American Journal of Epidemiology, 95,* 431-441.

Procidano, M., and Heller, K. (1983). "Measures of Perceived Social Support for Friends and Family: Three Validation Studies." *American Journal of Community Psychology, 11,* 1-24.

Rosenberg, M., Silber, E., and Tippett, J. (1965). "Self-Esteem: Clinical Assessment and Measurement Validation." *Psychological Reports, 16,* 1017-1071.

Surtees, P. (1980). "Social Support, Residual Adversity, and Depressive Outcomes." *American Psychiatry, 15,* 71-80.

Treas, J. (1977). "Family Support Systems for the Aged: Some Social and Demographic Considerations." *Gerontologist, 17,* 486-491.

23

Cross-Cultural Comparisons of Disability and Depression Among Older Persons in Four Community-Based Probability Samples

David E. Wilder and Barry J. Gurland

Because disability and depression are two of the most frequent problems associated with aging, they are often cited as being important causes of a diminished quality of life among the elderly. There is also the belief that because so many older persons have chronic disabilities, old age must be a depressing experience. This belief is just one component of the negative stereotypes held toward aging in our society; but it is an especially important aspect since it may become a self-fulfilling prophecy for many aging person. In addition, it may also prevent clinicians from providing therapeutic interventions that could be beneficial. However, neither the belief that aging is inevitably accompanied by disability nor the belief that disability must lead to depression is supported by the evidence, and the nature of these relationships in different cultures or populations is by no means adequately document nor understood.

It is well documented that rates of disability increase with old age and that these rates are highest among the oldest groups (U.S. Department of Health and Human Services, 1983). However, it has recently been suggested that rates of chronic disability in successive cohorts of older persons in the United States and in other industrial nations are changing and becoming lower (Fries, 1980; Katz, et al., 1985). Evidence also suggests that the onset of chronic disability among elderly persons is being delayed to older ages by advances in public health and in medical and social care: morbidity is becoming "compressed" into the last years of life, the span of active (nondisabled) life is increasing, and now only a minority of elderly are rendered dependent on others by their disability.

The relationship between depression and increasing age has been reviewed and questioned (Gurland, 1976; Gurland, Golden, Lantigua and Dean, 1984; Gurland and Toner, 1983). The use of different instruments and definitions and of data that are mostly cross-sectional all contribute to confounding the evidence about the relationship. While admitting to these limitations, prevalence rates of depression across many studies do appear to be higher among women than men, but the relationship with age is inconsistent. Prevalence rates also vary considerably depending upon whether symptom counts and broad concepts of depression were used or whether more restricted definitions, such as those based on psychiatric diagnosis of major affective disorders, were used. In all studies, no matter how inclusive the definition, depression affects only a minority of the elderly of their gender. Thus, it begins to appear that the closer the examination of the occurrence of depression and disability in old age, the more favorable the impression obtained and the more positive the expectations about the quality of life in old age.

There is no question that depression and chronic disability are associated more frequently with old age than can be accounted for by chance; that much is documented (Gurland, et al., 1984; Lader, 1983). However, it is less clear whether the association is universal or limited to certain groups of elderly; whether the association is determined by factors that can be brought under clinical or societal control; or what is the role of age itself in producing a relationship between the two conditions. In this spirit, some cross-cultural comparisons of the relationship between depression and disability are undertaken in this paper. The extent to which the relationship between disability and depression is a universal finding (i.e., identical across populations) can suggest the degrees to which inquiry into the relationship should be directed at general principles, or at local social and cultural characteristics, such as health services and health attitudes and beliefs.

DATABASE

Data on the relationship between disability and depression were taken from four samples of community-based populations. The first study was the U.S.-U.K. Cross-National Project, a collaborative project between the Columbia University Center for Geriatrics, Gerontology, and Long-Term Care and the Institute of Psychiatry in London (Gurland, Copeland, Kelleher, Kuriansky, Sharpe, and Dean, 1983). The second was a collaborative study done in 17 predominantly rural counties of New York State by the Health Systems Agency of Northeastern New York (HSANENY) and the Columbia Center (Stoller, Keane, and Earl, 1981). The third study was a collaboration of the Rancho Los Amigos Hospital in Downey, California, and the Columbia Center to study elderly Hispanics in Los Angeles, with most of the interviews conducted in spanish (Lopez-Agueres, Kemp, Plopper, Staples and Brummel-Smith, 1985). The selection and demographic characteristics of the study participants have been described in the citations noted earlier; all were probability samples of persons 65 years of age and older in the given community settings.

The interview data were derived from the Comprehensive Assessment and Referral Evaluation (CARE) or from one of its compatible versions, the "CORE CARE." (Gurland and Wilder, 1984). The CARE is a semistructured instrument with scripted probes, defined and coded responses, and a multidimensional scoring system producing 22 homogeneous scales covering psychiatric, medical, and social problems of the elderly. Global ratings and operational criteria are also used to assign subjects to classes of clinically relevant conditions.

Measures

There were several indicators of disability and depression that were used in collecting the study data under discussion and were incorporated in the CARE instrument. Both conditions were analyzed as continuous scale scores and as categories defined either by threshold scores or by operational criteria for diagnosis. The reliability, validity, and other psychometric properties of these measures have been described elsewhere (Golden, Teresi, and Gurland, 1984; Teresi, Golden, Gurland, Wilder, and Bennett, 1984; Teresi, Golden, and Gurland, 1984). Homogeneous scale scores with categorical cutoff points were used for this paper.

DISABILITY

There were 39 items in the Homogeneous Scale of Activity Limitations, which measured disability by using items on capacity for tasks of self-care, for carrying out household chores, and for range of movement. The 39 item were derived from a larger set of items by latent class analysis. A threshold cutoff score of nine or above was identified for membership in a statistically abnormal category.

DEPRESSION

There were 29 items in the Homogeneous Scale of Depression, which was also derived from a larger set of items using latent class analysis. The scale items included reference to mood, pessimism, suicidal ideation, diurnal variation, and vegetative symptoms. Other items covered the duration of symptoms, their persistence, and change for the worse. Scores were based on addition of numbers of symptoms rated as present. Latent class analysis also produced a threshold score of ten or above for membership in a statistically abnormal category.

FINDINGS

Disability

Employing a cutoff score of nine or above on the Homogeneous Scale of Activities Limitations, proportions above the cutoff level in the four community samples of elderly persons ranged from a high of 26.9 percent among the Hispanics in Los Angeles to a low of 17.5 in New York City (Table 23.1). Evidence that the Activities Limitations Scale is robust and measures a similar construct in all four cultural settings is provided by the high alphas, a measure of internal consistency, which were .90 and above in Los Angeles, New York City, and London and .71 in the rural New York setting. Disability rates increased with age within all four populations, and the Hispanics also had the highest proportion of disabled in the four populations when three different age groups were compared across samples. It should also be noted that even among the oldest groups (aged 75 years and above), only a minority scored above the cutoff score on the measure of disability in all four populations.

Comparisons of responses to individual items (not shown) in the activities limitations scale across the four samples were generally consistent with the results for the total scale scores, with the Hispanics most often indicating each limitation. There were some exceptions, however. For example, the highest proportion indicating that their health troubles interfered with desired activities was found in the New York City sample, the group with the lowest proportion scoring above the cutoff score for the scale as a whole; and the lowest proportion indicating that their health limited "other' activities (a residual category) was found in the Hispanic sample, the group with the highest proportion above the cutoff score for the scale.

Depression

Using the cutoff score of ten or above on the Homogeneous Scale of Depression, proportions at or above the cutoff level ranged from a high of 22.7 percent among the Hispanics to a low of 8.4 percent among those in rural New York (Table 23.1). The depression scale was also robust and internally consistent in all four samples with alphas ranging between .84 and .88. Overall, the proportions above the scale cutoff score were highest among the Hispanics and lowest for the Northeastern New York State group, and this was also found for each age group when compared across samples. However, unlike the disability measure, the depression scale was not related consistently to age across the four population samples.

Proportions with positive response ratings on individual items (not shown) in the Homogeneous Scale of Depression tended to repeat scale score rankings, with the Hispanics highest and the rural New Yorkers lowest. Again it should be noted that only a minority of elderly persons scored above the cutoff score on the depression scale in all four samples, with the range from 8.4 percent to 22.7 percent.

Relationships between Disability and Depression

The correlations between disability and depression were high within all four populations. They were highest in Los Angeles and in New York City (.50), somewhat lower in Northeastern New York State (.44), and lowest in London (.32) (Table 23.2). Using cutoff scores, differences between the proportions scoring high on the depression scale in the high and low disability groups within each of the four samples ranged from 34.0 percent in the Hispanic group to 11.1 percent in the London group. However, larger proportions with high depression scores were found in the more disabled group in all four cultural settings.

The robustness of the relationship between disability and depression across the four samples was further demonstrated when age was taken into consideration. Proportions at or above the cutoff level on the depression scale were higher for the more disabled group than for the less disabled group within each of the three age categories for all four samples (Table 23.3). Within samples, the relationship was strongest among the youngest of the elderly age groups in Los Angeles, London, and Northeastern New York State, but it was strongest in the oldest group in New York City.

DISCUSSION

The preceding findings are consistent with other studies that have found that rates of disability increase in a linear fashion with age among older persons. The fact that disability rates were highest among the Hispanics in Los Angeles is also consistent with recent suggestions that rates of chronic disability in old age are becoming lower, and that the active life span is increasing for older persons as a result of advances in public health and in medical and social care (Fries, 1980; Katz, et al., 1985). It should be noted that Hispanics would be the group least likely among the four populations to have benefited from those advances. However, even among the Hispanics aged 75 years and older, the proportion above the cutoff level on the disability scale was still a minority (41 percent). If persons in nursing homes or in other long-term care institutions were also taken into consideration, the proportions of disabled would no doubt constitute majorities among persons over the age of 85 years in some of these cultural groups; yet such advanced ages are still beyond the normal life expectancy in even the most advanced industrial nations.

Finding that a larger proportion of persons scored high on the depression scale in the Hispanic population than in the other three groups raises a number of questions. There are those who contend that depression may not be the same construct in some cultural groups (Kleinman and Goog, 1985), but the high internal consistency of the depression scale in the Los Angeles group indicates that was not true for them. There is substantial evidence that a great deal of the depression experienced by elderly persons is responsive to treatment (Blazer, 1985), and it is not entirely inconceivable that harsher life conditions may combine with a poorer service environment to produce more depressions among the Hispanics. It is also possible that expressing or admitting the type of feelings and other symptoms contained in the depression scale items is more socially acceptable among the Hispanics, or even that they subscribe more widely to the stereotype of aging as an inevitably depressing experience. However, our limited objective in this paper has been to focus on the fact that depression, like disability, although more common in some cultural settings than in others, is not a normative experience in any of the cultural settings we have studied.

While depression is more common among the disabled than the nondisabled elderly in all four populations, it is by no means inevitable for them either. In fact, only 12.7 percent of the Hispanic elderly were both disabled and depressed according to our measures, and proportions with both disability and depression were much lower in the other three populations (6.7 percent in New York City, 5.2 percent in London, and 4.3 percent in rural New York State). Moreover, substantial majorities of the older persons in all four settings (63.1 percent of the Hispanics, 68.4 percent in London, 75.5 percent in New York City, and 77.8 percent in rural New York State) were below the cutoff scores on both measures. Yet the belief persists that both disability and depression are inevitable in old age.

The cultural settings from which our samples were drawn were all in Western industrial nations, but the variability of rates of depression and disability was considerable even in these limited settings. At the very least, this supports the contention that both disability and depression among older persons are responsive to social factors, and that the rates found for either in any one particular cultural setting may provide poor estimates for rates in another setting. We know very little about how elderly persons experience disability or depression, what these problems mean to them, and how these are related to social and cultural factors. Why, for example, should depression rates be so low among disabled persons over the age of 75 years in London and in Northeastern New York and so high among their counterparts in New York City and in Los Angeles? Consideration of additional variables such as sex, socioeconomic status, household composition, service utilization, duration, and subtypes of disability and depression might also have an impact on the rates of disability and depression and on the strength of the association between them. Nevertheless, persistence of a strong general association between disability and depression among older persons across populations suggests that it is important for both researchers and clinicians to consider the two in conjunction no matter what the cultural setting. However, the market variability we have found in the strength of the relationship between the two within some subgroups should be a source of optimism about the potential for reducing the rates of both disability and depression, and thereby improving the quality of life of significant numbers of older persons.

REFERENCES

Blazer, D. (1985). "Depressive Illness in Late Life." In *America's Aging: Health in an Older Society,* sponsored by the Institute of Medicine and National Research Council, 105-128. Washing, D.C.: National Academy.

Blazer, D., George, L. K. , Landerman, R., Pennypacker, M., Melville, M. L., Woodbury, M., and Manton, K. G. (1985). "Psychiatric Disorders: A Rural/Urban Comparison." *Archives of General Psychiatry, 42,* 651-656.

Fries, J. (1980). "Aging, Natural, Death, and the Compression of Morbidity." *New England Journal of Medicine, 303,* 130-135.

Golden, R., Teresi, J., and Gurland, B. (1984). "Development of Indicator Scales for the Comprehensive Assessment and Referral Evaluation (CARE) Interview Schedule." *Journal of Gerontology, 39,* 138-147.

Gurland, B. J. (1976). "The Comparative Frequency of Depression in Various Adult Age Groups." *Journal of Gerontology, 31,* 283-292.

Gurland, B. J., Copeland, J., Kelleher, M., Kuriansky, J., Sharpe, L., and Dean, L. (1983). *The Mind and Mood of Aging: The Mental Health Problems of the Community Elderly in New York and London.* New York: Haworth Press.

Gurland, B. J., Golden R., Lantigua, R., and Dean, L. (1984). "Overlap between Physical Conditions and Depression in the Elderly: A Key to Improvement in Service Delivery. In *The Patient and Those Who Care: The Mental Health Aspects of Long-Term Physical Illness,* edited by D. Nayer, 23-36. Canton, MA: Watson Publishers.

Gurland, B. J., and Toner, J. (1982). "Depression in the Elderly: A Review of Recently Published Studies." In *Annual Review of Gerontology and Geriatrics,* edited by C. Eisdorfer, *Vol. 3,* 228-265. New York: Raven Press.

Gurland, B. J., and Wilder, D. E. (1984). "The CARE Interview Revisited: Development of an Efficient, Systematic, Clinical Assessment." *Journal of Gerontology, 39*(2), 129-137.

Gurland, B. J., Wilder, D. E., and Copeland, J. (1985). "Concepts of Depression in the Elderly: Signposts to Future Mental Health Needs." In *Aging 2000: Our Health Care Destiny,* edited by C. M. Gaitz and T. Samorajski, 443-451. New York: Springer-Verlag.

Katz, S., Ford, A. B., Moskowitz, R. W., Jackson, B. A., and Jaffee, M. J. (1963). "Studies of Illness in the Aged: The Index of ADL: A Standardized Measure of Biological and Psychological Function." *Journal of American Medical Association,* September, *185,* 914-919.

Katz, S., Greer, D. S., Beck, J. C., Branch, L. G., and Spector, W. D. (1985). "Active Life Expectancy: Societal Implications." In *America's Aging: Health in an Older Society,* sponsored by Institute of Medicine and National Research Council, 57-72. Washington, DC: National Academy Press.

Kleinman, A., and Goog, B., (Eds.) (1985). *Culture and Depression.* Berkeley, CA: University of California Press.

Lader, M. H., (Ed.). (1983). *Handbook of Psychiatry, Vol. 2, Mental Disorders and Somatic Illness.* New York: Cambridge University Press.

Lopez-Agueres, W., Kemp, B., Plopper, M., Staples, F., and Brummel-Smith, K. (1984). "Health Needs of the Hispanic Elderly." *Journal of the American Geriatrics Society, 32,* 191-193.

Stoller, E., Keane, J., and Earl, L. (1981). *Aging as a Rural Phenomenon.* Albany: Health Systems Agency of Greater New York.

Teresi, J., Golden, R., and Gurland, B. (1984). "Concurrent and Predictive Validity of Indicator Scales Developed for the Comprehensive Assessment and Referral Evaluation Interview Schedule." *Journal of Gerontology, 39,* 158-165.

Teresi, J., Golden, R., Gurland, B., Wilder, D., and Bennett, R. (1984). "Construct Validity of Indicator-Scales Developed from the Comprehensive Assessment and Referral Evaluation Interview Schedule." *Journal of Gerontology, 39,* 147-157.

United States Department of Health and Human Services, (1983). National Institute on Aging, National Institutes of Health, Public Health Service, *Special Report on Aging, 1983.* N.I.H. Publication, 83-2489. Bethesda, MD: National Institutes of Health.

Wilder, D. E., Gurland, B. J., and Bennett, R. G. (1986). "The Chronicity of Depression among the Elderly. In *Life Span Research on the Prediction of Psychopathology,* edited by L. Erlenmeyer-Kimling, and N. Miller. Hillsdale, NJ: Lawrence Erlbaum Associates.

Table 23.1

PROPORTIONS AT OR ABOVE CUT SCORES ON HOMOGENEOUS SCALES OF ACTIVITY LIMITATIONS

AND DEPRESSION IN FOUR COMMUNITY BASED PROBABILITY SAMPLES

	Los Angeles Hispanics	New York City	London U.K.	HSA NENY
Activity Limitations				
Age 65 - 69	17.3%	12.0%	13.7%	10.7%
70 - 74	22.4%	10.7%	14.3%	12.3%
75+	41.1%	25.1%	40.4%	27.9%
Totals	26.9%	17.5%	23.4%	18.2%
alpha	.93	.95	.90	.71
Depression				
Age 65 - 69	22.0%	13.3%	15.3%	8.4%
70 - 74	20.5%	11.5%	16.0%	7.1%
75+	24.7%	17.9%	10.6%	9.4%
Totals	22.7%	14.8%	13.4%	8.4%
alpha	.88	.87	.86	.84
N	(472)	(445)	(396)	(753)

Table 23.2

PROPORTIONS AT OR ABOVE CUT SCORE ON THE HOMOGENEOUS
SCALE OF DEPRESSION AND AT OR BELOW THE ACTIVITIES
LIMITATIONS SCALE CUT SCORE

ACTIVITY LIMITATIONS SCALE SCORE	LOS ANGELES HISPANICS	NEW YORK CITY	LONDON U.K.	HSA NENY
9 OR HIGHER	47.2%	40.0%	22.1%	23.5%
0 - 8	13.2%	9.0%	11.0%	4.9%
TOTALS	22.7%	14.8%	13.4%	8.4%
INTERCORRELATIONS OF TWO SCALES	.50	.50	.32	.44
N	472	445	396	753

Table 23.3

PROPORTIONS AT OR ABOVE CUT SCORE ON THE HOMOGENEOUS

SCALE OF DEPRESSION BY AGE AND ACTIVITY LIMITATION

SCALE CUT SCORE

	ACTIVITY LIMITATIONS SCALE SCORE		LOS ANGELES HISPANICS	NEW YORK CITY	LONDON U.K.	HSA NENY
AGE	65-69	9+	57.7%	29.4%	41.2%	41.7%
		0 - 8	14.5%	9.6%	11.2%	4.5%
	69-74	9+	38.9%	46.2%	29.4%	26.9%
		0 - 8	15.2%	7.3%	13.7%	4.3%
	75+	9+	47.7%	42.2%	14.8%	17.4%
		0 - 8	8.6%	9.7%	7.8%	6.3%
		TOTALS	22.7%	14.8%	13.4%	8.4%
		N	472	445	399	753

24

The Place of Age in Culture:
an Application of the Cultural Grid

Anne Pedersen and Paul Pedersen

No single definition of culture is accepted by all anthropologists for whom the concept is central. Agreement is not easily reached among other social scientists either, such as psychologists or sociologists, for whom culture is at best of peripheral concern. Artifacts, such as baskets, tools, and paintings, are commonly agreed upon products of culture. Dances, rituals, and so on demonstrate the processes of culture. However, the essence of culture itself defies definition. Is it an abstraction from group behavior with no indication of individual deviation as in funeral rites? Or is it a psychological construct by which we justify the peculiarities of an individual with little reference to the group (Segall, 1984)?

Despite the lack of definitional clarity, the term "culture" conveys sufficient explanation of the world around us to be retained in the social science vocabulary. Culture charts our life course and imbues it with meaning. It is the reason and way things are done. Therefore, any attempt to understand decisions and subsequent behaviors of an individual must include an interpretation of each behavior in terms of his or her personal cultural meaning.

The number of years and how we have lived is etched on our bodies and layers of our minds. In this sense, age describes both a group phenomenon of a same age cohort and individual characteristics interacting with a particular situation. By including age as a concept of culture, we acknowledge that age, like gender, socioeconomic status, and organizational affiliation, is a useful category in cross-cultural analysis. At times, age is even more salient than nationality or ethnicity in giving meaning to our behavior. There are advantages in treating age as a component of culture. The pattern of relationships between behavior and expectation can be seen in the larger context of group value and individually assigned meaning. This pattern can be captured on the framework of a cultural grid.

THE CULTURAL GRID

The Cultural Grid is a conceptual framework that captures both the complex and the dynamic aspects of culture. Social system variables are matched with individual cognitive categories, such as role behavior, expectation, and value-meaning, to illustrate a "personal cultural orientation." Characteristics of the social system include the following categories: demographic (e.g., age, gender, place, or residence); ethnographic (e.g., nationality, ethnicity, religion, or language); status (e.g., social, economic, or educational); and affiliation variables (e.g., formal, nonformal, or informal attributes). These, either individually or collectively, influence behaviors that the person deems appropriate to the situation. Certain expectations for a desired outcome are attached to this activity as is a sense of rightness or wrongness or value-meaning (Pedersen and Pedersen, 1985). Thus, many families would not consider placing an elderly grandmother in a permanent care facility for the aged. The grandmother would not expect this behavior; indeed, it might indicate a lack of love, responsibility, and ultimate betrayal of trust.

The Cultural Grid provides an open-ended analytical tool for understanding selected social system variables, such as age, within the kaleidoscope of personally generated experience. In this model, physical age is but one of many possible keys to a person's intrapsychic reality. The Grid serves: (1) to combine both the personal and group identity in a specific situation; (2) to help individuals portray their own cultural orientations; (3) to compare each person's orientation with those of other persons; (4) to account for and to predict changing priorities in relation to each situation; (5) to form hypotheses about cultural values versus personal differences in explanation; and (6) to provide a network of cues for guiding a comprehensive interview schedule.

The Cultural Grid, in Table 24.1, gives a comprehensive *intrapersonal* snapshot of one elderly person's (Mrs. Smith's) own culture by matching her social system variables with her behaviors, expectations, and values. A modified form of the Cultural Grid in Table 24.2 provides an *interpersonal* match between Mrs. Smith and the people around her.

The pattern of behaviors, expectations, and values most likely to be highlighted and displayed in any event or episode describes a personal cultural orientation.

The interpersonal Cultural Grid looks at the match between expectations and behaviors, defining cross-cultural conflict as occurring when both persons have the same expectation but different behaviors, and personal conflict as occurring when both persons do not share the same expectations. The conflicts between Mrs. Smith and the others around her will be analyzed using this interpersonal form of the grid.

For example, Mrs. Smith is 78 years old, Irish, a widow, and a grandmother. As she is chronically ill, she has lived in a Private Care facility for some years. Mrs. Smith used to keep copious notes on the deterioration of the facility. She frequently annotated these with estimated costs for repair and gave them to Mr. Thompson, the building coordinator. Mr. Thompson has since retired from the facility. Most people, however, deal with Mrs. Smith as though age was her primary culture in all settings.

To understand Mrs. Smith's personal cultural orientation is to take into consideration many other factors than her age, marital status, and nature of her illness. The social system variables to consider would be gender (female), age (78 years), ethnicity (Irish), status (private-care-facility resident and formerly a building inspector), and affiliation (widow and chronic patient). The role behaviors are: attends to maintenance costs and building repairs. The expectations are: to help make additions and repairs cost effective. The value is: efficiency.

In this situation, Mrs. Smith's former status as a building inspector is a more plausible explanation for her behavior than other, more concrete characteristics such as age.

Age: A Dynamic Aspect of Personal Cultural Orientation

A routine interview of Mrs. Smith (Slover, 1985), a rest-home tenant, by a social worker, can be analyzed through the Grid model. This analysis demonstrates the complex patterning of her personal cultural orientation. This orientation is ever-changing. It rotates according to the situation. For example, at one moment, she may display herself as an isolate with corresponding expectations to avoid contact with other elderly. In the next phase, she may speak as a grandmother regretful of decreased visits by her family. A careful interviewer should be able to detect and track the *salient cultural orientation* that she presents. Use of the Grid categories highlights the nature of psychic conflict in a cultural framework.

History

Mrs. Smith admits to being 78 years of age. Her early childhood was spent in a rural area of upstate New York. As a teenager she moved to New York City where she eventually married and had a son. He is now 54 years old. Mrs. Smith became a widow, but then remarried, moved to Syracuse, and gave birth to a daughter who is now 37 years old. Her second husband died about ten years prior to the interview.

At present, Mrs. Smith lives in a public housing facility for the aged and disabled. The following excerpts of an interview with her are taken from a transcript prepared for use in an introductory course on aging. These were selected to illustrate the different patterns highlighted by her particular cultural orientation.

Interviewer: Mrs. Smith, it is very nice to see you again.

Mrs. Smith: Nice to see you.

Interviewer:	The last time I talked with you, you told me a little bit about moving to Syracuse and where you went to school and where you grew up. One thing I forgot to ask you at that time was do you have any children?
Mrs. Smith:	Yes, I do. I have a boy and a girl. They're out of college now, both of them.
Interviewer:	A boy and a girl, and where do they live?
Mrs. Smith:	One lives in Wyoming, in Sheridon, right near Cheyenne, and the boy, he lives down in Kingston, Pennsylvania, and he works through that section for the government and I don't know what it is, nor nobody else does.
Interviewer:	I see. So you see your children very often?
Mrs. Smith:	My son was here twice in a month and that's a ..., oh my, and if I see him twice a year, I ... . Not because he don't want to come, but because he's too busy.

In order to understand the behaviors of Mrs. Smith and her son, it is important to consider the expectation behind the behaviors.

Mrs. Smith's perspective is as follows: (1) Behavior is "doesn't see son;" and (2) Expectation is "expects he is too busy but want's to come."

Mrs. Smith's perception of her son's perspective is as follows: (1) Behavior is "doesn't see mother;" while (2) Expectation is "wants to come but is too busy."

From this initial part of the interview, it is evident that the mother does not see the son often nor does she expect to see the son often even though the son-mother relationship might be highly valued by both persons. In addition, what constitutes "often" might be different for the son than it is for the mother.

Interviewer:	I see. How many grandchildren do you have?
Mrs. Smith:	I have two grandchildren and they are both graduates of the University of Washington.
Interviewer:	Hmm.
Mrs. Smith:	They're both married and one, the girl, my granddaughter, married the boy that was in school with her from Petersburg, Alaska. So they went up there on their honeymoon and they stayed there and she never came back. She has two children,

a boy and a girl. My grandson, he and his wife live there also and they have two boys.

Interviewer: Do you have any other relatives in this area?

Mrs. Smith: No.

Interviewer: Do you have any brothers or sisters?

Mrs. Smith: No, mine's the last of a long Irish gang.

Interviewer: I see.

Mrs. Smith: My grandmother come from Ireland in 1848. There were two brothers, they were both priests and they came on a grant of land. She was only eight years old. My mother couldn't leave her behind because their mother and father had died in that famine.

Interviewer: Umhm.

Mrs. Smith: The potato famine England created.

Interviewer: Yes.

Mrs. Smith: They almost starved to death. So quite naturally our whole family has no use for the English.

From this interaction, we add that Mrs. Smith is a grandmother and of Irish-American ethnicity to the pool of social system variables.

Mrs. Smith: For the way they treated us, you see, years and years ago my grandmother told us all, that if they found the books in our house they were absolutely -- well, you might just as well go hang yourself somewhere because they would get you.

Interviewer: Is that right?

Mrs. Smith: They didn't want them to have any education at all. And, you will find in the -- my generation, a great number of the professional people that are Irish. They were born in this country and their parents were knew what a terrible handicap it was not to be educated. They start right in and they call -- the old Irish people call it "book larnin."

It is now further apparent that education and independence are important values to Mrs. Smith. She connects the values of education and independence with the behavior of advancement by a generation of immigrants from Ireland.

Interviewer: Who else do you spend time with? Do you have any close friends in this area?

Mrs. Smith: Oh no, no. I have no close friends. I counted on my street where I lived for 21 years, on East Genesee St. There's 29 died. They're all older than me and they're all friends of mine.

Interviewer: How about in the building where you live? Are the people --

Mrs. Smith: No, I don't mix much with them.

A skilled interviewer would pick up on the salience of Mrs. Smith's being an isolate, in spite of her extremely active life previously.
Mrs. Smith's perspective is as follows: (1) Behavior is "inactive;" and (2) Expectation is "to do phone work or stamp sales." While Mrs. Smith's behavior was inactive, there is clear evidence that her expectation for herself is to be engaged in a project. It is also apparent that productivity is an important value in her life.

Mrs. Smith: Oh ho, ho! I read incessantly. But, then you see I have seven different kinds of medicines to take, counting 13 tablets a day. One of them, I have four to take. Another one, two, and I have acute illnesses so they know can't cure me. They do the best they can for me.

Interviewer: Yes.

Mrs. Smith: And, then they're a little pushy I have to sit down on them just like a bumble bee does. We have one doctor at the, ...ah...oh, what do you call that clinic over there...the neighborhood clinic. And he... going to have a cardiogram you're going to have a blood test, you're going to an x-ray, I...say, no I'm not. I'm not! And I won't! Just take your...and pull them up right down and send them bills to people like myself who don't need it.

Her expectations are different than her perception of her doctor's perspective. Mrs. Smith's perspective was as follows: (1) Behavior is "does not allow tests;" and (2) Expectation is "can't be cured." Mrs. Smith's perception of her doctor's perspective was as follows: (1) Behavior is "wants to give tests;" and (2) Expectation is "to send bills for money."

The priority of her role as a "patient" has now taken over the interview. It would be important for the interviewer to shift correspondingly and follow her lead to the salience of this identity. The possibility of her being over-medicated or otherwise dissatisfied with her role as a patient would be relevant.

Again the salient feature of Mrs. Smith's cultural orientation has shifted to her role as an isolate.

Mrs. Smith: I dread the lonesomeness.

Interviewer: Umhum.

Mrs. Smith: Very bad over there. Then they play cards and one won't play with the other. You die laughing, it kills me the class consciousness on them.

Interviewer: In what way?

Mrs. Smith: Why we got prima donnas over there. My God, they walk all around with their heads stuck up in the air and some poor old lady...speak to the poor woman...Oh no, don't you ever believe, that's the coldest place in the world.

Mrs. Smith's perspective is different from that of the other elderly. Her perspective was: (1) Behavior is "isolate;" and (2) Expectation is "avoids rejection." Mrs. Smith's perception of other elderly persons' perspectives was: (1) Behavior is "don't speak;" and (2) Expectation is "demonstrate superiority."

Her behavior may be seen as a coping mechanism to avoid rejection. This requires probing by the interviewer. An alternative explanation may be that her dislike of "class consciousness" is supported by a strong equalitarian value. The isolate behavior then serves the intent of disassociation with artificial social hierarchy.

Interviewer: You were very active in the building.

Mrs. Smith: Oh yes, I was. All the time he was there, when he went I quit.

Interviewer: Oh? Why is that?

Mrs. Smith: Because I didn't care about the activities they had. It was nothing that interested me. I can sew beautiful, I don't need to have a...I go to a sewing class, and as far as that making dogs and cats and stuff and marbles and the beads and all. No, that's kindergarten stuff for me.

Mrs. Smith's perspective was: (1) Behavior is "expert sewer refusing to sew;" and (2) Expectation is "to avoid simplistic tasks." Once again, her role as an expert seamstress leads her to continued isolation in order to avoid simplistic sewing tasks.

Interviewer: I wonder if you can talk a little bit about how you've changed in the last few years. Do you think you are very different?

Mrs. Smith: Oh, I think old age is terrible. I'd rather be dead.

Interviewer: Can you tell me why you feel that way?

Mrs. Smith: I don't know. Just the changes that come over me. I'm not able to do my work like I did and I developed a heart condition and, of course the high blood pressure is terrible with me. I was 200 over 100. There for a long time, they couldn't get it down. They finally got it down a little bit now and the emphysema alone was enough.

Mrs. Smith's perspective was: (1) Behavior is "inactive;" and (2) Expectation is "to avoid heart and blood pressure troubles." Her expectations for herself seem to be changing as she grows older and reinforces her isolation. Her role of patient again supports self-imposed inactivity.

Interviewer: Do you feel you've slowed down or stopped doing some of the things you used to do when your husband died?

Mrs. Smith: Oh my, I put on roofs and everything else on that big house. He couldn't put a nail in the wall without cracking his thumb. He was absolutely useless to me. I used to fix all our own plumbing, put on the washers on the sink to save all the plumbing bill, you know, the plumber was $6.75 an hour and his helper was $3.50 an hour. So be sure when you graduate from college that you are able to do practical things.

Mrs. Smith's perspective was: (1) Behavior is "thrifty, did manual work;" (2) Expectation is "to take care of what she needs;" and (3) Value is "independence and practicality."

Dramatic changes occurred in Mrs. Smith's life following the death of her husband, coupled with aging. She no longer can do manual work and is without a companion. She is now more helpless and more financially cautious. Judging from her enthusiasm for the past, her values may continue to support her expectations, which would make her present condition frustrating and stressful.

Mrs. Smith: I never think ahead. Give us this day our daily bread. Today!

Interviewer: How about now? Can I ask you to think ahead for a moment? How would you expect life to be like a few years from now?

Mrs. Smith: Well, I...I...would...want, in fact, I don't care about living any longer. I don't do a thing to prolong my life. Only take the medicine. I take that out of...I'm a coward, I don't want to suffer any more than I should. The way my husband went, he got up from the dinette and walked into his big chair in the living room and just went oh, just went that's all. That's a delightful way to go. You have no...nothing to think about. Everything is taken care of after you're gone, but it's an awful shock for those you leave, and you come from a big family and they're all dead too. I don't know what's keeping me old. But, I'm still here, for what I don't know. I don't like it, I tried to get out when Bruce did, but I couldn't do it. You see, people will not rent to old people and their liability insurance goes up. They're always afraid old people will fall, and I don't blame them, they do fall. We had this case where a woman was found on the floor, Friday, and she was dead Saturday night.

Mrs. Smith's perspective was: (1) Behavior is "to take each day as it comes;" and (2) Expectation is "the Lord will provide." Mrs. Smith's alternative perspective was: (1) Behavior is "to take medicine;" and (2) Expectation is "to die soon without suffering." She is reconciling herself to her new condition, however reluctantly. Given the changes in her life the future becomes less attractive and more uncertain. The shift in her expectations from an active optimism toward a passive realism is apparent. This is not totally incongruent with her strong value preference for practicality and a type of independence. She is "choosing," to some extent, to match her behavior with her assessment of the situation.

While she resists her isolation, she also values her privacy and her separateness from the worries of her son and daughter. She is willing to accept their inattention to her, but is not willing to maintain and continue their dependency on her for support on their terms. Elements of her valuing independence (for herself as well as her children) come through in her behaviors.

Interviewer: Do you have any boyfriends in the building?

Mrs. Smith: Me? You couldn't give me a boyfriend if he had 5 million dollars on his head.

Interviewer: No boyfriends? Why not?

Mrs. Smith: No, I have no use for them. I haven't got time. I got all the time in the world just for myself. I'm not going to tell some old duffer go take a bath, go comb your hair, go brush your teeth or something. I've got all I can do to do my own. And I, imagine...washing for somebody! They know that too. We are going to have a couple of weddings. There's one today, I guess. An old man marrying. He's all crippled up so he can't hardly move. But, he's got a Cadillac car. Some old lady and him are getting married, today.

Mrs. Smith's perspective was: (1) Behavior is "no boy friends;" and (2) Expectation is "to take care of herself." Mrs. Smith's perception of the elderly male perspective was: (1) Behavior is "wants to get married;" and (2) Expectation is "to be taken care of." Elements of her value of independence come through in many aspects of her life, specifically in terms of her resistance to have others depend on her.

If we were to do a content analysis of the interview with Mrs. Smith, the importance of "independence" as a foundation value would be very obvious. There is some conflict between her view of herself based on her once extremely active and full life, and her view of herself in her present situation. She is unwilling to give up her image as an independent and self-sufficient person in exchange for the view of herself by others, who describe her as less independent and self-sufficient. Understanding her personal cultural orientation should help the interviewer interpret accurately those behaviors that follow from independence and self sufficiency from those behaviors that follow from practicality and a sense of realism. Each add a richness to the understanding of Mrs. Smith's cultural identities beyond the singular description of "aged."

CONCLUSION

We have described how factors other than age function to alert an interviewer to a unique personal cultural orientation. It is necessary to understand the origin of Mrs. Smith's insistence on independence and self-sufficiency in her Irish background and to account for these values in interpreting her current isolationist behavior. It is then possible to separate those misunderstandings that are *personal* (where she deliberately, knowingly, and accurately opposes an action) from those misunderstandings that are *cultural* (where her perceptions and interpretations of others' expectations and theirs of hers are not accurate, or at best ambiguous).

We have compared differences in Mrs. Smith's interactions at two levels of analysis. We have first of all examined the intrapersonal and cultural differences between Mrs. Smith *as she once was* with Mrs. Smith *as she now is*. Both of these identities are part of Mrs. Smith's perception of herself, and the confusion of these two perspectives is frequent. Secondly, we have examined the interpersonal and or cultural differences between Mrs. Smith and those around her. Throughout the interview, our only access to the people around Mrs. Smith is through her presentation of them. In this level of analysis, we need to further distinguish between who the people around Mrs. Smith are in fact and who they are in her perception.

The Cultural Grid provides the interviewer with a conceptual map for diminishing the confusion of misunderstanding both within the person and between persons. The behaviors only have meaning in a cultural context through the expectations and values that give meaning to the behaviors. The feature of age then becomes merely one more characteristic of our complex cultural identity, which neither isolates us from others nor stereotypes us as being exactly the same as others.

REFERENCES

Chaffie, S., McLeod, J., and Guerrero, J. (1969). "Origins and Implications of the Coorientational Approach in Communication Research." In *Communicating and Organizing*, edited by R. Farace, P. Monge, and M. Russell. Reading, MA: Addison-Wesley.

Newcomb, T. M. (1953). "An Approach to the Study of Communicative Acts." *Psychological Review, 60*, 393-404.

Pedersen, A., and Pedersen, P. (1985). "The Cultural Grid: A Personal Cultural Orientation." In *Intercultural Communication: A Reader*, edited by L. Samovar and R. Porter, 50-62. Belmont, CA: Wadsworth Publishing Company.

Segall, M. H. (1984). "More than We Need to Know about Culture, but are Afraid Not to Ask." *Journal of Cross Cultural Psychology, 15*(2), 153-162.

Slover, D. (1985). Unpublished transcript for "Social Work 657: Process of Aging," Syracuse University School of Social Work. Syracuse, NY.

Table 24.1

The Cultural Grid: Personal Cultural Orientation

Cognitive Perspective

Social System Variable	Role Behavior	Expectation	Value Meaning
Demographic 　race 　gender 　age 　other			
Ethnographic 　nationality 　ethnicity 　language			
Status Level 　economic 　social 　educational			
Affiliation 　formal 　non-formal 　informal			

Table 24.2

Intrapersonal Cultural Grid

BEHAVIOR

	SAME	DIFFERENT
EXPECTATION SAME	no conflict	(cross cultural)
DIFFERENT	(personal)	total conflict

246

25

When Can We Say Memory Differs from Age to Age and/or Culture to Culture?

David S. Gorfein and Andrea Spata

We began our attempt to answer the question we had posed in the title by carefully searching the literature for previous attempts to answer this or similar questions. While there are a few cross-cultural studies on memory in the literature (Cole, Gay, Glick, and Sharp, 1971; Deregowski, 1970), cross-cultural research on memory and aging is virtually nonexistent. For literature on aging within our culture, the reader is referred to the *Journal of Gerontology, Psychology, and Aging,* and to an excellent volume on aging and memory based on the Talland memorial conference (Poon, Fozard, Thompson, Arenberg, and Cermak, 1980). For readers interested in a related topic, bilingualism, we recommend an article by Smith (1985). We must also acknowledge the thoughtful approach to a similar question: How do we know when a person has a memory deficit (Buschke, 1987)?

We found two very helpful books: one addressing the issue of aging, titled *Adult Cognition,* by Timothy Salthouse (1982); and another addressing the issue of cross-cultural differences, title *Comparative Studies of How People Think,* by Robert Cole and Barbara Means (1981).

THE MATCHING PROBLEM

It is agreed by both Salthouse (1982) and Cole and Means (1981) that any attempt to develop matched groups on the basis of individual and/or demographic variables will be unsuccessful. Persons of differing ages are different in experience, just as persons of differing cultures have had different experiences. A college-educated 70-year-old Westerner or a college-educated Mid-Easterner is not the same as a 20-year-old person by virtue of the fact that the selection criterion for college varies from age to age and culture to culture. Therefore, matching on a given variable, in our example, education, does not necessarily mean that, experientially, the two groups are equivalent. Salthouse goes even further: we cannot match in cross-sectional studies, but he further suggests that longitudinal studies may have little or no generality. In effect what he suggest is that, at least in a rapidly evolving culture, changes attributed to aging may in effect be due to cultural evolution.

Salthouse points out that the researcher should be aware that any cultural or generational differences will influence the variable being studied. When making cross-sectional (or ontogenetic) comparisons, therefore, one should be aware that the behavioral differences observed between different age groups may be the result of different experiences accrued over the years, rather than the result of increased age.

Another problematic issue raised by Salthouse is representativeness, namely, how do we ensure that the sample selected is indeed representative and unbiased? In other words, how do we ensure that all age groups are equally representative samples? A potential problem of all cross-sectional research is confounding representativeness with age differences.

On the other hand, longitudinal studies, while allowing us to follow individual aging trends in the absence of individual differences variables, are also subject to confounding cultural variables. Even within the same culture, cultural and societal factors change. According to Salthouse, separating age effects from the effects of cultural and societal change is as difficult in longitudinal as in cross-sectional research.

Salthouse offers several approaches to teasing out environmental effects from maturational ones. First, he suggests a comparison sample in a culture not undergoing such a rapid change. Unfortunately, we are offered no guidelines as to how to pick such a culture. Second, he proposes that one should redo an original study at some other point in time using a different but comparable sample. For example, if a study was conducted in 1930 comparing 20-year-olds to 70-year-olds and then it was repeated in 1980, comparing the 20-year-olds to the 70-year-olds at either date could lead to results where maturational and environmental factors were confounded. By comparing the 20-year-olds from 1930 to the 20-year-olds in 1980, the observed differences could be attributed to environmental changes over the 50 years and not to maturity. The same, naturally, would be true for the 70-year-olds. On the other hand, if no differences were observed between the same two age groups, then we could conclude that environmental changes had little or no effect on the variable under study. The third and final approach proposed by Salthouse is to compare cross-sectional samples at the same time from populations that are known to differ on some important cultural characteristic, such as young and old in an urban, Western culture versus young and old in a rural underdeveloped culture. If the magnitude of observed differences between the young and old are pretty much the same in the two societies, then environmental factors probably do not play an important role in influencing developmental differences for that particular variable.

THE MATERIAL PROBLEM

A second area of agreement exists regarding other problems of control; whether we are talking about aging or cross-cultural comparisons, the problem associated with equivalence of stimulus materials exists. In cultural comparisons, we have the questions of equivalency in translations. The issue of translation touches upon all aspects of cross-cultural research. Problems with translation can arise at any stage: from initial planning and the preparation of verbal materials to the interpretation and explanation of results (Cole and Means, 1981; Osgood, 1971).

An important aspect of language is what is sometimes referred to as "connotative meaning" -- the feelings, images, and relationships that words arouse. Charles Osgood (1964) undertook one of the most extensive and systematic cross-cultural investigations of language and thought, with specific regard to testing the generality of the connotative aspect of language. Osgood found that three dominant factors, or dimensions of meaning, could describe concepts, namely, evaluation, potency, and activity.

Osgood next asked whether this semantic framework is shared by all people, regardless of language and culture. Osgood prepared a 100-item list, accepted by anthropologists and linguists as culturally fair. The list was then translated into various languages and tested. The same three dimensions of meaning describe the rating judgments in each language studied. However, individual concepts are rated differently from culture to culture on these semantic factors. In other words, the structure of connotative meaning is the same from culture to culture, but the connotative meaning of certain concepts are culture-specific.

The problem of using instruments developed in one culture when assessing another has long been recognized (Brislin, 1976; Berry and Dasen, 1974; Triandis, 1976). Brislin points out that materials prepared in one culture, usually middle-class American, may have limited usefulness in another culture. During the development of the materials, the experimenters draw upon the common experiences shared by the people of the culture in which the instruments are being developed. The comparative group's members, on the other hand, may not attach the same value and meaning to those experiences.

THE TASK PROBLEM

Typically, in studies of aging in the United States, free recall is a preferred method of study as it shows large influences of age (Smith, 1980). However, the procedure may have limited application in cross-cultural research as several investigators have shown (Cole, Gay, Glick, and Sharp, 1971; Cole and Means, 1981; Cole and Scribner, 1974).

Cole et al. (1971) used the free recall technique to study cultural differences in memory among the Kpelle people in Liberia. According to Cole, the clustering of related items in free recall to study processes of organization in memory is an appropriate approach for determining how people of different cultures go about a memory task. Since the subjects are free to recall the material learned in any manner they choose, insight into memory mechanisms, with specific regard to organizational processes, may be gained. In other words, if a subject recalls the items in the order of the original presentation, then we may say that performance is by rote. On the other hand, if items are recalled in "clusters," or as taxonomic categories, then we may infer that active reorganization of the material has occurred (Cole and Scribner, 1974).

In their study, Cole, et al. (1971) presented the subjects with a list comprised of items from easily identifiable semantic categories. Following the presentation of the list, subjects were asked to recall as many items as they could remember, in any order. This procedure was then repeated five times. The results were as follows: overall, the Kpelle subjects recalled fewer items than their American counterparts, there was no evidence of semantic organization, and there was no increase in recall with successive trials. In contrast, American subjects tended to recall in "clusters," showing evidence of reorganization of material learned, and their performance improved significantly with trials.

Cole, et al. (1971) found that any standard manipulation -- giving incentives, using lists based on functional rather than semantic classes, showing the actual objects to be remembered, or extending the number of trials -- did not improve the Kpelle group's performance. However, when the items to-be-remembered were incorporated into folk stories, or when subjects were given explicit verbal cues, or when recall was constrained, performance of the Kpelle with regard to organization and the amount recalled improved.

According to Cole and Scribner (1974), the cultural difference in memory performance in free recall is based upon the fact that educated subjects respond to the task by imposing a structure upon which performance rests. Noneducated subjects do not spontaneously engage in this structure imposition. When they do, either as result of being instructed to do so, or because the task itself structures the material, cultural differences are eliminated or at least greatly reduced.

Cole and Scribner (1974) and Cole and Means (1981) raise the important point that underlying a great deal of cross-cultural research, is the assumption that poorer performance by non-Western groups is the result of some sort of "deficiency." The poorer performance of a special group, be it the Kpelle, the aged, or any other group under study, on some experimental task is frequently taken as support for what has been referred to as the "deficiency hypothesis" (Cole and Scribner, 1974), namely, that the members of that group lack a specific ability or skill. This deficiency interpretation is often misleading, as we can see from the results of the Cole, et al. (1971) study.

Berry and Dasen (1974) also caution that performance differences observed on some cognitive task should not be automatically be interpreted as "differential cognitive competence." According to Berry and Dasen, the specific goals and aims of cultures vary, and therefore the cognitive abilities of the members of a given culture will be oriented toward meeting the goals of that culture. Therefore, it behooves the investigator to go beyond the deficiency interpretation and look for possible alternative explanations, such as the failure of the group to utilize that skill or ability in a particular task, under specific circumstances (Cole and Scribner, 1974).

THE INADEQUACY OF PROPOSED SOLUTIONS

Having considered the reasons that any causal conclusions we draw from our designs will be limited, we may go on to see the positive recommendations our authors offer us. Both books (Cole and Means, 1981; Salthouse, 1982) suggest that our research needs to be conducted from the perspective of theory, although they differ on what is the appropriate area of theory. Cole and Means suggest that group differences will be understood if we have a good theory of the task, what they call a "model-based" approach. They would seek in a task's performance changes in parameters of the model that are associated with intergroup differences. In contrast, Salthouse believes that what is needed is an appropriate theory of aging and that experiments need to be designed to separate what he deems "maturational" effects from "environmental" effects.

It is worth mentioning here that Salthouse's position raised the interesting speculation that it might be easier to compare memory of people of the same age group across cultures than people of differing ages within a culture. According to his analysis, people of different ages within a culture vary both in maturation and culture, whereas people of the same age in differing cultures only vary on a single factor, that of culture.

We would like to comment first on the Cole and Means approach, which advocates studying group differences in terms of a model of the task. We should note that wile Salthouse advocates an approach based on a theory of aging, he makes extensive use of models of the task. This approach is dependent on a adequate theory of the task under study.

We will draw an illustration from the memory literature to demonstrate a possible failing of such a model-based approach. We will begin with a clear-cut case where theory has misled us. The commonly held theory of recall versus recognition, until relatively recently, was that the two processes differed in terms of a single stage, that is recall involves a retrieval stage and recognition does not. When someone can recognize but not recall an item, we interpret this as successful encoding of the item, but as a failure of retrieval. When we cannot recognize a previously studied item, we argue that there has been a failure in encoding or a loss from storage. We believed that Korsakoff's patients were unable to encode items since they failed at recognition memory of recently presented list words.

A number of recent studies cast doubt on the model that says recognition does not require retrieval. In a study by Jacoby and Witherspoon (1982), patients and controls in a pretest situation were asked questions such as: "name a musical instrument that employs a *reed*." The key word "reed" is a homophone and the less common of the two homophones "read-reed." In phase 2 of the experiment, which was presented to the subjects as another experiment altogether, they were asked to spell a number of words, including homophones that had been presented to phase 1 and others that had not. In a third phase, a recognition memory test was given for phase 1 words.

In the recognition test, the normals recognized 76 percent of the homophones heard in phase 1 of the experiment, while the patient group only recognized 25 percent of the items. Normally, such an outcome is attributed to failure of registration of storage on the part of the Korsakoff's patients (an amnesic effect). However, if we look at performance on the spelling test, it is the patient group who shows the greater influence of the phase 1 experience. They spell 63 percent of the words in the direction of the phase 1 experience (i.e., "reed" not "read") whereas the normals show an influence of phase 1 on only 49 percent of the items. Both groups spell control words (words not presented in phase 1) at the same level. If the spelling test is our measure of registration (encoding), it is the normal population that turns out to be amnesic.

The Jacoby and Witherspoon study illustrates a failure in theory, or rather an instance in which a process-model approach has failed in the past for these populations. Influence of registration (encoding) and recognition performance are independent processes, contrary to prior models. One failure does not require our elimination of an approach. However, it is necessary to recall that very little of our current theorizing resembles that of 10 or 20 years ago. In this period, such views as the modal model of Atkinson and Shiffrin (1968) have come and gone, as have numerous other models of behavior. Clearly, use of such an approach would leave our understanding of culture and aging only as illuminating as our most recent theories.

The alternative approach of Salthouse is not immune to the problem of theoretical interpretations changing. As an illustration of the problem, we will consider one of the possible aging interpretations offered by Salthouse, who suggests that as aging is accompanied by a general slowing of processes, it is this slowing and not any loss of capacity per se, that results in the decrements observed in normal aging. In giving credit where credit is due, we should indicate that this view has been well articulated by Nancy Waugh and Robin Barr at the Talland conference. We will review a small aspect of the data addressing that theory to indicate how we are limited by similar problems to those of the model-based approach. A number of studies have made use of one or another variation of the high-speed scan method developed by Saul Sternberg (1969).

In this approach, a memory search set of one to six digits (words or letters) is presented to the participant. Then a single probe item of the memory class is presented with the instructions to decide if that item is a member of the memory set. Participants are asked to make their YES - NO decision as quickly as they can while maintaining a high level of accuracy. The dependent variable of interest is response time.

It is the case that performance in this task is linearly related to size of memory set. We can therefore extrapolate two parameters from the experiment: the intercept of the line and the slope of the line.

The experiments reviewed by Salthouse computed the slope and intercept of data drawn from different age groups. In a meta-analysis, Gorfein and Spata (1985) compared the age samples in each study. Following a suggestion of Salthouse, they expressed each set of slope and intercept parameters as a percent of the youngest group in each experiment. (Note that a higher percent indicated a poorer performance.) In interpreting the results of these studies, Salthouse focused on the slope values because Sternberg's model of the task singled this out as the "memory scan" portion of the performance. The intercept, which is unaffected by set size, is interpreted as the result of a number of other nonmemory factors, including encoding time for the probe, decision time, response selection time, etc. If we accept the interpretation that the slope is the memory portion, it is important to note that there are large increases in slope ("scanning rate" time) in these studies -- about 185 percent on the average from the youngest to oldest group. However, we may be puzzled why this decrease in speed is often a much larger percent of the younger groups' performance than the corresponding increase in intercept -- a process thought to involve more stages of processing. With respect to intercept, the average of the older times is 144 percent that of the younger times. The more stages involved should result in a greater increase in time since each stage will add its effect. It is, in short, unclear what we are to make out of the data since our understanding of the task does not conform to the observed performance.

SOME SUGGESTED APPROACHES

To this point, we have spent a great deal of time answering the question of why we cannot say anything about memory from age to age. We believe the answer reflects the state of the art. Given the limitations of matching subjects and stimuli, we now have to decide what can be done. Following the suggestions of Underwood (1957), we may attempt to match subjects and materials on a few significant variables (such as vocabulary level for subjects and frequency for word materials), namely, variables that have been shown to be highly related to performance. Attempts to match other variables will only lead to restrictions on the generalizability of our results. We will look first at solutions for the language problem.

An often-used methodological approach to cross-cultural research is the etic-emic distinction developed by Pike (1966) based on the distinction between phonemics and phonetics in linguistics (Brislin, Lonner, and Thorndike, 1973). According to Pike, the emic approach studies behavior from within the system and examines only one culture, and criteria are relative to internal characteristics. In contrast, the etic approach studies behavior from outside the system and compares and studies many cultures; in addition, the criteria are absolute and universal.

The previously mentioned work on affective meaning systems by Osgood (1964) could be interpreted in terms of the etic-emic distinction. The basic invariant dimensions of meaning, namely, evaluation, potency, and activity, could be taken as representing the etic aspects. These major factors were derived by means of factor analysis after ratings have been gathered in each culture by using the emic procedure.

Brislin (1970, 1976) and Werner and Campbell (1970) have suggested the methods of back-translation and decentering as ways to control for potential translation problems. Back-translation has the advantage of "decentering" the material away from the original source, namely, changing the source material so that the product in the second language is not stilted and artificial, yet still conveys the original meaning (Brislin, 1976).

The back-translation and decentering method may also be employed to yield etic and emic dimensions. Material that is retained during the decentering process could be said to reflect the etic aspects of the material, while items that are eliminated would reflect the emic aspects.

In memory studies, poor performance may result when the to-be-remembered materials are not representative of what Cole and Scribner (1974) refer to as "dominant culture themes," namely, things that are important and meaningful to the people of the culture under study. In studies on memory and aging, it has been found that memory differences between younger and older adults (namely, a deficit in recall for older subjects) may not be due to aging per se, but may in fact be limited to recall for meaningful material (Barrett, 1978; Barrett and Watkins, 1980). These authors have found that given appropriate conditions, older adults show higher recall than younger adults. Barrett and Watkins (1980) found that generational word familiarity is an important variable that affects both the magnitude and the direction of recall differences. Barrett (1978) hypothesized that decrement in recall is due not to maturational factors but rather to task variables such as word familiarity.

Barrett (1978) used common words as stimuli, but manipulated the generational appropriateness of the materials. Two lists were prepared: one was comprised of items more familiar to the older adults, such as "fedora" and "poultice," and one list with items more familiar to the younger subjects, such as "afro" and "disco." Barrett found that recall was a function of age of subject and the list ("young" list or "old" list). When the "old" list was presented, older subjects showed a higher recall than younger subjects. The opposite was true for the "young" list. This is a further manifestation of the etic-emic problem. Materials need to be selected appropriate to age as well as to culture.

Cole and Scribner (1974) suggest a possible solution to the task problem, namely, training groups on the task under study. They found that effective use of strategies such as clustering and recall by categories can be elicited if subjects are given explicit instruction and/or training. Similarly, Cole, et. al. (1971) constrained recall by instructing subjects, for example, to "recall all the clothes," etc. The constrained recall made the stored items accessible. It had the added benefit of training subjects to use this technique in other tasks.

Given then that we can improve our studies by attending to the emitetic problem with respect to language (back-translation, etc.) and the task problem by appropriate training, we still have not been able to say anything at a theoretically meaningful level. However, our title promised that we would tell you *when* we would be able to say something. We are going to begin to sketch an answer to that. We believe the answer to our problem will come from two sources: first a more thorough analysis of the extant literature than even the commendable job of Salthouse, to assess which tasks show performance differences from young to old people. Second, we need a serious attempt to study a number of these tasks in the same populations (preferably, the same individuals) to assure ourselves that the results are consistent within a population. This is particularly crucial in that it is very difficult to separate the normal aging from persons who have suffered minor strokes, etc. Finally, we must try to control the experience factor, which differs so much from study to study. Only a very few studies make any attempt to consider the experience component. What we have in mind are studies like those used to evaluate incipient Alzheimer's disease by Grober (1985). In her work, five cognitive tasks are used and the crucial finding is that the groups differ on some tasks and not on others, indicating that they were well matched. Those studies lead to a new understanding, in this case of the disease process, and from another viewpoint of the nature of memory.

A similar line of research in our own lab has involved embedding a task within another. In this design, a final free recall is given after the subjects have performed in a standard short-term memory (STM) task. Gorfein and Shanahan (1984) have demonstrated that even where no memory differences existed between age groups in the Brown-Peterson short-term memory task, the participants did differ as a function of age in terms of on attempts to freely recall the items presented in STM immediately following the STM task. This research thus has the advantage of showing that the age groups are the same in the immediate task, indicating that they registered the items equally well. This study led to analytic attempts to understand the differences between *STM* and *Free Recall* and to understand why well-matched individuals, as illustrated by equality of performance on one aspect of a task, differ on another aspect. Such double tasks would seem to be quite useful in the study of aging across cultures, since we could see if a similar pattern exists in each culture.

CONCLUSION

We have argued that a full approach to the study of memory and aging in a cross-cultural design will require careful selection of materials, both across and within cultures, training of the subject populations in the tasks employed, the use of a variety of tasks to develop a taxonomy of tasks, and wherever possible, the use of one task embedded within another. If such detailed procedures are undertaken, it is possible that cross-cultural research in aging and memory will help to clarify our understanding of aging as well as culture.

REFERENCES

Atkinson, R. C., and Shiffrin, R. M. (1968). "Human Memory: A Proposed System and Its Control Processes." In *The Psychology of Learning and Motivation: Advances in Research and Theory,* edited by W. K. Spence and J. T. Spence, Vol. 1, 89-195. New York: Academic Press.

Barrett, T. R. (1978). "Aging and Memory: Declines or Differences." Paper read to the Psychonomic Society, at San Antonio, TX.

Barrett, T. R., and Watkins, S. K. (1980). "There are Age-Related Declines in Recall Following Semantic Processing: True or False?" Paper read to the Psychonomic Society, at St. Louis, MO.

Berry, J. W., and Dasen, P. R., (Eds.) (1974). *Culture and Cognition: Readings in Cross-Cultural Psychology*. London, GB: Methuen and Co., Ltd.

Brislin, R. (1970). "Back-Translation for Cross-Cultural Research." *Journal of Cross-Cultural Psychology, 1,* 185-216.

Brislin, R. (1976). "Comparative Research Methodology: Cross-Cultural Studies." *International Journal of Psychology, 11,* No. 3, 215-229.

Brislin, R., Lonner, W., and Thorndike, R. (1973). *Cross-Cultural Research Methods*. New York: John Wiley and Sons.

Buschke, J. (1987). "How Do We Know when a Person Has a Memory Deficit?" Paper read at the Ebbinghaus Centennial Conference, at Adelphi University, Garden City, NY.

Cole, M., Gay, J., Glick, J., and Sharp, D. W. (1971). *The Cultural Context of Learning and Thinking*. New York: Basic Books.

Cole, M., and Means, B. (1981). *Comparative Studies of How People Think*. Cambridge, MA: Harvard University Press.

Cole, M., and Scribner, S. (1974). *Culture and Thought*. New York: John Wiley and Sons.

Deregowski, J. B. (1970). "Effect of Cultural Value of Time upon Recall." *British Journal of Social and Clinical Psychology, 9,* 37-41.

Eriksen, C. W., Hamlin, R. M., and Daye, C. (1973). "Aging Adults and Rate of Memory Scan." *Bulletin of the Psychonomic Society, 1,* 259-260.

Gorfein, D. S., and Shanahan, G. (1984). "Aging and the control of Short-Term Memory." Paper read at the Annual Meeting of the Eastern Psychological Association, at Baltimore, MD.

Gorfein, D. S., and Spata. A. (1985). "Problems Associated with Studying Memory and Aging Cross-Culturally." Laboratory Report, Adelphi University, Garden City, NY.

Grober, E. (1985). "Early Identification of Dementia." Paper read at the symposium on Memory in Non-Normal Populations, 4th Annual Adelphi Applied Experimental Psychology Conference, Garden City, NY.

Jacoby, L. L., and Witherspoon, D. (1982). "Remembering without Awareness." *Canadian Journal of Psychology, 36,* 300-324.

Osgood, C. E. (1964). "Semantic Differential Technique in the Comparative Study of Cultures." *American Anthropologist, 66,* 171-200.

Osgood, C. E. (1971). "Explorations in Semantic Space: A Personal Diary." *Journal of Social Issues, 27,* 5-64.

Pike, K. L. (1966). *Language in Relation to a Unified Theory of the Structure of Human Behavior.* The Hague, The Netherlands: Mouton.

Poon, L. W., Foxard, J. E., Cermak, L. S., Arenberg, D., and Thompson, L. W. (Eds.) (1980). *New Directions in Memory and Aging.* Hillsdale, NJ: Lawrence Erlbaum Associates.

Salthouse, T. (1982). *Adult Cognition: An Experimental Psychology of Human Aging.* New York: Springer-Verlag.

Smith, A. D. (1980). "Age Differences in Encoding, Storage, and Retrieval." *In New Directions in Memory and Aging,* edited by W. Poon, J. L. Foxard, L. S. Cermak, D. Arenberg, and L. W. Thompson. Hillsdale, NJ: Lawrence Erlbaum Associates.

Smith, M. (1985) "Evidence for Bilingual Activation Using Word Fragment Completion." Paper read at the Annual Meeting of the Psychonomic Society, at Boston, MA.

Sternberg, S. (1969). "Memory-Scanning: Mental Processes Revealed by Reaction-Time Experiments." *American Scientist, 57,* 421-457.

Triandis, H. C. (1976). "Methodological Problems of Comparative Research." *International Journal of Psychology, 11*, No. 3, 155-159.

Underwood, B. J. (1957). *Psychological Research*. New York: Appleton-Century-Crofts, Inc.

Werner, O., and Campbell, D. T. (1970). "Translating, Working through Interpreters, and the Problem of Decentering." In *A Handbook of Method in Cultural Anthropology*, edited by R. Naroll and R. Cohen, 398-420. New York: American Museum of Natural History.

26

Cross-Cultural Comparability

Lars H. Ekstrand and Gudrun B. Ekstrand

EPISTEMOLOGICAL PROBLEMS IN CROSS-CULTURAL RESEARCH

Recently, several authors have stressed the need for more idiographic approaches in addition to the prevalent nomothetic ones. The nomothetic approach is the quantitative statistical approach that is often called positivistic or neopositivistic. The idiographic approach holds that social science findings are valid in their cultural or social setting only. Taft (1987) has argued that cross-cultural researchers tend to rely too much on nomothetic approaches. They should, to a larger extent, apply idiographic methods.

Particularly interesting for cross-cultural psychology is the ethnic component in the idiographic/nomothetic debate. Husén (1986) gives examples how survey research has been denounced as "an instrument of methodological imperialism" or as "the elitist approach of industrialized countries." Consequently, the IEA (International Association for the Evaluation of Educational Achievement) is now reorienting its cross-national comparisons toward more idiographic approaches (Husén, 1986). These contemporary ethnic strivings to a large extent coincide with the approach that was argued by early anthropologists such as Malinowski (1922) and Boas (1943) and later became known as "emic."

It may at this stage be appropriate to say a few more words about the nomothetic/idiographic and the emic/etic distinctions. It was Wilhelm Windelband who coined, towards the end of the nineteenth century, the term idiographic for the methodology in the humanistic and social sciences that describes phenomena *sui generis*, and nomothetic for the natural science methodology as primarily establishing laws for observed phenomena. The idiographic approach wants to describe what is unique, whereas the nomothetic approach is looking for universals. The idiographic approach often uses so-called "soft-data" methods. Later on, Allport (1942) used this distinction to assert the identity of humanistic psychology as separate from behaviorism and test psychology. He thereby broadened the concepts to comprise virtually all "hard data" methods versus all "soft data" methods. This broad conceptualization is also used by Husén (1986).

Superficially similar to the nomothetic/idiographic dichotomy is the emic-etic distinction (Jahoda, 1983; Ekstrand and Ekstrand, 1986a, 1986b). However, although the ways of using the dichotomies are often similar in contemporary jargon, the two dichotomies are only partially overlapping.

The terms "emic" and "etic" were coined by Kenneth Pike (1967) to designate a number of meanings of two major approaches in cultural research. Emic may mean "internal view, from the inside, internal criteria, culture-specific, studying one culture at a time," and etic may mean "comparative, universal, from the outside, external criteria;" see Ekstrand and Ekstrand (1986a) for closer description and analysis. All idiographic research is not, however, necessarily emic, and not all nomothetic research etic, and vice versa. Nor is research carried out by native researchers necessarily idiographic and/or emic. Particularly, much intracultural research in developing countries is performed by native researchers with nomothetic methods or in an etic way.

As Eckensberger (1979) and Eckensberger and Burgard (1982) have pointed out, there are many ways to operationalize a given concept. First, this is true within a given paradigm. When there is a question of choice between paradigms, the number of potential operationalizations increases drastically. In terms of the nomothetic/idiographic controversy, there are many ways to conduct both idiographic and nomothetic research. A major question, then, for the researcher who wants to take an idiographic course, is to decide which approach to apply. Second, within the selected approach, or combination of approaches, modes of operationalization must be decided. In practical work, this can be a slow and painstaking process, filled with trial and error.

CROSS-CULTURAL COMPARABILITY

If idiographic or emic methods become more widely used in cross-cultural comparisons, this will immediately accentuate the problem of cross-cultural comparability, in a number of ways. First, how can idiographic data from different cultures be compared? Second, how can results, obtained with different epistemological approaches, be compared? Third, can different epistemological approaches be combined?

Thus, idiographic approaches do not exclude or diminish the need for cross-cultural comparisons. In fact, the more we learn about specific cultures, the greater the need for comparisons, juxtapositions, and analyses. By definition, they will have to be made between "uncomparable" groups. However, even with nomothetic methods, the question is how comparable "comparable" groups really are.

As Eckensberger and Burgard (1982) point out, there has long existed research questioning whether data are automatically comparable just because they are generated with the same method. As the authors stress, there are many types of data equivalence, namely of measurements, scores, stimuli, responses, concepts, functions, and many others. Some authors claim that the first concern is to establish equivalence in *meaning*, that is, of the concepts that are being operationalized. Obviously, there are also types of equivalence with regard to subjects, experimental setup, research design, methods, and instruments.

Thus, in cross-cultural comparisons, equivalence of data cannot be taken for granted. In intracultural research, groups of subjects are thought to be equivalent if they have the same composition with regard to age, sex, socioeconomic status (SES), occupational structure, urban/rural setting, etc., and if they have similar results on variables of intelligence, academic achievement, and so on. Whereas such an assumption may be true in the intracultural situation, it may not be so in the cross-cultural situation, even if different cultural groups should happen to be alike with regard to the aforementioned variables. The cultural background and circumstances of living of the various groups may be very different, and also their world view, their concepts, and their metaphysical categories.

If the differences in income and material standard, occupational structure, cultural background, etc., are huge, it may not at all be possible to obtain groups that are even superficially comparable. On the other hand, if one were to select samples that are very similar, they might be highly unrepresentative for one or both cultures. Nevertheless, comparisons between "uncomparable" groups may be of great scientific interest. For instance, the psychosocial situation of children in highly different cultures may be of the utmost interest, not in spite of but because of the cultural differences. In a world that rapidly shrinks because of improved means of communication, cross-cultural understanding becomes increasingly important. Domestic social, economic, or technological problems may find their solutions in ideas from other cultures.

Cross-cultural comparisons also constitute a practical research tool. Hidden cultural traits in one's own culture often become visible first when this culture is contrasted with another. Adding more cultures to the comparisons provide new dimensions to the interpretations of patterns made visible by the contrasts.

SOME SUGGESTED SOLUTIONS TO CERTAIN PROBLEMS OF COMPARABILITY

One solution may be actually to obtain as high a degree of statistical comparability as possible between two or more groups from different cultures. These data should be combined with rational consideration of other relevant factors. Demands on "equivalence of meaning" or other similar demands are disregarded. Instead, we study if the methods work the same way, that is give the same practical results in all groups. If they do, we assume that differences we have not discovered or eliminated are of less practical consequence in the given situation.

For instance, Ekstrand (1976, 1983) compared tests of intelligence in the Thurstone Primary Mental Abilities (PMA) factors R, N, and S for more than 2,000 immigrant students from 36 different nations to the results for a major Swedish group. It was found that the means, dispersions, distributions, reliability, intercorrelations between tests, point-biserial item/test correlations, and difficulty of items were practically identical between the immigrant group and the Swedish group. For certain research purposes, and also for some practical school psychological work, this may be considered a sufficient degree of comparability. For example, if there is a research purpose, such as studying the cognitive development among immigrant students in relation to native students, the degree of comparability may be assumed to be sufficient for the measurements chosen. Likewise, if an immigrant student is said to be backward, and the tests show him to be of average or even superior intelligence, we assume that the tests function in a valid way.

For other purposes, the degree of comparability may not be sufficient, for the reasons discussed above by Eckensberger and his coworkers. For example, if the assumed backwardness in our aforementioned immigrant student were confirmed by the tests, we should be cautious in relying on the result, because there might be hidden dimensions -- unfamiliarity with test-taking, or whatever -- that may distort results in some situations, but not in others. There are obvious parallels in research situations.

Another way of making a meaningful comparative evaluation of results from quite dissimilar groups is not to compare them directly, but to relate the results to independent criteria. For instance, features in the psychosocial situation of children in two very different cultures may be evaluated with respect to how well these features satisfy criteria derived from basic research on affective development. Such research and the derived criteria should, furthermore, be culture-free, or shown to be universal to several cultures. If one of the cultures under study is a touch culture and the other a nontouch culture, we might assume that the touch culture will better satisfy results demonstrating that touch is essential for a harmonious affective development (Harlow, 1958; Harlow and Suomi, 1970). Such a procedure, obviously, is not conclusive, but may generate important hypotheses that can be tested in direct studies. The scientific value would thus still be high.

The simplest solution may be to compare data from "incomparable" cultures without striving at statistical or any other comparability at all. Instead, what is typical for each culture is directly compared, without regard to any equivalence demands. This may be expressed thus: every culture is described in an emic way, and these descriptions are the basis for the comparison.

The rationale is that the usual strict demands for comparability with regard to background variables are, in fact, an overinterpretation of experimental requirements. Comparability is necessary in experimental and quasi-experimental designs in order to avoid confounding effects of certain background variables with the treatment to be studied.

Many cross-cultural research studies are not of the experimental or causality-seeking nature, however. Certainly, in some studies, if culture, or cultural differences, constitute the independent variable, comparability may still be necessary. Yet if we are merely interested in studying the differences, there seems to be no reason at all for striving to make incomparable cultures comparable. It may actually be a disadvantage to make samples comparable.

Let us say that a developing country is being compared with an industrialized country. In such a case, with the solution sketched here, what is typical for each culture would be selected to represent the culture in question. For instance, the occupational structure in one country would contain many highly educated persons, while the other would contain many poorly educated or illiterate persons. This difference would be taken into consideration when interpreting results, and so would other cultural differences. Samples that were equivalent with regard to occupational structure might, in fact, remove existing differences, and hence remove the basis for any meaningful interpretation of cultural differences that nevertheless exist.

Consider the following situation. In on-going research, norms and sanctions for child rearing are being compared in the four very different cultures of Sweden, India, reindeer-herding Lapps, and the religious sect of Laestadians (Ekstrand and Ekstrand, 1985, 1987, Ekstrand, 1986, 1987). Now, first, should parent samples be equal with respect to SES, occupation, and income? We argue that this would be misleading for all four cultures. Instead, samples should be representative for each culture (with some modifications). In other words, the occupational, SES and income. Distributions should be typical of each culture, that is, should be very different in the four samples.

If samples are typical of each culture, they are clearly more emic. Effects of background variables should be studied *within* each culture. For instance, in India, caste breaks the pattern of SES differences. A Brahmin is usually highly educated and has a high status, but may very well be poor. However, in this situation we need to make sure that we compare the same *kind of data*, on the same level of detail.

If data have been collected in survey-type studies, their relative frequency and importance in each culture may be established. However, sooner or later, a qualitative analysis is necessary to describe the roots and closer meaning of the different cultural data. The same words, even similar concepts, may be so loaded with different values and roots that the survey descriptions are incomplete, and important observations remain unexplained. The main thing is that the cultural patterns from each culture become reflected in one another to bring out hidden dimensions. This approach might yield results that would be totally different from those obtained in monocultural studies. In this perspective, statistical comparability might well ruin results, rather than produce safe data.

A BRIEF DISCUSSION OF NOMOTHETIC
VERSUS IDIOGRAPHIC APPROACHES

Basically, three varieties of nomothetic/idiographic applications in cross-cultural research may be discerned, and two modes of applying these varieties. The three varieties are: (1) the purely nomothetic approach; (2) the purely idiographic approach; and (3) any combination of nomothetic and idiographic approaches.

The two modes of application are: (1) the Static Mode of Application (SMA); and (2) the Interactive Mode of Application (IMA).

An idiographic/nomothetic combination can be made in many ways, but not in any one way. For instance, in certain projects, positivistic psychological techniques have been combined with anthropological methods. However, it is important to observe that a coupling of paradigms cannot be made in any way whatever. It is perfectly feasible to analyze the same data with very different types of method. It is also possible to start a study with one paradigmatic approach, and make the next step with another. However, statistical data cannot be *interpreted* from the basic postulates of another paradigm. If questions with fixed response alternatives have been used, it is impossible to make any deeper interpretation of the results. The subjects have not had the opportunity to give any other answers. Even if there has been space for subjective comments, the technique does not allow for further exploration of the meaning of those comments. Thus, combination of paradigms must be carefully considered.

By the Static Mode of Application, we mean that once the design is decided on, it is followed in any of the three varieties. By the Interactive Mode, we mean that experiences from one culture may affect the procedure in another, and vice versa. Methods may be developed and changed as the research goes on. As new knowledge is obtained and understanding deepens, this is allowed to affect the subsequent procedure. Although the interactive mode in principle could be applicable to any of the three varieties, it is very much against the way that positivistic procedures are usually applied. Interactive studies are rare, as they presuppose a step-wise, continually changing research process, such as may be found as a principle in hermeneutic or semi-hermeneutic approaches, so far rarely applied in cross-cultural settings.

A problem with the quantitative, statistical, positivistic approach is that it requires a fair amount of knowledge upon which to base hypotheses or assumptions. It also requires a basis for the construction of instruments, preferably on the interval scale level. It moreover requires a solid base for making a tenable design. Unless instruments or design are enough advanced, strict sampling techniques are not meaningful to apply. The positivistic approach is also static. When the design, instruments, sampling, data collection, etc., are decided on, there is not much that can be changed. When the interviewers, coders, etc., have been trained and put to work, they cannot take an on-the-spot decision of following up new leads, make a new data collection when a suitable occasion unexpectedly turns up, and so on. Also, positivistic work is often expensive, because it takes several employees.

In many situations, it may be profitable to switch to another research paradigm. The study of a problem often takes a developmental course, so that it is better to start with some nonpositivistic paradigm, and to introduce quantitative techniques as the research procedure proceeds. This, naturally, often is a matter of several years.

There are at least three epistemological approaches that do not presuppose a prior body of knowledge upon which to base the design and instruments, and that allow a developing course of research, similar to the "hermeneutic spiral" (Dilthey, 1914-1936; Åkerberg, 1986). As new knowledge is gained, the same data may be reinterpreted, and/or new data added to the first collection. The increased knowledge is allowed to lead to modifications of the research procedures. These approaches are the ethological approach, the anthropological approach, and the hermeneutic or interpretative approach.

Ethology applied to humans requires detailed observations repeated at short intervals. Ethological techniques may be applied without much theory or assumptions, thus being at variance with most nomothetic behavioral methods (Lorenz, 1965, 1969). This is a distinct advantage for an idiographic approach. Some interesting human ethological applications have been done on social learning and personality development in deaf and in blind children (Preisler, 1983; Preisler and Palmer, 1986). However, the close observation and recording is too painstaking a method for the purpose of cross-cultural comparisons.

Anthropology provides several suitable methods and approaches that may readily be adapted to the needs of the behavioral sciences, such as psychology, education, and psychiatry. They are too well-known and too extensive to be discussed here. Instead, we refer to current textbooks on anthropological methodology, such as those by Otterbein (1972) and others. However, there is rarely a subsequent switching to another paradigm, for instance, a quantitative analysis of the primary data, or the development of more positivistic instruments from the knowledge obtained. Anthropologists are rarely trained in test construction and quantitative data analysis.

Hermeneutics provides very interesting clues for an idiographic approach. The concepts of preunderstanding and understanding, the stepwise gaining of understanding, the progressive work, and gradually increased knowledge according to the hermeneutic spiral are all well suited to idiographic approaches (Dilthey, 1914-1936; Åkerberg, 1986). However, it is not necessary to completely adopt the hermeneutic mode of analysis. Rather, certain principles may be adopted. There is a variety of hermeneutic applications along the continuum between behaviorism and pure hermeneutics, from semihermeneutic to semibehavioristic.

Finally, it may be said that in many situations, it may be necessary to compare and discuss cultural data, obtained with different methods and sometimes also different epistemological approaches. Positivistic multivariate methods may, like other approaches, ultimately yield data that allow conclusions in very broad terms.

REFERENCES

Åkerberg, H. (1986). *Hermeneutik och Pedagogisk Psykologi.* (Hermeneutics and Educational Psychology.) Stockholm, Sweden: Norstedts.

Allport, G. W. (1942). *The Use of Personal Documents in Psychological Science,* Bulletin No. 49. New York: Social Science Research Council.

Boas, F. (1943). "Recent anthropology." *Science, 98,* 311-314.

Dilthey, W. (1914-1936). *Gesammelte Schriften.* (Collected Works.) Leipzig, Germany.

Eckensberger, L. (1979). "A Metamethodological Evaluation of Psychological Theories from a Cross-Cultural Perspective." In *Cross-Cultural Contributions to Psychology,* edited by L. H. Eckensberger, W. J. Lonner, and Y. H. Poortinga, 255-275. Lisse, Holland: Swets and Zeitlinger,

Eckensberger, L., and Burgard, P. (1982). "The Cross-Cultural Assessment of Normative Concepts: Some Considerations on the Affinity between Methodological Approaches and Preferred Theories. In *Human assessment and Cultural Factors,* edited by S. H. Irvine and J. Berry. New York and London: Plenum Press.

Ekstrand, G. (1986). "Familjemönster i Sverige och Indien." (Family patterns in Sweden and India.) *Pedagogisk-Psykologiska Problem,* No. 468, Malmö, Sweden: University of Lund, School of Education.

Ekstrand, G. (1987). "Gud och Trollen. Intervjuer med Samiska och Laestadianska förlädrar om barn." (God and the Trolls. Interviews with Lappish and Laestadian Parents about Children.) *Pedagogisk Dokumentation,* No. 87. Malmö, Sweden: University of Lund, School of Education.

Ekstrand, G., and Ekstrand, L. H. (1985). "Patterns of Socialization in Different Cultures: The Cases of Sweden and India." In *Cross-Cultural and National Studies in Social Psychology,* edited by R. Diaz-Guerrero, Vol. 2, 225-244. Amsterdam, Holland: North-Holland.

Ekstrand, L. H. (1976). "Adjustment Among Immigrant Pupils in Sweden. *International Review of Applied Psychology, 25*(3), 167-188.

Ekstrand, L. H. (1983). "Tvärkulturella Mätningar." (Cross-Cultural Measurements.) Mimeographed Report. Malmö, Sweden: University of Lund, School of Education.

Ekstrand, L. H., and Ekstrand, G. (1985). "Barn/Vuxenrelationer: Ett Tvärkulturellt Projekt för Studiet av Psyko-sociala Relationer i Skilda Kulturer." (Child/Adult Relations in Different Cultures. An account of a Research Program.) (Revised 1987) Mimeographed. Malmö, Sweden: University of Lund, School of Education.

Ekstrand, L. H., and Ekstrand, G. (1986a). "Developing the Emic/Etic Concepts for Cross-Cultural Research. In *Ethnic Minorities and Immigrants in a Cross-Cultural Perspective*, edited by L. H. Ekstrand, 52-65. Berwyn and Lisse, Holland: Swets North America Inc., and Swets and Zeitlinger.

Ekstrand, L. H., and Ekstrand, G. (1986b). "Epistemological and Metamethodological Applications in Cross-Cultural Studies." *Educational and Psychological Interactions*, No. 87. Malmö, Sweden: University of Lund, School of Education.

Ekstrand, L. H., and Ekstrand, G. (1987). "Children's Perceptions of Norms and Sanctions in Two Cultures." In *Growth and Progress in Cross-Cultural Psychology*, edited by C. Kagitcibaci, 171-180. Berwyn and Lisse, Holland: Swets North America Inc.

Harlow, H. F. (1958). "The Nature of Love." *American Psychologist, 13*, 673-685.

Harlow, H. F., and Suomi, S. J. (1970). "Nature of Love -- Simplified." *American Psychologist, 17,* 161-168.

Husén, T. (1986)."'Comparing the Uncomparable': Paradigm and Criterion Problems in Conducting Cross-National Comparisons of 'Quality' in Education." In *Ethnic Minorities and Immigrants in a Cross-Cultural Perspective,* 24-34. Berwyn and Lisse, Holland: Swets North America Inc.

Jahoda, G. (1983). "The Cross-Cultural Emperor's Conceptual Clothes: The Emic-Etic Issue Revisited." In *Explorations in Cross-Cultural Psychology,* edited by J. B. Deregowski, S. Dziurawiec and R. C. Annis, 19-37. Berwyn and Lisse, Holland: Swets North America Inc.

Lorenz, K. (1965). *Evolution and Modification of Behavior.* Chicago: University of Chicago Press.

Lorenz, K. (1969). "Innate Bases of Learning." In *On the Biology of Learning,* edited by K. Pribram, 11-93. New York: Harcourt, Brace and World.

Malinowski, B. (1922). *Argonauts of the Western Pacific.* London, GB: Routledge.

Otterbein, K. F. (1972). *Comparative Cultural Analysis.* New York: Holt, Rinehart and Winston.

Pike, K. (1967). *Language in Relation to a Unified Theory of the Structure of Human Behavior,* 2nd ed. The Hague, Holland: Mouton.

Preisler, G. (1983). *Deaf children in Communication.* University of Stockholm: Department of Psychology.

Preisler, G., and Palmer, C. (1986). "The Function of Vocalization in Early Parent-Blind Children Interaction." In *Precursors of Early Speech,* edited by B. Lindblom, and R. Zetterström. Basingstoke, GB: McMillan and Co.

Stevens, S. S. (1956). "The Suprising Simplicity of Sensory Metrics." *American Psychologist, 11,* 29-39.

Torgerson, W. S. (1960). *Theory and Methods of Scaling,* 2nd ed. New York: John Wiley and Sons.

Taft, R. (1987). "Cross-Cultural Psychology as Psychological Science." In *Growth and Progress in Cross-Cultural Psychology,* edited by C. Kagit-cibaci, 3-9. Berwyn and Lisse, Holland: Swets North America Inc., and Swets and Zeitlinger.

INDEX

Abdel Gafar, A. M., 20
academic performance, father
    absence and, 51-52
Adams, G. R., 50
addiction, therapeutic management
    of, 93-100
Adler, L. L., 3-10, 112-16, 165-68
adolescents: addiction and drug
    abuse, 93-100; brain-damaged,
    78-84; in Jamaica, 61-68; self-
    actualization and, 74-77;
    Thalidomide effects on, 85-92
adult development: in China,
    205-11; friendship relations,
    193-200; middle age studies,
    164-68; religiosity and, 173-78;
    stages of, 155-161
Africa: Fruit-Tree Experiment in,
    4-6; Sudanese children's
    cognitive development, 17-26
Agbayewa, M. O., 52
Ahmed, R. A., 17-19
Åkerberg, H., 265
Aldons, J., 121, 205
Allport, G., 259
Almeida, R. M., 88
Amman, S., 49-50
Angelini, A. L., 88
antisocial behavior, father absence
    and, 50-52
applied behavior analysis, cross-
    cultural variations in, 40-42
Arbman, E. 175
Arenberg, D., 247
Argyle, M., 112
Arling, G., 194
Asia, Fruit-Tree Experiment in, 4
Askham, J., 135
assertive behavior, ethnic and
    gender differences in, 103-7
Atkinson, R. C., 252
Attia, S., 49
attitudes: Fruit-Tree drawings and,
    5-10; types of, 5-6
Australia, Fruit-Tree Experiment
    in, 4

Baer, D. M. 42
Bain, H. C., 51
Bandura, A., 40
Bannon, J. A., 50
Barnes, M. L., 67
Baron, R. Y., 103
Barrett, T. R., 254
Basseches, M., 155
Beck, A., 218
Beddoe, I. B., 67

Beit-Hallahmi, B., 175
Bell, R., 193
Belz, H. F., 51
Bem, D. J., 136
Bem, S. L., 7, 103, 136
Benchekroun, M. F., 50
Bender, L., 4
Berman, W., 37
Berry, J. W., 249-50
Bieliauskas, V. J., 50-51
Bik, E. L., 27
Birren, J. E., 155
Blazer, D., 228
Boas, F., 259
Boersma, F. J., 51
Bonaventura, E., 27, 30
Bond, A., 38
Boone, S. L., 50
Booth, A., 193
Boss, P. G., 48
Bourdin, C. M., 50
Bow, E. C., 104
Bradley, R. H. 48
brain-damaged adolescents, 78-84
Brazil, adolescent development in, 85-92
Bringle, R. G., 51
Brinich, P., 50
Brislin, R., 249, 253-54
Broden, M., 38
Brody, E. M., 205
Bronfenbrenner, W., 38
Brook, J. S., 50
Brummel-Smith, K., 224
Bruner, J. S., 132
Bruno, E., 48
Buckley, N. K. 38
Buck, P. L., 112
Burgard, P., 260
Buschke, J., 247
Butler, R. N., 199
Byrne, D., 103

Campbell, D. E., 180
Campbell, D. T., 37, 254
Candy, S. G., 193

Canty, E. M., 104
Caplan, R., 216
Caplow, T., 135-36
Carlson, R., 121, 205
Carp., F. M. 180
Cassel, J., 216
Cermak, L. S., 247
Chapman, J. W., 51
Chen, L., 121
Chiland, D., 52
childhood: cross-cultural research on, 3-60; intervention strategies, 37-42; in Sudan, 17-26. *See also* children.
children: Chinese and child-parent behaviors, 121-26; father absence effects, 47-52; Fruit-Tree drawings of, 3-10; in Jamaica, 61-68; moral development, 61-68; reasoning of by Sudanese schoolchildren, 17-26; teacher rating scales used to assess, 27-32
China, old age care in, 205-11
Chinese child-parent behaviors, 121-26
Civcivelli, B. G., 205
Cobb, S., 216
cognitive development: brain-damaged adolescents and, 79-83; father absence and, 51; in Sudanese children, 17-26; teacher rating scales used in measuring, 27-32
Cohen, C. I., 193
Cole, M., 247-55
Coleman, J. S., 42
Cole, R., 247
Colletta, N. D., 48
Copeland, J., 224
Coriandoli, E., 85
Coult, A. D., 121
Covell, K., 50
Crain, W. C., 157
cross-cultural research: on addiction, 93-100; on adolescent development, 61-100; on adult development, 103-75; on

assertive behavior and dominance, 103-7; on brain-damaged adolescents, 78-84; on childhood, 3-60; on Chinese child-parent behaviors, 121-26; on disabilities, 223-28; on early childhood intervention, 37-42; epistemological problems in 259-65; of in-law relations, 131-41; memory and old age, 247-56; moral reasoning in Jamaican children, 61-68; nomothetic approaches, 259-65; on old age, 179-266; on old age care in China, 205-11; on religiosity, 173-78; on residence environment for elderly, 179-91; RIPIS used in, 26-32; self-actualization and adolescents, 74-77; social support of elderly, 216-21; teacher rating scales used in, 27-32; Thalidomide effects on adolescents, 85-9
Crutchfield, R. D., 200
Cuellar, J. B., 121, 205
cultural grid, old age and, 234-44
Cunningham, W. R., 155

D'Amico, G., 30
Darrow, C. N. 157
Dasen, P. R., 249-50
Daum, J. M., 50-51
Davidson, S., 216
Davis, W. M., 165
Dawson, M., 121
Daye, C., 257
Dean, J., 112-
Dean, J., 223
Deaton, H. S., 50
Deaux, K., 103
Décarie, T. G., 88
Deitch, I., 165
Dennis, W., 3, 5, 10
depression, disability and, 223-28
Deregowski, J. B., 247
development of by Sudanese

children, cognitive development, 17-26
Dilthey, W., 265
disability, cross-cultural research, 223-28
distance, in social and interpersonal behaviors, 112-16
Dittes, J., 173-74
divorce, father absence effects on children, 47-52
dominance, ethnic and gender differences in, 103-7
Donoghue, K. C., 48-49
Douki, S., 49-50
dowry system, in India, 133-34
Doyle, A., 48
drug abuse, therapeutic management of addiction, 93-100

Earl, L., 224
early intervention, cross-cultural differences, 37-42
Eberhardt, C. A., 50
Eckensberger, L., 260
education: early intervention in, 37-42; as social influence, 38
Eisenberg, L. A., 193
Ekstrand, G., 260, 262-63
Ekstrand, L. H., 260, 262-63
Elardo, R., 48
Ellis, S., 38
emotions, social behavior and interpersonal distance, 113-16
epistemology, in cross-cultural research, 259-65
Erbaugh, J., 218
Erikson, C. W., 257
Erikson, E. H., 138
ethnic differences: in adult development, 156-61; on assertive behavior and dominance, 103-7; on friend relations, 193-200; and in-law relations in India 131-41
Europe, Fruit-Tree Experiment in, 4

familiarity hypothesis, children's drawings and, 3-4

father absence: clinical consequences, 50-52; cross-cultural research on, 47-52; psychoanalysis of Greco-American man, and 143-53; stress on children and, 48-49

Festinger, L., 175

Flavell, J. H., 20

Fleshman, R. P., 50

Foot, N., 121, 205

Fozard, J. E., 247

Frank, J. C., 40

French, J., 216

Freud, S., 50, 143

Friend, J. H., 48

friendship, ethnic and gender differences, 193-200

Fries, J., 223

Fruit-Tree drawings: of children, 3-10; familiarity hypothesis, 3-4; Fruit-Tree Experiment described, 4-5; value hypothesis, 3

Gallimore, R., 39, 41

Gauvain, M. 38

Gay, J., 247-249

Geary, D. C., 51

Geiwit, J., 155

gender differences: on assertive behavior and dominance, 103-7; on friend relations, 193-200; and in-law relations in India, 131-41; retirement residence and women, 179-91

Gettner, J., 64

Gielen, U., 65, 68

Ginsburg, H., 19

Gispert, M., 50

Glick, J., 247, 249

Goffman, E., 113

Golden, R., 225

Goldstein, J. S., 50-51

Goller, W. L., 112

Golub, S., 104

Gongla, P. A., 48

Goog, B., 227

Gordon, A. S., 50

Gore, S., 216

Gorfein, D. S., 253, 255

Gorsuch, R. L., 67

Gottman, J. M., 104

Graubert, J. G., 113-14

Greek-americans, cultural influences on, 143-53

Grober, E., 257

Grossman, S. M., 50

Guadagnoli, E., 27

Gullotta, T. P., 48-49

Gurland, B. J., 223-28

Gutmann, D., 156

Hacker, H. M., 193

Haffani, F., 49-50

Hall, R. V., 38

Hamlin, R. M., 257

Hanson, C. L., 50

Harburg, E., 121, 123-25, 208-10

Harlow, H. F., 262

Hau, K. T., 67

Haven, D., 217

Hebenstein, R., 121

Heller, K., 218

Henggeler, S. W., 50

Hess, B., 193

Hess, R., 42

Hill, O. O. 165

Hill, R., 121, 123, 205

Himmelfarb, S., 48

Hindu behaviors: and in-law relations, 131-41; social and interpersonal distance, 112-16

Hogan, J. D., 164

Holmes, T., 216

Hsaio, c., 121

Hsu, F.L.Y., 135-36, 210

Husén, T., 259-60

Huttunen, M. O., 49-50

identification, in psychoanalysis of Greco-american man, 145-50
idiographic approaches, to cross-cultural research, 259-65
India: in-law relations in, 131-41; social behavior and interpersonal distance, 112-16
Ingham, J., 216
Inhelder, B., 17
in-law relations, in India, 131-41
Ino, S., 103-4
interpersonal distance, cross-cultural differences, 112-16
intervention, models of and cross-cultural research, 37-42
Iverson, M. A., 112-14

Jacoby, L. L., 251
Jahoda, G., 260
Jamaica, child development in, 61-68
Japan, Fruit-Tree Experiment in, 9
Jensen, A. R., 37
Johnson, R. C.
joint family system, in India, 133
Jones, R. T., 38
Jordan, C., 39, 41

Kakar, S., 133-136
Kamehameha Early Educational Program (KEEP), 39-42
Kaplan, B., 216
Kappes, B. M., 48
Kashkoush, I., 20
Katz, S., 223, 227
Keane, J., 224
Kelleher, M., 224
Kemp, B., 224
Kessen, W., 38, 156
Kimmel, D. C., 164
Kleck, R., 112, 114
Kleemeier, R., 179-80
Klein, E. B., 157
Klein, V
Kleinman, A., 227

Koehn, H., 121
Kohlberg, L., 61-68
Krasner, L., 39
Kreiger, L., 50
Kubany, E. s., 41
Kumar, U., 132, 137-38
Kumar, W., 8
Kuriansky, J., 224

Lacan, J., 152
Lang, O., 121
Lantigua, R., 223
Lawton, M. P., 179-80
learning, brain-damaged adolescents and, 79-83
Lefcoe, D., 139
Lemke, S., 180
Lerner, R. M., 156
Levenson, R. W., 104
LeVine, R., 156
Levinson, D., 165
Levy, M., 121
Levy, S. G., 193
Levy-Shiff, R., 50
Lewittes, H., 50
Linn, M. W., 50
London, R. S., 112
Lonner, W., 253
Lopata, H. Z., 194
Lopez-Agueres, W., 224
Lorenz, K., 265
Lowe, J. C., 158, 164
Lowenthal, M., 217
Lowenthal, M. F., 193

McCarthy, E., 48
MacDonald, R., 121, 205
MacDonald, W. S., 39, 41
McElrath, D., 139
McKee, B., 157
McKinley, D. G., 121
McLanahan, S. S., 48
McLaughlin, J. E., 51
Ma, H. K., 67
Maijer, A., 48

Malinowski, B., 259
Manosevitz, M. 50
Maruani, G., 50-51
marriage, and in-law relations in
    India, 131-41
Matalon, B., 17
Mazo, P., 88
Means, B., 247, 249-50
Medelson, M., 218
memory: of brain-damaged
    adolescents, 79-83; old age and,
    247-56
Merenda, P. F., 27, 30
Miao, E., 27
middle age: cross-cultural research
    on, 103-5=75; perceptions of,
    164-68^R
Miller, J. B., 138
Miller, P., 216
Miller. T. W., 50
Mindel, C. H., 200
Mines, M., 158
Mock, J., 218
modern attitudes, versus traditional
    in Fruit-Tree drawings, 5-10
Montare, a., 50
Monte-Serrat, S., 88
Moon, U. L., 61, 67-68
Moore, J. W. 158, 164
Moos, R. H., 179-184
moral development, in Jamaican
    children, 61-68
Moss, J. J., 121
Mrinal, N. r., 165

Neugarten, B. L., 158, 164, 168
Neugarten, D. A., 168
Niskanen, P., 49-50
nomothetic approaches, to cross-
    cultural research, 259-65
Northman, J. E., 50
Novack, H. S., 27, 30
Nuckolls, C., 216
number, development of reasoning
    and, 17-26

old age: in China, 205-11; cross-
    cultural research on, 179-266;
    cultural grid and, 234-44;
    depression and, 223-28;
    friendship relations, 193-200;
    memory and, 247-56; perceptions
    of, 164-68; social support of,
    216-21
O'Leary, D. K. 38
O'Leary, S. G., 38
O'Neill, M., 88
Opper, S., 19
Ortega, S. T., 200
Osgood, C. E., 249, 254
Oshman, H. P., 50
Otterbein, K. F., 267

Palmer, C., 265
Panyan, M, 38
parental behavior: of Chinese, 121-
    26; in Jamaican families, 61-68;
    self-concept and, 75-76
Parikh, B. S., 62
Parish, T. S., 48, 51
Park, J. Y., 67
Pedersen, A., 235
Pedersen, P., 235
perseverance, in brain-impairment,
    80
Pfeiffer, J. R., 112
Phillips, J. E., 194, 198
Piaget, J., 17, 88
Pike, K., 260
Pike, K. L., 253
Pincus, A., 180
Pinneau, S., 216
Plopper, M., 224
Poon, L. W., 247
Preisler, G., 265
Pringle, R., 90
Procidano, M., 218
Pruitt, J. A., 50
psychiatric disturbances, father
    absence and, 50
psychoanalysis, of Greco-American
    man, 143-53

psychopathology: addiction and drug abuse, 93-100; depression, 223-28; father absence and, 50-52

quantity, development of reasoning and, 17-26

Rabinowitz, V. C., 104
Rabushka, A., 194, 198
Radcliffe-Brown, A. R., 131
Rahe, R., 216
Rajkowski, H., 193
Ray, J. W., 165
reasoning, development of abilities by Sudanese children, 17-26
religiosity: cross-cultural research, 173-78; retirement residence and, 179-91
Rembowski, J., 48-49
Renner, W., 50
Rest, J., 61, 64-68
retirement, real-ideal residence environment research, 179-91
Rhode Island Pupil Identification Scale (RIPIS), 27-32
Riccards, M., 175
Roach, D. A., 51
Robin, M. W., 47, 51
Rogoff, B., 38
Rohner, R., 64
Rosamilha, N., 88
Rosenberg, M., 218
Rosenkrantz, P., 103
Rosenthal, D., 48
Rubin, D., 38
Rushing, W. A., 200

Safilios-Rothschild, C., 194
Salafia, W. R., 113
Salthouse, T., 247-53
Sarason, S. B., 38
Schaie, K. W., 155
Schenenga, K., 51

Schill, T., 50
Schwarz, J. C., 64
Scobie, G., 175
Scribner, S., 249-51, 254
Searles, H., 151
Segall, M. H., 234
self-actualization, in adolescents, 74-77
self-concept, factors influencing, 75-76
Shanahan, G., 255
Sharp, D. W., 247, 249
Shea, J. A., 50
Sheehy, G., 156
Sheltered Care Environment Scale (SCES), 179-91
Shiffrin, R. M., 252
Shill, M., 50
Shinn, M., 51
Silber, E., 218
Sinclair, J., 88
Singh, N., 133
Skinner, B. F., 40
Slater, E. J., 50
Slogett, B. B., 41
Slover, D., 246
Smilansky, S., 50
Smith, M., 247
Snarey, J., 61, 68
social behavior, distance differences, 112-16
socioeconomic status, cognitive development and, 20-21
Souberain, G. B., 88
Soules, B. J., 85
Southern, M. L., 50
space, concept of and reasoning, 17-26
Sparacino, R. R., 27, 30
Spata, A., 253
Speicher-Dubin, B., 62
Spires, R. C., 47, 51
Staats, A. W., 40
Stack, C. B., 200
Staples, F., 224
Stein, A., 42
stereotyping, 103-5

Stern, E. E., 48-50
Sternberg, S., 252
Sterne, R., 194-198
Stewart, J. J., 50
Stokes, T., 42
Stoller, E., 224
stress, father absence effects on
    children and, 48-49
Sudan, child development in, 17-26
Sue, D., 103-4
Sue, D. M., 103-4
Sue, S., 121
Sullivan, N. D., 50
Suomi, S. J., 262
Surtees, P., 216, 218
Svanum, S., 51
Sweetser, D. A., 133
Szeminska, A., 19

Taft, R., 259
Tanaka-Matsumi, J., 40
teacher rating scales, in cross-
    cultural research, 27-32
Teresi, J., 225
Thalidomide, effects on
    adolescents, 85-92
Tharp, R. G., 39
thinking, development of abilities
    by Sudanese children, 17-26
Thompson, L., 247
Thorndike, R., 253
Tietjen, A. M., 50
Tippett, J., 218
Tolor, A., 113
Toner, J., 223
Tormena, M. E., 80
Torrey, E. F., 40
traditional attitudes, versus
    traditional in Fruit-Tree
    drawings, 5-10
Treas, J., 221
Triandis, H. C., 249
Trickett, P., 38-39
Troll, L., 193
Turnbull, W., 50

Ullmann, L. P. 39
underachievers, early intervention
    for, 37-40
Underwood, B. J., 253

Vaillant, G. E., 161
value hypothesis, children's
    drawings, and 3-4
van der Lans, J., 175
Van Harrison, R., 216
Van Slyck, M. R., 50
Verghese, J., 131
Vernon, P. E., 18
Vincelet, P., 48
Vukcevic, D. P., 112

Wadley, S., 132
Walker, H. M., 38
Ward, C., 218
Waring, E., 139
Watkins, S. K., 254
Wechsler, D., 86
Weeks, J. R., 121, 205
Weisz, G., 139
Werner, O., 254
Wheeler, K., 50
Wickes H., 139
Wiehe, V. R., 50
Wilder, D. E., 224-25
Witherspoon, D., 251
Wirths, C. G., 121
Wojciechowska, L., 48
Wolff, M., 42
Wright, P. H., 194
Wu, P., 121, 123-26

Yamamoto, K., 155
Yorke, G.G.F., 164
Yu, L. C., 121-26, 205-211
Yu-Wen, H., 27

Zigler, E., 37-40

Contributors

Helmut E. Adler

HELMUT E. ADLER received his Ph.D. in Experimental Psychology from Columbia University. He is Professor of Psychology at Yeshiva University, where he is the Chair of the Department of Psychology at Yeshiva College. Dr. H. E. Adler published many articles, several chapters and five books. Currently he is a Member of the Editorial Board of the *International Journal of Group Tensions*. Dr. Adler's research in Comparative Psychology over the years included birds, cats, dogs, dolphins, whales, and sea lions. His publications in the History of Psychology deal with G. T. Fechner, W. Köhler, H.L.F. v. Helmholtz (in progress), and C. G. Carus.

Leonore Loeb Adler

LEONORE LOEB ADLER received her Ph.D. in Experimental Social Psychology from Adelphi University. She is a Member of the Faculty in the Department of Psychology and the Director of the Institute for Cross-Cultural and Cross-Ethnic Studies at Molloy College. Dr. Leonore Loeb Adler is President of the Academic Division, Former President of the Social Psychology Division, both of the New York State Psychological Association, and the recipient of both the N.Y.S.P.A. Kurt Lewin Award and the N.Y.S.P.A. Wilhelm Wundt Award. She was the Treasurer of the International Council of Psychologists and is Past President of the Queens County Psychological Association. For six years she was the Managing Editor of the *International Journal of Group Tensions*, for which she is currently on the Editorial Board and on the Executive Board of the International Organization for the Study of Group Tensions. Dr. Adler is involved in several cross-cultural and cross-ethnic research projects. She has attended and organized psychological conferences, workshops, colloquia, and symposia nationally and internationally. She has published over 50 professional papers and chapters; she is the author, editor, and coeditor of seven books.

Ramadan A. Ahmed

RAMADAN A. AHMED received his M.A. degree from Alexandria University in Egypt and his Ph.D. degree from the Karl Marx University, Leipzig, D.D.R. (East Germany) in Psychology, specifically in a cross-cultural context investigating the cognitive development in children with different cultural, national, and socioeconomic backgrounds. Dr. Ramadan A. Ahmed is affiliated with the Faculty of Arts of Cairo University Khartoum Branch in the Sudan. He is currently a visiting faculty member in the Department of Psychology at Kuwait University in Kuwait. Before embarking on a professional career in psychology, Dr. Ahmed received a law degree and worked for the Government as a lawyer. His present research activities include studies in developmental and social psychology, such as the perception of age, attitudes toward family members, as well as moral development. Dr. R.A. Ahmed has presented his research and participated at international psychological congresses, conferences, and conventions.

Joseph Avellani

JOSEPH AVELLANI received his Ph.D. from Teachers College, Columbia University. He is currently Director of Institutional Research at Teachers College. Dr. Joseph Avellani is one of the collaborators in a study of moral reasoning in students, which includes, at this point in time, 12 countries around the globe.

Elaine C. Bow

ELAINE C. BOW is a Doctoral Candidate in Industrial/Organizational Psychology at the Graduate School of the City University of New York. She is currently employed at the Port Authority of New York and New Jersey as a Tests and Measurements Specialist. Elaine Bow also was an Adjunct Lecturer at Baruch College and at Hunter College, both of the City University of New York.

Alice T. Carey

ALICE T. CAREY, M.A., M.D., founded the Westchester County Methadone Maintenance Treatment Program sponsored by St. Vincent's Hospital and Medical Center and established it as an internationally recognized model for effective treatment of narcotic addiction. For the past ten years, her primary work has been with the New York State Office of Mental Health.

Justin P. Carey

JUSTIN P. CAREY, Ph.D., Ed.D., J.D., former Visiting Professor of Psychology and Sociology at the State University of New York at New Paltz and Visiting Professor of Psychology at the College of New Rochelle, is now on the College of Business Administration faculty of St. John's University. Dr. Justin P. Carey is a Former President of the New York State Psychological Association and was for many years the editor of the *New York State Psychologist*. He is currently the Chair of the Committee on Ethics and Social Responsibility for the American Psychological Association Division on Religious Issues.

S. Patricia Clark

S. PATRICIA CLARK, O.P., received her Ed.D. from Teachers College, Columbia University. She is currently the Chairperson of the Gerontology Department and Director of the Institute of Gerontology, both at Molloy College. She is actively involved in sponsoring, organizing, and often chairing workshops and conferences for professionals, as well as for students. Dr. Patricia Clark, a Dominican Sister, is most interested in environmental studies.

William M. Davis

WILLIAM M. DAVIS received his Ph.D. from Hofstra University in Rehabilitation Research. He is Associate Professor of Psychology at Molloy College, as well as Adjunct Associate Professor of Psychology at York College of the City University of New York. Dr. William Davis is a consultant in Industrial/Organizational Research, and is also affiliated with the Nassau Psychological Services Institute. His primary area of academic interest is the teaching of psychology and the use of computers in education and industry. Dr. Davis' current research activities are in the area of cross-cultural and cross-ethnic issues, nutrient replacement in learning disabled children, and in human visual perception, as well as in the misperceptions of illusions.

Florence L. Denmark

FLORENCE L. DENMARK received her Ph.D. in Social Psychology in 1958 from the University of Pennsylvania. She was the President of the American Psychological Association, 1980-1981; the Eastern Psychological Association, 1985-1986; the New York State Psychological Association, 1972-1973; the International Council of Psychologists, 1989-1990; of Psi Chi, the National Honor Society in Psychology, 1978-1980. Besides that, she served as Vice President for the New York Academy of Sciences and the International Organization for the Study of Group Tensions among other committee positions. Dr. Florence L. Denmark has been the Thomas Hunter Professor of Psychology at Hunter College, City University of New York. Currently, she is the Robert Scott Pace Professor of Psychology at Pace University where she Chairs the Department of Psychology. She has authored and edited eight books and wrote numerous chapters and articles.

Chavannes Douyon

CHAVANNES DOUYON, Ph.D., is Chairperson and Professor in the Psychology Department at the University of Haiti. He is also the Director of the Main Power Division of the Ministry of Social Affairs; and he is Consulting Psychologist to the Psychiatric Center of Port-au-Prince, as well as a Clinical Psychologist in private practice. Dr. Chavannes Douyon is the founder of the Haitian Association of Mental Health.

Gudrun B. Ekstrand

GUDRUN B. EKSTRAND was trained as an actress at the State Actors College in Norrkoping in 1961. She was a drama teacher at the Malmö School of Education from 1969, made her M.A. in 1973, and is currently working toward her Ph.D. degree in Cross-Cultural Comparisons between India and Sweden. Gudrun Ekstrand has been a Lecturer in Education since 1978. Her bibliography contains about 25 titles.

Lars H. Ekstrand

LARS HENRIC EKSTRAND received his Ph.D. in Education in 1964, and in International Education in 1978. He has worked on Bilingualism, Immigrant Adaptation, and Cross-Cultural Comparisons since 1958. As a School Psychologist and Research Associate, Dr. L. H. Ekstrand was affiliated with the Swedish National Board of Education from 1958 to 1966. He has been a Professor at the Malmö School of Education, University of Lund, Sweden, since 1966 to date. His bibliography contains about 130 articles and books. Presently he is also a Research Associate.

Maria Emilia Tormena Elias

MARIA EMILIA TORMENA ELIAS received her M.Psy. from the Pontificia Universidade Catolica de Campinas, Brazil (PUCCAMP). She is currently on the Faculty of the PUCCAMP Institute of Psychology. Maria Emilia Tormena Elias teaches Child Assessment and serves as a Clinical Psychology Practicum Supervisor.

Jefferson M. Fish

JEFFERSON M. FISH received his Ph.D. in Clinical Psychology from Columbia University. He is a Professor of Psychology at St. John's University, where he previously was the Director of the Ph.D. Program in Clinical Psychology as the Chairperson of the Department of Psychology. From 1974 to 1976, he was a Visiting Professor at the Pontificia Universidade Catolica de Campinas, Brazil, where he returned as a Fullbright Scholar in 1987. Dr. Jefferson Fish has published two books and many papers. Currently, he is on the Editorial Boards of four journals and one international newsletter. He is a Former President of the Academic Division of the New York State Psychological Association and a former Chair of the Section of Psychology of the New York Academy of Sciences. Presently, he is the Treasurer for the International Council of Psychologists.

Cynthia L. Frazier

CYNTHIA L. FRAZIER, Ph.D., is a Clinical Psychologist and a Gerontologist who serves as the Director of the Clinical Programs and Education for Morningside House Nursing Home and Aging in America, Inc. Dr. Frazier maintains a private practice and is the consultant for hospitals and nursing homes. She lectures internationally on treatment issues pertaining to the older adult.

Machiko Fukuhara

MACHIKO FUKUHARA received her Ph.D. in Counseling and Educational Psychology from the University of Tokyo, though she spent some time studying at several colleges in the United States of America. Dr. Machiko Fukuhara is currently a Professor of Psychology at Jissen Women's University in Tokyo. She is involved in the activities of International Associations, and her interests include cross-cultural communication and research. Dr. Fukuhara has published widely in both Japanese and English, including many research papers and 15 books.

Uwe P. Gielen

UWE P. GIELEN received his M.A. degree from Wake Forest University and his Ph.D. degree from Harvard University. He is currently a Professor of Psychology and the Chair of the Department of Psychology at St. Francis College. Dr. Uwe Gielen has studied moral reasoning in a wide variety of cultures. He has traveled extensively, and his research includes 12 countries. Dr. Gielen conducted field work in Ladakh (NW-India), where he investigated religious and moral values in a Tibetan culture. At present, he is coediting a book on moral values in Chinese cultures.

Joan Goldberg

JOAN H. GOLDBERG received her B.A. degree in Psychology and Mathematics from Molloy college in 1974. Currently, she is pursuing her graduate studies in psychology. In the interim, Joan Goldberg worked as a teacher in various disciplines, initiating courses, and organizing programs. Recently, she was a Research Assistant at Molloy College, participating in research that was sponsored by the Institute for Cross-Cultural and Cross-Ethnic Studies.

David S. Gorfein

DAVID S. GORFEIN completed his undergraduate training at the City College of New York, of the City University of New York, and received his doctorate in Social Psychology from Columbia University in 1962. In 1966, he undertook post-doctoral training in memory with the late Arthur W. Melton at the University of Michigan. After 10 years at the New College in Florida, David Gorfein came to Adelphi University in 1975, where he is Professor and Chairperson of the Department of Psychology. He is the editor of two books and numerous articles in the area of memory.

Jean G. Graubert

JEAN G. GRAUBERT, received her Ph.D. in clinical Psychology from Adelphi University, where she was a Professor of Psychology until she retired. She had a Private Practice for many years. Dr. Graubert's areas of research included attitudes toward mental patients cross-culturally and cross-nationally, as well as investigations of some correlates of sex role stereotypes.

Barry J. Gurland

BARRY J. GURLAND, M.D., is Director of the Columbia University Center for Geriatrics and Gerontology of the Faculty of Medicine and the New York State Office of Mental Health. He is John E. Borne Professor of Research and Clinical Psychiatry at Columbia University; a Fellow of the Royal College of Physicians, and a Fellow of the Royal College of Psychiatrists. Since 1966, he has conducted a series of studies comparing the health problems and treatment of the elderly in New York and London.

John D. Hogan

JOHN D. HOGAN received his Ph.D. in Developmental Psychology from Ohio State University, and is on the Faculty of Psychology at St. John's University. Dr. John Hogan's publication topics include reading, Piaget, humor, creativity, developmental disabilities, professional issues, and the history of psychology. He is currently coediting a volume on International Psychology.

Eric and Margo Kahn

ERIC and MARGO KAHN are a husband/wife-team who are the founders of Maric Productions. Both were born in Germany and educated there and in Switzerland and immigrated to the United States of America. They are members of the Photography Society of America, the Photography Federation of Long Island, and the Great Neck Color Camera Club. Margo and Eric Kahn, individually, are multi-star exhibitors in International Salons. Together they are world travelers and produce Multi-Media Slide Shows (Travelogues). Both have photography as their hobby. However, in addition, Margo spends her time transcribing books into Braille.

Usha Kumar

USHA KUMAR received her Ph.D. from the Ohio State University in the field of Counseling/Clinical Psychology. After two years of Internship at the University of the Michigan Counseling Centre, she returned to India and joined the Faculty of the Department of Humanities and Social Sciences, at the Indian Institute of Technology, Kanpur. Dr. Usha Kumar is currently Professor of Psychology at the same university, where she pursues her research in the areas of development of Indian women, and in the middle-age crisis of managers in cross-cultural comparisons.

Hedva Lewittes

HEDVA LEWITTES received her Ph.D. from Stanford University. She is a Professor of Psychology at the State University of New York at Old Westbury, where she teaches developmental psychology, gerontology, and women's studies. Dr. Lewittes recently completed two articles titled "Just Being Friendly Means a Lot: Women, Friendship and Aging," and "Grown-Up Steps: Reflections on Two Generations of Adult Stepdaughters and Their Stepmothers."

Junko Tanaka-Matsumi

JUNKO TANAKA-MATSUMI received her Ph.D. from the University of Hawaii. She is a Clinical Psychologist and an Associate Professor of Psychology at Hofstra University. She was a scholarship student at the East-West Center in Hawaii, where she conducted cross-cultural research on depression and taxonomy of basic emotion words. Currently, Dr. Junko Tanaka-Matsumi serves on the Editorial Board of the *Journal of Cross-Cultural Psychology*.

Peter F. Merenda

PETER F. MERENDA received his Ph.D. from the University of Wisconsin in Madison. He is Professor Emeritus of Psychology and Statistics in the Department of Psychology as well as Computer Science and Statistics, at the University of Rhode Island. Dr. Peter Merenda is a Former President of: the International Council of Psychologists; the Division of Psychological Assessment of the International Association of Applied Psychology; the New England Psychological Association; and the Rhode Island Psychological Association. He is an Affiliate Representative to the International Union of Psychological Sciences; and Chair of the Committee on International Relations in Psychology of the American Psychological Association. Dr. Merenda was the Invited Lecturer and/or Research Collaborator at major Universities and Research Institutes in eight countries in Europe and Asia.

Halina Grzymala-Moszczynska

HALINA GRZYMALA-MOSZCZYNSKA received her M.A. degree in Clinical Psychology and her Ph.D. in Social Psychology, both degrees from the Jagiellonian University. Dr. Grzymala-Moszczynska is teaching courses in the field of psychology of religion at the Institute for the Science of Religions at the same University. Currently, she is completing a project on the therapeutic and pathogenic aspects of religious systems.

Nihar R. Mrinal

NIHAR RANJAN MRINAL received his various degrees at different Universities in India: his M.A. from Agra, his D.M. and S.P. from Ranchi, and his Ph.D. in the Experimental Social Psychology from the Indian Institute of Technology, Kanpur. Dr. Nihar R. Mrinal is currently a member of the Faculty in the Department of Applied Psychology at Nagpur University. His areas of interest include clinical, community, cross-cultural and research methodology. He is a Practicing Therapist and a Resource Person (personality development) at the Indian Institute of Youth Welfare, Nagpur, and Bharatiya Adim Jati Sevak Sangh, Nagpur.

B. Runi Mukherji

B. RUNI MUKHERJI received her Ph.D. from the State University of New York at Stony Brook. She is an Associate Professor of Psychology at the State University of New York at Old Westbury and is currently the Director of a Grant in Health Professions Training. Dr. Runi Mukherji's major research area is cognitive processes and neurophysiology of depression. However, she is also on the Faculty for the Centre for Aging and is currently engaged in research on changes in the perception of life events as a function of age and cultural transitions, and in patterns of friendship among the elderly.

Anne Pedersen

ANNE PEDERSEN has been Adjunct Professor at the School of Education, Syracuse University, from 1982 to the present. She has also been Visiting Professor at the Harvard Summer School, from 1984 to date. Dr. Anne Pedersen has Chaired the Science Communication and Education Committee of the Pacific Science Association since 1980 to the present. She is the author of numerous publications on international organizational communication and communication management.

Paul Pedersen

PAUL PEDERSEN has been a Professor of Education and Chair of Counselor Education at Syracuse University since 1982. He has also been Visiting Professor at the Harvard Summer School from 1984 to date. Dr. Paul Pedersen taught for years in Indonesia, Malaysia, and Taiwan, and directed an East-West Center Project at the University of Hawaii, from 1978 to 1981. He has authored or edited 16 books on multicultural counseling.

Claudette Reid

CLAUDETTE REID received her M.A. degree from Teachers College, Columbia University and is an Adjunct Lecturer at St. Francis College. Claudette Reid grew up in Jamaica, one of the Caribbean Islands, where she returned to collaborate and conduct the present research.

Mitchell W. Robin

MITCHELL W. ROBIN holds a Ph.D. degree and is an Associate Professor in Psychology at the New York City Technical College of the City University of New York. Dr. Mitchell Robin is also a Member of the Faculty at the New School for Social Research and a Staff Therapist at the Institute for Rational Emotive Therapy. His interests include the activities as an Associate Member of the Dramatists Guild, the professional organization of playwrights.

C. Edward Robins

C. EDWARD ROBINS, S.T.D. Ph.D., is Adjunct Associate Professor, Excel Division, at Fordham University, Lincoln Center, as well as a Member of the Faculty of the Long Island Institute for Contemporary Psychotherapy. Dr. C. Edward Robins is a member of many professional organizations and associations. In addition, he is a Psychoanalyst in Private Practice.

Marshall H. Segall

MARSHALL H. SEGALL trained mostly at Northwestern University, with input from Yale and l'Université de Genève, is an internationalist social scientist, and the recipient in 1987 of the New York State Psychological Association's Kurt Lewin Award. Best known for his work in cross-cultural psychology, including a study of visual perception done with Donald Campbell and Melville Herskovits and a widely used text, of which a revised and much expanded version is to be published in 1989, he has spent more than twenty years in the Maxwell School at Syracuse University, where he is now the Associate Dean of the College of Arts and Sciences. His recent innovations in the undergraduate curriculum include a course that challenges the universality of psychological findings generated mainly by research performed on American undergraduates.

Saulo Monte Serrat

SAULO MONTE SERRAT received his M.Psy. from Pontificia Universidade Catolica de Campinas, Brazil (PUCCAMP). He is currently Graduate Dean at PUCCAMP, where he served previously as Director of the Institute of Psychology. Saulo Monte Serrat joined the Institute's Faculty and teaches Community and Institutional Psychology in the Clinical Psychology Master's Program. He has published a number of papers and served on the Editorial Board of *Estudos de Psicologia*.

Andrea V. Spata

ANDREA V. SPATA received her B.A. degree in Psychology from Molloy College in 1984. She continued her studies at Adelphi University, where she received her M.A. degree and is currently pursuing a doctoral degree in Experimental Psychology. Andrea Spata is also Adjunct Assistant Professor of Psychology at Molloy College.

Regina C. Spires

REGINA C. SPIRES holds an M.S. degree and is currently continuing her studies for a Ph.D. degree at the Graduate Center of the City University of New York. She is an Assistant Professor at the New York City Technical College of the City University of New York, where she teaches Anthropology and Sociology. Regina Spires is also a member of the Faculty at the New School for Social Research in the Anthropology curriculum. Her research interests include the impact of mythology upon cognitive development, with particular interest in the mythology of Meso-America.

Manny Sternlicht

MANNY STERNLICHT received his Masters degree in School Psychology and Experimental Psychology and his Ph.D. in clinical Psychology from Yeshiva University, where he is currently a Professor of Psychology. Dr. Manny Sternlicht is also in Private Practice and is a Diplomate in Clinical Psychology, American Board of Professional Psychology. He has published many books, chapters, and articles, extensively in the area of developmental disabilities.

Gwendolyn Stevens

GWENDOLYN STEVENS received her Ph.D. in Educational Psychology from the University of California, Riverside. She is currently on the Faculty at the U.S. Coast Guard Academy, teaching courses in Psychology and providing Counseling at the Cadet Counseling Center. Dr. Gwendolyn Stevens has conducted social psychological research on hyperkinesis and its assessment, biographical studies of women important to the history of psychology, and numerous other studies on feminine issues. She co-authored, together with Dr. Sheldon Gardner, three books.

S. Patricia Walsh

S. PATRICIA WALSH, O.P., is a Certified Music Therapist. She is a Dominican Sister, who received her M.S. Degree from Queens College, City University of New York. After teaching elementary (primary) and secondary school levels for 30 years, she continued her studies and received her M.A. from New York University, which was followed by a clinical internship at Bellevue Psychiatric Hospital. Currently, S. Patricia Walsh is continuing her research with a geriatric population at the New York Geriatric Center. She is also the Executive Director of Activities at the Lawrence Nursing Home in Arverne, New York.

David E. Wilder

DAVID E. WILDER, Ph.D., is Deputy Director of the Columbia University Center for Geriatrics and Gerontology of the Faculty of Medicine and the New York State Office of Mental Health. Dr. David Wilder is also an Adjunct Professor of Sociology at Teachers College, Columbia University. He has conducted research and published widely in sociology of education and in social and mental health aspects of aging.

Shu-Chen Wu

SHU-CHEN WU, Ph.D., is a biostatistician who has been involved with a number of research projects. Currently, Dr. Shu-Chen Wu is an Assistant Professor in the Department of Epidemiology at the University of Minnesota.

Gary G. F. Yorke

GARY G. F. YORKE is a Doctoral Candidate in Clinical Child Psychology at St. John's University. He holds a Master's degree from Duquesne University. Gary G. F. York has written and lectured on Self-Psychology, Interpersonal Psychology, and Existential-Phenomenological Psychology. His research interests include assessment and the training of social and personal competence in children.

Lucy C. Yu

LUCY C. YU received her Ph.D. from the University of Michigan. She is Associate Professor in the Department of Health Policy and Administration and Senior Research Associate in the Institute of Policy Research and Evaluation at The Pennsylvania State University. Dr. Lucy Yu's research has been in the following areas: support of aged parents among Chinese Americans and Chinese in the People's Republic of China; urinary incontinent elderly in long-term care institutions; cognitive and functional status of institutionalized elderly, and occupational stress of nurses.

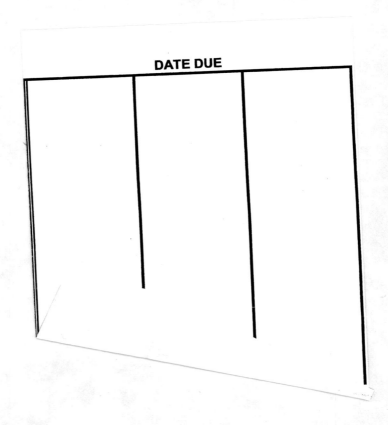

DATE DUE